American Letters and the Historical Consciousness

American Letters and the Historical Consciousness

Essays in Honor of
Lewis P. Simpson

Edited by
J. GERALD KENNEDY AND
DANIEL MARK FOGEL

Louisiana State University Press
Baton Rouge and London

A B V-1651

PS
169
H5
A44
1987

5/1988
Am. Lit

Copyright © 1987 by Louisiana State University Press
Manufactured in the United States of America

Designer: Laura Roubique Gleason
Typeface: Linotron Trump
Typesetter: G & S Typesetters, Inc.
Printer: Thomson-Shore, Inc.
Binder: John H. Dekker & Sons

10 9 8 7 6 5 4 3 2 1

Library of Congress Cataloging-in-Publication Data

American letters and the historical consciousness.
    Bibliography: p.
    1. American literature—History and criticism.
2. Literature and history.   3. History in literature.
4. Historical fiction, American—History and criticism.
5. United States—Historiography.   6. Simpson, Lewis P.
I. Simpson, Lewis P.   II. Kennedy, J. Gerald.   III. Fogel,
Daniel Mark, 1948–
PS169.H5A44   1987   810'.9   87-13547
ISBN 0-8071-1416-2

John Crowe Ransom's "In Process of a Noble Alliance" and "Vision by
Sweetwater" and excerpts from his *Selected Poems: Third Edition, Revised and Enlarged, Chills and Fever,* and *Two Gentlemen in Bonds* are
reprinted courtesy of Alfred A. Knopf, Inc.

Contents

vi   Contents

Acknowledgments

This volume is the work of many hands, and the editors extend thanks to those who have had a part in its making. Our colleague James Olney, Henry J. Voorhies Professor of English and Co-Editor of the *Southern Review,* has from the beginning of the project generously offered advice and encouragement. William J. Cooper, Jr., Professor of History and Dean of the Graduate School, also offered valuable suggestions about editing a collection of essays. Beverly Jarrett, Associate Director and Executive Editor at LSU Press, enthusiastically supported the undertaking, provided wise counsel, and kept the book on schedule. John Easterly at LSU Press improved the book immeasurably by his attentive copyediting, and Mike Davros, then a graduate assistant in humanities, diligently checked all quotations and footnote references for accuracy. The editors, however, accept responsibility for any errors that remain.

Finally, we wish to thank our distinguished contributors for the timely completion of their essays and their cooperation during the editing and proofreading processes. We have been bound together in this enterprise by our esteem and affection for the one whom we would honor.

American Letters and the Historical Consciousness

J. GERALD KENNEDY AND
DANIEL MARK FOGEL

Introduction: Letters and History

At the end of *All the King's Men*, Robert Penn
Warren speaks (through Jack Burden, the "student of history") of sin, death, and historical consciousness. Jack con-
templates the life he and Ann Stanton must reconstruct
upon the wreckage of the past: "Soon now we shall go out of
the house and go into the convulsion of the world, out of history into history, and the awful responsibility of Time." With
Jack's realization of his own role in the deaths of Judge Irwin,
Willie Stark, and Adam Stanton, his "history lesson" culminates in a new perception of the human situation. Jack dis-
cards his theory of blind instinct—the stimulus-response
model that he calls the Great Twitch—for a theory of will
and moral culpability. And by acknowledging "the awful responsibility of Time," he manifests an awareness that history constitutes the ineluctable ground of being; tainted by
the sins of the past, the present generation must confront
the mortal consequences of living in time. Jack arrives at an
agonizing sense of complicity with his forebears, perceiving
himself at last as a fated being caught in the web of history.

Warren's metaphor for the inescapability of time and
death—the spider web—seems (apart from its strictly Cal-
vinistic aspects) a useful emblem for the historical consciousness we have come to associate with the southern
writer and, more broadly, with the American literary mind.
For we have long recognized in our native letters an acute
and often ironic sense of history, a preoccupation with the
"usable past," rooted in a sometimes oppressive sense of his-

torical impoverishment and cultural immaturity. Hawthorne
once calculated the obstacles for an American writer of romances whose own country could offer "no shadow, no antiquity, no mystery, no picturesque and gloomy wrong, nor
anything but a commonplace prosperity." The awareness of
a foreshortened tradition—or rather the absence of tradition—has from the beginning produced a contradictory consciousness of both the history-making nature of American
experience and its fundamental discontinuity with history.
American writers have consequently tended to see themselves as caught in time, yet bereft of origins—orphans pre-
occupied with an obscured past.

This brooding concern with antecedents—with ancestry,
authority, paternity, genealogy—may be the psychological
burden of a problematic and literally unprecedented begetting. It has produced generations of American writers obsessed with forerunners, compelled to search for familial
and cultural roots. T. S. Eliot's quest led him to renounce his
midwestern upbringing and New England lineage to complete a historical circuit; his journey to East Coker brought
him back to the family's ancestral home, to his own psychic
origins. Many years after assuming British citizenship, he remarked (in language perhaps reflecting upon the American
dilemma):

> A people without history
> Is not redeemed from time, for history is a pattern
> Of timeless moments.

The "timeless moments" embedded in English history afforded Eliot a glimpse of the enduring order masked by temporal experience. He perceived time (history) as essentially
"unredeemable" and deterministic; however, only the movement of history enables one to apprehend the timeless "still
point" at the center of Being.

The succession of American writers attracted to Europe
by a yearning for history and tradition stretches from Irving
to Eliot. Not all American writers, however, have sought the
past amid the ruins of the Old World. Discovering the persistence of history in the Mississippi delta country, Faulkner
remarked (in *Requiem for a Nun*): "The past is never dead.
It's not even past." Yet, Faulkner's insistence on the present-
ness of the past and his fictional enactments of that theme
must be measured against his portrayal of the modernization—that is, the dehistoricizing—of the South. Nowhere is

this dismantling of the past more evident than in *The Sound and the Fury;* the selling of the mirror in the Compson home epitomizes the loss of that memory and reflection through which the past continues to live. Such moments in Faulkner's fiction reveal the paradox of the historical consciousness: the past is always simultaneously present and absent.

In some basic way, the past must remain imponderable, unthinkable, precisely because it manifests itself only in vestiges and remnants, as a residue of the irrecoverable—as memory, testament, artifact, or ruin. No doubt this irrecoverability explains, at least in part, the fascination, even the irresistibility of the study of history. The sense of loss or mutability compels reflection; the longing to retrieve the presence and plenitude of the past finally yields to the more modest desire to comprehend its distinctiveness. Yet, the past is paradoxically always present insofar as it inheres in the blood and bones of the living and in the patterns of human action. Eliot formulated the immanence of history as a circularity.

> Time present and time past
> Are both perhaps present in time future,
> And time future contained in time past.

The problem of the American writer's relationship to the past has also been the intellectual province of a distinguished contemporary man of letters. For better than thirty years, Lewis P. Simpson has been writing graceful and incisive essays about the modern literary consciousness. His numerous publications comprise an ambitious project of philosophical and critical understanding, directed at nothing less than a comprehensive vision of the human fall into history and the ascendancy of the secular, rational mind. If his work has been concerned largely with the character of American culture, that focus derives not from any indifference to European thought and experience but from a perception that the formation of our national literary imagination has typified the general loss of belief, tradition, and wholeness in Western life. Simpson's major studies—*The Man of Letters in New England and the South, The Dispossessed Garden,* and *The Brazen Face of History*—bring together essays composed over two decades and unified by the author's attention to the historical consciousness implicit in American letters.

Virtually from the outset, the American writer sensed a special relationship to history—indeed, sensed the singularly historical nature of the attempt to construct a new order out of the timeless wilderness. But Simpson contends that both the New England Puritan and the southern planter conceived of their colonizing activities as a version of pastoral experience, that is, as a denial of history and (patently) as an escape from time. The Puritan aimed to build a New Jerusalem, the "garden of the covenant," while the southerner endeavored to create what Simpson wryly calls the "garden of the chattel," an unprecedented pastoral world contingent upon slavery. Both of these projects foundered upon historical impossibility: the very effort to invoke the pastoral as "an idealized reaction to modernity" acknowledged the presence and pressure of history. In both New England and the South—in fact throughout the United States—the image of the New World garden persisted into the nineteenth century, but the conception of America as a privileged pastoral scene, exempt from the ordinary catastrophes of history, from the beginning carried a dubious metaphorical claim.

If the mythology of the garden marked an initial and futile desire to escape history, the proclamation of national identity in 1776 signaled the country's belated recognition of its intractably historical status. Concerning the Declaration of Independence, Simpson writes that "its unstated intention [was] more profound than the overthrow of a monarch, being nothing less than the transference of society and its government out of the dominion of a hierarchical world of custom and tradition into the dominion of independent rational mind." This enshrinement of reason as the guarantor of social and political relations effected "the radical displacement of the traditional community centered in Church and State, and in hierarchy, custom, and ritual" by a new model of social organization based upon "public mind or public opinion." Through this repudiation of tradition, the nation assumed its fundamentally historical character—as a product of time and change, subject to the vagaries of popular mind and will.

Simpson regards the American break with Europe as one facet of the more comprehensive process by which the "traditional world was replaced by modern society." In the broadest perspective he sees the emergence of the modern mind as a consequence of the "breaking apart of Christendom," beginning in the early Renaissance. The eroding authority of the Church, the emergence of scientific thought (which through Galileo and Copernicus radically altered man's conception of the cosmos), the foundation of modern nation-states, and the rise of secular rationalism all conspired to produce an acute awareness of individual consciousness and an "apprehensive sense of estrangement from the earth homeland." Although this summary does not do justice to the subtlety of Simpson's analysis, it suggests the main phases by which the modern mind acquired its characteristic fascination with its own operations. The exploration of self-consciousness—which may be said to have begun with the *cogito* of Descartes—leads to the subjectification of history and experience and to a fateful questioning of the relation between sensory evidence and truth: "In the subsequent loss of the equation between appearance and reality, the Western society joined in blood and cosmic mystery, and made real in image and icon—the sacramental, hierarchical, corporate, prescriptive community of Christendom, a society of myth and tradition—was displaced as the model of consciousness." One major outcome of this transformation is the redefinition of history, which is "no longer to be regarded as a story but as a process or series of processes" in some way emulating the "processes of consciousness." That is, mind itself becomes the model of history and assumes the task of defining its ordering principles.

Simpson contends that "American writers have a unique relation to the modern internalization of history" by virtue of the peculiar conditions under which America was settled and civilized. Without custom and tradition, much less a sustaining literary community, the American writer experienced "the increasing isolation of the self and . . . the ever-growing burden of self-consciousness in a society existing in and constantly being transformed by the cognitive processes of the human mind." An early concern for the relationship between American letters and an estranging modernity informs Simpson's 1960 essay "'Touching the *Stylus*': Poe's Vision of Literary Order." In this seminal discussion, Poe emerges as a representative figure, for his scheme to establish a journal to support "the general interests of the republic of letters"—in the language of Poe's prospectus for the *Stylus*—proved impossible precisely because he was, as Simpson remarks, "attempting to reverse history," trying to superimpose a literary order upon an already decentered, chaotic, and anti-intellectual society. For Poe lived in an age in which (as Simpson notes) "the literary mind of the Western tradition was undergoing a radical process of displacement." The combined forces of democracy, capitalism, and technology had already effected a dispersion and leveling of culture that isolated the writer and rendered his authority problematic. For Simpson, Poe's inveterate sense of alienation—figured in such texts as "The Fall of the House of Usher"—testifies to the predicament of the modern artist-writer who knows no community and must perforce inhabit the lonely realm of mind, the "monarch Thought's dominion."

Ranging from Puritan history to modern southern fiction, Simpson has developed an inclusive vision of American writing. His studies of literary thought and practice in New England include two early editions (*Profile of Robert Frost* and *The Federalist Literary Mind*) as well as the four essays that open *The Man of Letters in New England and the South* and the first portion of *The Dispossessed Garden*. His essays in *The Brazen Face of History* discuss such diverse figures as Franklin, Brown, Brackenridge, James, Hemingway, and Malcolm Cowley. Yet from the outset, Simpson has concerned himself most closely with southern letters (a fact suggested by the title of yet another edited collection, *The Poetry of Community: Essays on the Southern Sensibility of Literature and History*). From the early writings of Captain John Smith, through Robert Beverley and Thomas Jefferson to Faulkner, Tate, Warren, and contemporary writers, Simpson sees the southern struggle with history as a key to its unique literary attitude. His essays elaborate a persuasive theory of the stages through which southern writing has passed: an initial denial of time and historical consciousness through the pastoral imagery in early narratives of colonization and the nineteenth-century plantation novel; an eventual "recovery of memory and history"—a veritable project of reclamation—during the Southern Literary Renaissance of the early twentieth century; and a more recent rejection of "the historicism of consciousness" in the apocalyptic fiction of Flannery O'Connor and Walker Percy. Simpson's forthcoming study, *The Fable of the Southern Writer*, promises to bring the problem of letters in the South into definitive focus.

Simpson has long perceived the irreversible breakdown of the southern preoccupation with memory and history as itself symptomatic of a larger spectacle—"the progressive drama of the closure of history in the finitude of human consciousness." He sees the subjectification of literary thought—particularly apparent in the great works of high modernism—as a sign of "the final stage" in the "dissolution of the Western moral and spiritual culture." Indeed, the formation of what Simpson calls the "Third Realm," the Republic of Letters, as a "polity of secular letters" distinct from both Church and State (a development that coincides with the invention of the printing press) itself manifests a condition of alienation and a growing tendency to conceive of experience along historical rather than theological lines. In effect, the rise of the Republic of Letters institutionalizes the dissociation of thought and belief, encouraging the process by which the mind comes to interiorize history as a product of consciousness. By the time the self has fully assumed the burden of history—a circumstance enacted in *All the King's Men*—it has become "a creature of historical time" and can only contemplate through an act of imagination what it must mean to transcend its own historical condition. Through his intricate analysis of the Republic of Letters, Simpson shows how the internalization of history reveals a relentless subjectivity that culminates in the despair of one's own historical (that is, mortal) condition. Despite this bleak assessment, Simpson insists that the writing self can endure if not prevail over the forces of history by recognizing the prison house that is the modern historical consciousness. Only then can the writer begin to explore "the possibility of the reopening of the metaphysical dimension of reality" and the promise of "a participation in the mystery of history."

Each of the twelve essays published here examines the historical consciousness of American civilization as it has been shaped and manifested in the work of our major writers. As various as are the authors and topics of these excursions into American identity, the reader will perhaps discover what we have found to be an astonishing continuity as well, indicative perhaps of something irreducible and recurrent in the encounter between the national myth and the literary mind. That enduring element is the typology of a special destiny, equally present, for example, in the Puritan figuration of divine promise and the errand into the wilderness proclaimed by John Cotton, Cotton Mather, and others through the changing forms of the American jeremiad and in the explicit history and implicit prophecy conveyed by Ernest Gaines through his portrait of Miss Jane Pittman as a black Everywoman.

It is fitting that in a volume devoted to explorations of the idea of history in American letters the arrangement should be chronological. And so the reader who takes up these essays in order will move from colonial New England through the nineteenth century and on to the modern South into which the almost biblically long-lived Miss Jane survives. There is, however, one exception to the chronological order, "The Cultural History of Southern Slave Society: Reflections on the Work of Lewis P. Simpson." Because the authors, Elizabeth Fox-Genovese and Eugene D. Genovese, have devoted this essay to the work of our honoree, we have placed it at the beginning of the volume, almost as an extension of the present introduction. Fox-Genovese and Genovese hail Simpson as "our greatest cultural historian of the South." They detail the major elements of Simpson's reading of southern history, including his account of the evolution of Mind, his examination of the alienation of southern intellectuals from the international Republic of Letters, and his description of the antebellum South as something new in history, neither feudal nor bourgeois, but a unique "slave society inscribed in a modern (capitalist) world." The authors of this challenging essay offer not only a rich and illuminating appreciation of Simpson's work but also a provocative critique of certain ideas and readings that they would modify. While they accept Simpson's argument for the historical novelty of the antebellum South, they do not "accept the implication that the southern struggle for a new mind precluded a legitimate quest for continuity with European civilization"—that is, they argue, Simpson is in danger of obscuring the southerners' "sense of a strong link to medieval feudalism." And yet what their essay demonstrates throughout is the enduring structure of Simpson's analysis, within which they develop their valuable response. Fox-Genovese and Genovese testify above all to the seminal power of Simpson's thought, to the breadth and clarity that have made him, in their words, "our prime interpreter of southern letters."

The first of the essays in chronological sequence, Sacvan Bercovitch's "The Modernity of American Puritan Rhetoric," also testifies to the influence of Simpson's work, which in this case has inspired a major reformulation of Bercovitch's own view of the Puritans. He notes that Simpson has characterized the first settlers of Massachusetts and Virginia as "reactionaries to modernity"; not until the Revolution does Simpson see a shift from a religious to a literary consciousness, from "the minister in reaction against modernity" to the "man of letters confronting modernity." Writing "in tribute to Professor Simpson's sustained, enriching, and fortifying influence on [his] work, and that of a whole generation of Americanists," Bercovitch mounts a counterargument for "the profound modernity from the start of Puritan New England." In Bercovitch's view, the literary and religious have always been fused in the American historical imagination. Underlying that imagination is the "proposition that prophecy is history antedated, and history, postdated prophecy." The strategy of blurring the distinction between the literary and the religious, originating with the Puritans, is sustained over three centuries "through virtually every major event in the culture, from the Great Awakening through the Revolution and the westward movement to the Civil War, and from that Armageddon of the Republic to the Cold War and the Star Wars of our latter days." Thus, Bercovitch argues that "America" as a cultural symbol and modernist concept is essentially "the discovery of Puritan New England."

J. A. Leo Lemay also demonstrates the American foundations of the modern. In "Robert Beverley's *History and Present State of Virginia* and the Emerging American Political Ideology," Lemay refutes the notion that the rhetoric and ideology of the Revolution derived from English "seventeenth-century commonwealthmen" and "eighteenth-century opposition writers" by tracing the emergence of a distinctively American political thinking. Beverley's *History* is an exemplary document, Lemay contends, precisely because the author's attitudes were not original or unique; they express, rather, the emotional and philosophical bases for the struggle for independence—attitudes discoverable in key Virginia documents during the half century before the *History*. Beverley's insistence on the primacy of legislative bodies and his attention to the evil of "Rapacious and Arbitrary Governors" clearly foreshadow the ideology of the Revolution, but these ideas are perhaps less crucial to Lemay's argument than the beliefs shared by Beverley and the patriots of the Revolution but not by the English opposition writers: an American identity that entailed the rejection of English material culture, a colonial opposition to the English mercantile system, a devotion to the legal traditions of Virginia in explicit opposition to English practices, and an anti-aristocratic, egalitarian bias.

The next two essays deal with nineteenth-century fiction. In "The Romance of the Colonial Frontier: Simms, Cooper, the Indians, and the Wilderness," Louis D. Rubin, Jr., examines Simms's *The Yemassee,* using *The Last of the Mohicans* as a point of comparison and contrast. In Cooper, Rubin observes, we witness "the pathos inherent in the fall of timeless innocence in nature before human complicity in history." For Cooper, the imaginative remove to the unspoiled forest is an escape from history, from time, and from the obligations of authorship and ownership. Despite the superficial similarity of the two authors' fiction, Simms's position is antithetical to Cooper's, for the former never romanticizes life in nature, and his frontiersmen pursue a dream not of escape from society but "of the right to pursue one's objectives and to make the most of one's abilities within society." Simms's historical fiction thus becomes a vehicle for his Jacksonian democracy, which is sharply distinguishable from Cooper's commitment to patrician values and social subordination.

In "Reflections on Hawthorne's Nature," James M. Cox presents a complex, multifaceted meditation on Hawthorne's art, both in its "secret" personal origins and in its undervalued political dimensions. From his position of retirement in the Old Manse, Hawthorne looked through a window— etched with his own signature—"upon both nature and history." Cox finds at the heart of Hawthorne's "power to conceive fiction . . . both a wish and inhibition to violate, and sexually violate, the taboo and trust of his nearest, and presumably dearest, feminine relations." Wracked by both the pride and shame of authorship, Hawthorne adopted a voyeuristic relation to life and preferred to work from indirect sources—literary and historical texts—rather than from lived experience. Cox sees Hawthorne as balancing the gloom of inherited Puritanism with an eighteenth-century disposition: "Hawthorne, born on July 4, 1804, was close to that century, to its balance of mind, to its skepticism, to its detachment, and to its own deep passion for freedom—freedom, we must remind ourselves, from tyranny and not from slavery." While Hawthorne had, consequently, "the freedom truly to imagine" the Puritan past, he eschewed transcendentalism and the antislavery movement because he saw in them a "threat of the tyranny of the imagination in literature and of righteous morality in politics." Cox's meditation culminates in a consideration of Hawthorne's desire to democratize literature and to achieve intellectual freedom.

The next two essays seem transitional, for both move from nineteenth- to twentieth-century texts. In "Telling the World Over Again: The Radical Dimension of American Fiction," Terence Martin describes a sustained project in our literature, according to which novelists attempt imaginatively to re-create radical beginnings, unspoiled origins, firsts in collective and in individual history that imply a subsequent movement through time. Martin explores this ambition to "tell the world over again" in the work of Cooper, Willa Cather, and Faulkner. The movement toward genesis is always both a movement out of time and the recovery of a point of departure into time, thus enabling narrative. In all three authors, moreover, the shaping power of beginnings is sought in unspoiled nature, among the grand and elemental forms of landscape: in Cooper's forests, in Cather's prairie and Southwest, and in Faulkner's Mississippi delta wilderness, shrinking, in Isaac McCaslin's view, so that its life will be coterminous with his own.

In "The Unholy City: A Sketch," Daniel Aaron offers an excursion into literary history, tracing a pattern in American letters very nearly antithetical to the one delineated by Martin. To our nineteenth-century writers, Aaron observes, the city was wicked, corrupt, dirty, and disease-ridden. Writing in 1819, Richard Henry Dana, Sr., pronounced the city "unsuitable" for romance. Later in the century, the writers who brought the city within the scope of fiction—William Dean Howells, Robert Herrick, and Hamlin Garland, among others—did so with distaste for metropolitan corruption and disorder. It remained for a new breed of American writers to embrace the city imaginatively; these "neo-Natty Bumppos" were of late immigrant stock, and the city was their own briar patch. Dreiser was the first in this line; the city "de-

lights and dazzles him" and "coerces his imagination." He
was followed by such figures as Michael Gold, Henry Roth,
Alfred Kazin, James T. Farrell, Nelson Algren, and Richard
Wright. In terms of the analyses by Rubin and Martin (in
which one escapes time through nature), it might be said
that the acceptance of the city traced by Aaron signifies an
embrace of modernity and the force of history.

Only one of the essays in the present collection treats
American poetry, a consequence of authorial preference
rather than editorial design. We might speculate that the sequential narrative of fiction is more intrinsically historical
than the ordering principles of poetry, though Whitman,
Eliot, and Hart Crane come instantly to mind as poets whose
work is informed by a consciousness of history. Whatever
the reasons for this preponderant attention to fiction, we are
especially pleased that one of the essays is devoted to John
Crowe Ransom, a great southern poet and, among the mod-
ernists, arguably one of the least adequately appreciated. In
"Innocent Doves: Ransom's Feminine Myth of the South,"
Louise Cowan identifies Ransom's "dominant metaphor: the
victimization of women." The southern myth of woman-
hood, the ideal to which Ransom is steadfastly committed,
falls under the threat of the "primordial," which is sometimes masculine lust, a necessity that inheres in nature, and
sometimes, in its historical dimension, brute power—the
encroaching power of modernity—threatening to ravish traditional culture. Because Ransom's myth is always subject to
displacement, to the violent disruptions of the primordial,
his poems, Cowan suggests, display a "grotesque and sometimes weird distortion." Although the "jarring features of his
style" have often been faulted, Cowan argues that the grotesque elements stem "from an art that is adapted with astonishing consistency to his purpose," for that art expresses
"an insight that is itself grotesque."

The next two essays treat the historical consciousness of
other writers of the Southern Renaissance. Cleanth Brooks,
in "The Past Alive in the Present," observes in the major
southern writers of this century a commitment to bear the
burdens of the past honestly and unflinchingly, to accept the
past, and, if possible, to redeem it. Brooks sketches this concern in Faulkner and in Robert Penn Warren, and he concen-
trates the last half of his discussion upon Allen Tate's *The
Fathers*. While conceding that Tate's late vision raises prob-

lems that his own analysis cannot resolve, Brooks sets forth a reading of the novel that casts Major Buchan and George Posey as opposing figures. Posey is the purely destructive antitraditionalist, whereas Major Buchan is a traditionalist disabled because he lacks a historical consciousness—an "awareness of change and of the need to cope with it."

Walter Sullivan remarks in "The Novelist as Historian: Andrew Lytle's *Forrest*" that Robert Penn Warren and Allen Tate, like Lytle, wrote biographies before they completed their first novels. All of these writers clearly felt a need to possess history, "to establish themselves more firmly in the tradition out of which they had come and which they could now see slippping away." For Lytle, Nathan Bedford Forrest was not only an ebullient military leader but also a type of the yeoman farmer whom Lytle wished to celebrate. Once Forrest's antagonist, Braxton Bragg, enters the biography, "it ceases to be historical study . . . and becomes historical narrative with a hero and a villain as distinctly identified as those in any novel." Lytle schooled himself in narrative technique in the course of writing *Forrest*, and he also discovered in the biography the major theme of the fiction that was to come, the "conflict between and coincidence of public and private duty."

Our volume closes with essays on two great fabulists of the southern imagination, William Faulkner and Ernest Gaines, writers whose work everywhere testifies to their intense cultivation of the historical consciousness. In "History as Myth, Myth as History, in Faulkner's Fiction," Daniel Hoffman explores the relation between "historical data and the transcendent and legendary meanings that inhere in them." Hoffman shows that Faulkner played changes on a series of mythic and folkloric paradigms: the " 'myth' of southern history, a secularization of the biblical theme of the Garden of Eden and the inescapable presence therein of original sin"; the motif of a ruined aristocracy, centered in self-made men, versions of the metamorphic hero of folklore, as exemplified by Thomas Sutpen and as grotesquely mirrored on another social stratum by Flem Snopes (whom Faulkner views "with loathing"); and finally an "executive image of the human condition . . . the *imitatio Christi*." The last of these paradigms, in Hoffman's analysis, suffers a disastrous "allegorical simplification" in *A Fable* and assumes a distorted "parodic bitterness" in *Light in August*. But in *Go Down*,

Moses Hoffman finds a complex, masterful fusion of Faulkner's "mythic prototypes—the doom of an aristocratic family, exile from Eden, the imitation of Christ—in the historical matrix of the South." Here, "history becomes myth and myth becomes history."

Since Ernest Gaines became a fictional historian of his people—the poor blacks of the rural South—under the inspiration of Faulkner's example, it is not surprising that in "Jane Pittman Through the Years: A People's Tale" Blyden Jackson should seek to establish *The Autobiography of Miss Jane Pittman* as "an exercise in historiography," fictive, to be sure, but nevertheless profoundly true, visionary, documentary, and prophetic, the work of "an artist of a large and unclouded vision." Jackson shows how Gaines's novel covers "all of Afro-American history from its inauguration until the early 1960s," with each of its four books "conforming closely in every vital essential to a chapter in a good history of black America." And Jackson also shows that, beyond historiography, the novel is mythic: "above all, a morality play," a "history of a people," but also, "like the medieval *Everyman* . . . a message meant for those who have ears to hear about their own salvation," black and white alike.

Taken together, the essays collected here reflect the diverse and profound ways in which the historical consciousness has infused American letters. As such, they represent an effort to honor one who has enriched our understanding of this important connection. The editors of this volume have been privileged to be colleagues of Lewis P. Simpson, albeit for barely a third of his forty-year career at Louisiana State University. We have marveled at his wisdom and acuity as well as his unwavering gentleness of manner. In admiration and gratitude, we present these essays to him, on behalf of their authors and of all students of American civilization, as a tribute to one who has so brilliantly illuminated the historical nature of the Republic of Letters.

ELIZABETH FOX-GENOVESE AND
EUGENE D. GENOVESE

The Cultural History of Southern Slave Society: Reflections on the Work of Lewis P. Simpson

Whoever undertakes to write the much-needed comprehensive cultural history of the Old South will have to build on the seminal work of Lewis P. Simpson, which interprets southern letters as a distinct tradition in critical tension with the Atlantic bourgeois tradition that spawned it. A comparable tension informs Simpson's own project. For, as our premier interpreter of southern letters, he appears to cherish the unrooted—more charitably, the universal—"Republic of Letters" that stands as the preeminent identification of what he calls the modern mind. Withal, he peerlessly delineates the ways in which the antebellum southern mind differed from its bourgeois counterpart.[1]

Simpson's preoccupations with the relation between tradition and modernity and with southern distinctiveness have rendered him uncommonly sensitive to the nature and character of antebellum southern society. Never nostalgic, he rejects the easy view that the South embodied some form of traditional or seigneurial social relations and its corollary that southerners espoused unmediated traditional values. Instead, he eloquently argues, most notably in *The Dispossessed Garden*, that the Old South represented something new under the sun: a slave society inscribed in a modern (capitalist) world that had extruded but could not control it.

Simpson has rejected the interpretation of the Old South as in some way residually feudal, but he has also rejected the much more popular interpretation of it as "middle-class." The Old South, he insists, must be understood as a novel slave society under the aegis of a master class. *Middle-class* alone designates nothing. Small and middling slaveholders and propertied nonslaveholders lived in a society based upon slave property and did not constitute the same kind of middle class or classes that small and middling property holders did in a society based upon bourgeois property. The middle-class interpretation could only make sense if by "middle-class" were meant "bourgeois," but those who wish to view the Old South as "middle-class" eschew the term *bourgeois.* For the substitution of *bourgeois* for the less precise *middle-class* would come perilously close to exposing the interpretation as implausible. The South did have a modest bourgeoisie, and more important, it could never fully isolate itself from the conquering bourgeois ideology and, more broadly, the culture of the larger Atlantic world. The South remained a battleground for warring tendencies but, as Simpson stresses, a battleground increasingly dominated during the eighteenth and nineteenth centuries by a master class with overwhelming power over material production and human reproduction—a master class that commanded the regional political economy.

According to Simpson, the southern intellectuals' membership in this distinct society alienated them from the international Republic of Letters, to which they aspired and from which they sought recognition. For Simpson, this Republic of Letters amounts to the transnational polity of mind that has, at least since Petrarch, ostensibly embraced "free" intellectuals. From Petrarch and the Renaissance humanists to Sir Francis Bacon on to the luminaries of the Enlightenment and beyond, Western civilization has enjoyed—some might say suffered—the emergence and expansion of an intellectual elite that has proclaimed itself independent of and superior to the time-honored realms of Church and State, which it has aimed to supersede. This Third Realm long saw itself as the carrier of a Golden Age of the future and has always tried to render unto Mind—in short to itself—the things previously rendered unto Caesar and God.

Simpson's concept of Mind, which merits more extended discussion than we can provide here, in essence emphasizes—and even distills into archetypal form—the general transition in Western thought from a view of truth as inscribed in the mind of God and only partially and episodically revealed to man to a view of truth as the product of the human mind itself. The men of the premodern world institutionalized access to God's Mind in Church and State. Their modern, not to mention postmodern, successors, lacking the conviction of an absolute, transcendental, or prior truth, also cast doubt on the authority of institutions that could only draw their legitimacy from their custodianship of transcendent Mind. In this perspective, the Republic of Letters emerges as their quintessential institution—without enforceable boundaries or laws and especially without authority. For the laws of the Republic of Letters, bereft of roots in particular societies, reduce to opinion and fashion, their pretensions to higher standards notwithstanding. Thus, the Republic of Letters has mocked traditional institutions, which it has also dismissed as arbitrary, and has elevated the alienation of the individual to its own privileged version of citizenship. Simpson understands as much and can be acutely critical, but he also displays deep sympathy with the tradition of enlightened and combative alienation.

Simpson cogently argues, in *The Man of Letters in New England and the South,* that southern men of letters differed from their New England peers because of their relation to their own qualitatively different society. Southern slave society differed from New England society and from all other nascent bourgeois societies by resisting the tendencies toward the universalism—the rootlessness—that defined those societies' distinct character. The very logic of the triumph of the Mind of man over the Mind of God dictated alienation as the condition of the intellectual. Southern intellectuals also participated in that logic, but they did so as men and women firmly committed to the society in which they lived—a society imbued with particularism, not as nostalgia but as practice.

New England transcendentalism, Simpson observes, shared with the growing philosophies of skepticism an alienation from "the homeland of man and the community of men who make the world a household."[2] Simpson does not elaborate on the household metaphor he introduces, but it should be clear from his discussions of the southern pastoral that slavery engendered a formidable myth of the South as a world of extended households. That myth was no idle creation of self-serving proslavery ideologues. It arose from the essential nature of the political economy, which counterposed the organic social relations of its interior life to the market relations of its exterior connection to the world market and the Atlantic bourgeois world.[3] The southern intellectuals could not follow Emerson and other northern intellectuals into a celebration of Self, no matter how "individualistic" they were in their own way. "Family, friends, servants," Simpson writes of Emerson and others, "all fade as the Self in the flow of the currents of the Universal Being becomes part and parcel of God. The flow of Being is away from the human community of the world and never toward it."[4] The moral imperatives of a modern slave society grounded in extended plantation households demanded the reverse. As the slaveholders' ethos matured, it became steadily more communitarian.[5]

Southern writers, according to Simpson, completely lost their capacity for ironic detachment and disaffection, for the crisis of the literary order in the Atlantic world never reached the South. "Literary pastoralism," he writes, "became devoted wholly to the defense of slavery instead of the defense of poetry. . . . The literary realm virtually disappeared."[6] Simpson is referring to the literary realm strictly defined. As he acknowledges, the Old South had a considerable number of impressive intellectuals who doubtless considered themselves men of letters: theologians, social theorists, historians, political scientists, and political economists. The political economists are especially instructive, for several ranked among the ablest in the United States. George Tucker, perhaps best known today for his novel *The Valley of the Shenandoah*, made significant contributions to the theory of economic development and to economic statistics. Jacob N. Cardozo displayed an unusually high level of technical sophistication in his studies of rent, international trade, and related subjects. Among others, Thomas Cooper, Louisa Susanna McCord, J. D. B. De Bow, and especially Thomas Roderick Dew did work worthy of respect. All, with the controversial exception of Tucker, strongly supported slavery while espousing the political economy of Adam Smith and his successors.[7]

Therein lay the problem, for the logic of their political economy, worked out splendidly by Tucker, led them to project the eventual demise of slavery and advance of free labor and bourgeois social relations or, alternatively, to project the gradual restriction of slavery to specified geographic areas on the periphery of a world economy based on free labor. Any moral or philosophical defense of slavery they may have wished to make had to end, even in the no-quarter polemics of the redoubtable McCord, as a gratuitous superimposition on their political economy. They might, that is, flirt with criticism of slavery itself without suffering ostracism, for their essential loyalty to the South remained unquestioned. But their specific economic writings faded into the background of southern intellectual life when the proslavery intellectuals moved to the high ground of a positive defense of slavery as the necessary and proper basis for civilized society. During the 1850s the moral and social philosophers and those who began to call themselves sociologists effectively assumed the task of defending slavery and of speaking for the South in its ideological war with the North.[8]

Simpson plausibly dates the beginning of the image of the South as a dispossessed world from John Randolph of Roanoke.[9] We should recall that while Randolph defended southern institutions and values passionately, he was no friend to slavery. Men of his generation were the last who could admire and defend the world the slaveholders were making even while they considered slavery itself a problem, a misfortune, a curse. Those who followed, including Randolph's half brother Nathaniel Beverley Tucker, had to face the hard truth that slavery itself provided the social basis for the interests, institutions, and values that Randolph had courageously and eloquently espoused throughout his life. Thomas Jefferson may well have seen the light, for how else can we explain the last years of the author of the *Notes on the State of Virginia?* Having penned a searing indictment of slavery, he recoiled at the implications of the Missouri debate, fell silent on emancipation, and ended his life staunchly defending the South against alleged northern aggression. The men of 1830–1860 shed Jefferson's qualms and retreated from his vision of a democratic republic of freeholders. Their republicanism, closer in spirit to Randolph's proud identification with aristocracy, accepted as essential the subordination of the laboring classes in a stratified society and celebrated slavery as the proper foundation of moral as well as social order.

The proslavery intellectuals knew perfectly well that the South was not a "traditional society" and that its slave society had been spawned by the expansion of capitalism and fueled by the Industrial Revolution. George Fitzhugh's invocation of Ecclesiastes notwithstanding, they even seemed to glimpse that it was a new thing under the sun. Their intellectual effort, especially their literary effort, constituted a massive attempt to "create" the missing tradition by relating the plantation community to the organic communities of premodern Europe. They struggled to create a culture that would stand as a worthy heir to the best in the Western Christian tradition and would prove a bulwark against the disintegrating tendencies of the modern world. They perceived their project not as reactionary or restorationist but as progressive—as a morally superior, socially cohesive, alternate road to modernity. Their defense of traditional values and their assertion of continuity with the organic European community of earlier times ranked not as bad faith, as superficial critics often charged, but as a heroic, if deeply contradictory, attempt to build what Simpson has wryly called "a plantation on a hill."

The dream of the plantation as the encompassing model of social order, like the New Englanders' dream of the ideal city of two centuries earlier, had an inescapably utopian and reactionary cast. Above all, it opposed—even tried to deny— the countervailing forces that threatened to engulf it from without and erode it from within. It left, as Simpson maintains, little room for the unfolding of the Third Realm—for the expansion of autonomous Mind. In this respect, social relations and intellectual tradition converged. The consolidation of southern slave society in opposition to northern bourgeois society occurred during the early years of the republic, when southern intellectuals were suppressing their doubts about slavery. During the late eighteenth century, attacks on slavery had gained wide currency in the Third Realm, less because of intellectuals' deep concern with the condition of laboring people than because of their deep concern with their own status as individuals. Slavery represented the absolute antithesis of the freedom of being for which they fought for themselves. Slavery in this respect constituted an existential rather than a material condition. Yet, in the decades following the Revolution, material conditions regained their paramount role as guarantors of the life of Mind.

Northerners, having cast their material lot with free labor, found ample justification for their continuing, indeed growing, preoccupation with the freedom of the Self. Southerners, having cast theirs with slavery, beat a retreat from what they would increasingly call the antisocial and irresponsible claims of that Self. The northern way, like the bourgeois way in general, permitted, even invited, a simultaneously narrower and broader view of the Self and its claims than anything the world had previously known, or anything southerners could accept. The Self of Mind Triumphant joined the narrowly personal to the broadly abstract and universal. Arrogantly subjective and rationalistic, that Self could claim uniqueness and universality for its own experience, could claim absolute authority both for its discrete perceptions and its universalizing rational powers. In so doing, it abstracted itself from time, place, and society. Hence its perception of itself as everywhere and always alienated. Southern slave society left little room for that alienation and its critical distance on its dominant social system.

Yet, if the South left little room for a Third Realm, it also left little for a First or Second. As Simpson suggests, "Church, State, and Letters were all three absorbed by the rise of a society dominated by a class convinced that its existence depended on fostering a social order centered in 'only one opinion and one interest.'"[10] There is much to be said for this formulation, if properly qualified, but its starkness risks distortion. The Old South was by no means a totalitarian or a "closed" society, and it is surprising to find Simpson, here and elsewhere, conceding so much ground to this favorite shibboleth of liberal criticism. The hegemony of the master class presupposed a wide range of shared culture with the yeomanry but also exhibited deep strains of class antagonism. The South, at least the cotton states and substantial parts of the border states, did close on the slavery question, but it remained remarkably tolerant of heterodoxy in religion, politics, and philosophy. If southern poets and novelists were suffocated by their commitment to slavery, the reasons lay elsewhere than in censorship or self-censorship.

We might project a loss of critical nerve, but if we do, the question may arise whether any society that attaches its intellectuals to its social relations and primary institutions and values could possibly produce a great literature. And then we should have to explain away Elizabethan England and seventeenth-century France. And suppose that that society and its social relations, institutions, and values deserve adherence? On what grounds could we condemn the result? Simpson's remarks on the cultural exigencies of the master class remain heuristically valuable and contain more than a grain of truth, but they say too much. For it could be argued that the "alienation" of northern and other bourgeois intellectuals wondrously conformed to the exigencies of their own societies, however much they whined about the consequences.

Public opinion did not prevent southern writers from criticizing the realities of southern life from the vantage point of its highest professed ideals. Eminent jurists and legal scholars like John Belton O'Neall of South Carolina and T. R. R. Cobb of Georgia did just that in demanding reform of the slave codes. The theologians peppered their communicants with calls for higher Christian standards and with slashing attacks on the unchristian personal and social behavior of all too many slaveholders. Agricultural, industrial, and political reformers preached long and hard against the cultural backwardness of the master class as well as the people at large. In most cases they failed to effect the desired reforms, and slavery did lie at the root of their failure. For in most respects slavery as a social system prevented deep structural reform and sooner or later discouraged critical thought or, as with the political economists, swept it aside.[11]

Simpson, of all people, does not need the brittle formulation of an incipient totalitarian society; much less does he need to comfort those who find totalitarianism wherever they encounter a broad social consensus. He has advanced further than anyone—and by a good deal—in laying bare the specific contradictions into which a commitment to slavery plunged the southern writers. Throughout his work, especially in his extraordinary book *The Dispossessed Garden*, he has analyzed their dilemma. Their alienation from the world of industrial capitalism led them into a reassertion of the pastoral, which at first glance looks like no more than a regional variation of the transatlantic conservative critique of marketplace values. But they lived in and supported an alternate social system, which flowered in the wake of the rise of the world market and yet extruded a plantation society that in material interests and spirit and ideals counterposed to the marketplace a system of extended households and organic social relations. Perhaps Simpson's own sympathy for the highest ideals of the Third Realm encouraged his too-ready toleration of the view of the South as incipiently totalitarian, but such a view ends as of a piece with the spurious concept of the human mind as transcendentally free.

Southern writers' use of the pastoral simultaneously reveals their kinship to and their differences with the discourses of the Third Realm. As early as William Byrd of Virginia, they could invoke the pastoral and proclaim the South a garden. Yet, as Simpson insists, that pastoral image imperfectly masked its dark underside: The master of the garden was no gardener. Nor did that role fall to sturdy yeomen or to loyal dependent peasants; it fell to degraded beings who were legally classified as chattel. The moral justification for assigning the labor of the garden to slaves proclaimed their moral as well as intellectual and even physical inferiority but, in so doing, threatened to render preposterous the southern version of the myth of the garden: "If virtue is rural, if it stems from labor in the earth, then the slave should be as virtuous as the master—acting in some sense as the peasant was imagined to act in the capacity of an intermediary between the virtue conferred by direct contact with the soil and the lord's supervision of his labor and his life. But the slave was a chattel, in brutal economic terms, a thing." [12]

The contradiction haunted the intellectuals of the Old South and led some of them to question, if feebly, the perpetuity of chattel slavery. But in daring to question, they only succeeded in deepening their dilemma. Simpson astutely assesses southern intellectuals' effort as directed toward the creation of a world view—philosophy, social theory, ethos—appropriate to a slave society and appropriate as a standard for a worldwide Christian renewal. In one of his foremost contributions, he dissects, as no one else has, the betrayal of Mind toward which the southern intellectuals were inexorably led. For their commitment to property in man arose within a transatlantic culture that was establishing a Third Realm firmly and necessarily committed to the antagonistic principle of property in oneself.

In this context Simpson delineates and elaborates the way in which the southern intellectuals separated themselves from the Republic of Letters and condemned themselves to a measure of literary paralysis at the very moment in which, and by the very process through which, they were impressively struggling to create an alternate road to modernity. Indeed, Simpson goes further and suggests that, had the war not intervened, subsequent generations would probably have created a reasonably well-rounded world view. Yet, ever sensitive to the nuances and complexities of an inherently contradictory cultural process, he makes a necessary concession to Louis Rubin and others who deny the special slaveholding nature of antebellum southern society and culture. He acknowledges that the vision of a "plantation on a hill" constantly ran afoul of the entrepreneurial, acquisitive, and commercial-bourgeois realities of a slaveholding society based upon commodity production for a world market. For the exigencies of that market threatened to make a mockery of the vision and to subvert the organic social relations essential to its material foundations.

The southern intellectuals themselves recklessly forged ahead and almost ruined themselves by widening and deepening their commitment to slavery, which Simpson sees suggestively, if problematically, as an assimilation of slavery to Mind. Yet Simpson, having carried the analysis to unprecedented heights, stops short. Many among the ablest strove to overcome the contradiction between their organic vision and the subversive realities of the world market. In so doing, they retreated all the more from the Republic of Letters and its assertion of the primacy of the Third Realm. In effect, they foresaw as social tendency and advocated as social policy the evolution of chattel slavery into one or more forms of labor dependency reminiscent of medieval serfdom but adapted to life in an increasingly industrial world. Henry Hughes of Mississippi, whose ideas were winning attention and respect, called for "progress" in a modern, developing world in which all labor would be assigned to "warrantors" regulated by a corporate state.[13]

The moral and ethical foundations for the emerging vision were being laid by the enormously influential theologians, who, among other advantages, guided the South's educational system. During the 1850s their leading spokesmen—the Presbyterian James Henley Thornwell, the Baptist Thornton Stringfellow, the Methodist William A. Smith, and others—embraced one or another version of a corporatist solution to the "social question." Yet, in vigorously defending slavery and pronouncing it ordained of God, they denied that it was destined to last forever in its southern form. God had ordained social stratification and had included slavery among the appropriate forms of the subordination of labor, but even in the reading of the strictest adherents of the literal interpretation of the Word, God had not required that chattel slavery, in contradistinction to less rigorous systems of servitude, remain forever in a morally progressing Christendom. The militantly proslavery Frederick A. Ross, pastor of the Presbyterian church of Huntsville, Alabama, opened his powerful tract *Slavery Ordained of God* by chiding those who unwisely insisted that slavery as then practiced in the South must be rendered perpetual. God might well guide his people toward an emancipation that, on close inspection, would mean not bourgeois freedom but some more humane, socially safe form of the subordination of labor to personal authority.[14]

The theologians thereby instructed the secular intellectuals in the art of having and eating their cake—in defending slavery, not merely Afro-American slavery but slavery in the abstract, and yet in holding out the promise of progress toward a more recognizably Christian system of social relations that would be free of the undeniable evils of the present system. Those theologians were, more or less consciously, combating extreme racism by suggesting that Afro-Americans could be raised to the level of most white workers, who they thought should also occupy a subordinate position in society.

This vision threatened to play havoc with the realities of the political economy of the world market, which had engendered New World slavery in the first place and which alone could sustain it. Every southern political economist and every economically literate theologian—and many were in fact economically literate—understood that the southern social system rested on commodity production for a world market and that, historically, slave labor but not serf labor had proved adaptable to the fierce competition engendered therein. Thus, the projected evolution of southern social relations, which would ostensibly open an alternate road to modernity and progress, disguised the very reaction and premodern restoration it was designed to avoid. Among the southern intellectuals, only George Fitzhugh took the full measure of the contradiction and proposed to resolve it by repudiating much of the modern world and destroying the world market. That insight marks the originality of his thought, not his advocacy of slavery in the abstract, which had been advocated by many others for a long time and which, by the 1850s, had become common fare in the South.

That contradiction assailed the thought of the late antebellum southern intellectuals in ways that bear directly upon Simpson's analysis. In the early 1970s Simpson described the literary situation as one in which the commitment of the antebellum southern men of letters to slavery tended to isolate them from the Republic of Letters and to lead them toward a repudiation of the Third Realm. Alone among the intellectual strata of the Atlantic world, they identified with their society in a manner that precluded identification with the Third Realm. The exigencies of a slave society embedded in a hostile bourgeois world compelled denial of moral legitimacy to the autonomy of the Republic of Letters and especially to its claims of preeminence as a Third Realm. The southern men of letters were deprived, as it were, of the right, duty, and even possibility of suffering the alienation that increasingly characterized the intellectuals of Western civilization and that liberated them to assimilate the material and social world to Mind.[15]

Simpson subsequently modified his thesis and especially praised Drew Gilpin Faust's *A Sacred Circle*, which demonstrated a strong sense of alienation among a particularly significant group.[16] Simpson's salutary modification has enriched his analysis, but it has also threatened to veer into a cul de sac. Its strength lies in its much fuller appreciation of the tension in southern thought and, in particular, of the intellectuals' desperate, sometimes pathetic, struggle to feel part of the Republic of Letters and to assume a critical stance toward the slave society they were celebrating. It permits, that is, an appreciation of the extent to which they, and all modern intellectuals, remained bound by the ideological and moral revolution that inhered in the world conquest of the transatlantic bourgeoisie.

The weakness of Simpson's modification lies in its tendency to conflate the southern critics of marketplace values with the conservative and even radical critics of the rest of the Atlantic world. Faust herself, in *A Sacred Cricle*, but not in her later works, fell into this trap. For alone in the West,

the southerners criticized "getting and spending," repudiated the "cash nexus," and protested that "things are in the
saddle and ride mankind" from the vantage point of a society
based on organic social relations. They shared with others
in the Atlantic Republic of Letters a vocabulary of alienation from the bourgeois marketplace that was absorbing the
world, but unlike the others, including Europe's conservative
traditionalists who nostalgically dreamed of restoring the
ancien régime, they spoke for a social class that held power
in a large, rich region that was increasingly aspiring to become a nation-state. Hence, they felt alienated in precisely
the same way as the slaveholding class as a whole felt alienated from a modern world it sought to join but only on its
own unacceptable and war-provoking terms.

The southern intellectuals' alienation partook directly of
the tensions that rent their identities as intellectuals and
as southerners. They inescapably worked within the dominant discourse of Western bourgeois culture, and they used
the same words, especially the same groupings of words, to
describe, analyze, justify, and criticize the world around
them.[17] They proved especially comfortable in turning to
Shakespeare or other Renaissance and early modern forerunners of the dominant tradition of their own day. But the
Republic of Letters had not preserved its own history graven
in stone. It had modified it with changing experience. The
truths that southerners, like northerners and Western Europeans, accepted as the grounding of human experience had
been applied to changing situations and, accordingly, modified by living cultures. Understandably, the southerners
claimed that legacy as their own, but increasingly during the
late eighteenth and early nineteenth centuries, they began
to adapt it to their own circumstances and commitments.
Their attempts led them ever further from the substance
of the general bourgeois interpretation of man in society,
but they never forsook the vocabulary that they continued
to share with their bourgeois rivals. The results provoked
confusion.

Southern intellectuals, like literate southerners in general, could readily embrace the bourgeois critique of industrial society. In "getting and spending," they could concur
with Wordsworth, "we lay waste our powers." In the same
spirit, they could enthusiastically second the Romantics'
celebration of nature. But in the hands of the bourgeois Ro-

mantics that celebration had moved beyond the tradition of the pastoral. The bourgeois Romantics turned to nature in personal nostalgia, as a temporary and personal retreat from the hustle and bustle of the capitalist world to which they belonged. Raymond Williams has convincingly argued that by the early nineteenth century bourgeois culture's view of the country constituted a direct extension of its acceptance of the city, understood as proxy for capitalist social relations. Yet, southerners could still claim the country as an alternate way of life, as the embodiment of admirable social relations. Whereas in the North and in Western Europe, the city was irreversibly conquering the country—in reality and in the forms of imagination—in the South the country struggled, with considerable success, to conquer the city. Indeed, the low level of southern urbanization, the slow growth of a free labor force, and the persisting commercial, in contrast to industrial, character of the majority of large southern cities all lent aid and comfort to those who nourished the prospect.[18]

Hence, the alienation of southern intellectuals had a distinct cast. For northern intellectuals and Western European intellectuals alienation meant the individual's homelessness in the world. That sense of alienation primarily expressed personal psychological malaise or, as the French symbolists would have it, ennui. The intellectuals did draw upon an older pastoral tradition to forge an apparent opposition between nature and society, but they did not seriously propose a return to older systems of social relations. Even the French Romantics' infatuation with the Middle Ages had more to do with style and with their revolt against a constraining rationalism—with the celebration of personal feeling—than with a projected re-creation of a traditional society. No more than the French did the southerners propose to rebuild medieval society in Virginia's or Carolina's "green and pleasant land." Indeed, they largely borrowed their view of medieval society from Scott and other Romantics. Many nonetheless understood that they were attempting to create a modern defense of a system of values that placed society and its order above the feelings of the individual. Thus, when they turned to the pastoral to express their distinct imagination, they were groping for a way of expressing a system of social relations and values that differed radically from those cherished by bourgeois denizens of the Third Realm.[19] In sum, while bourgeois intellectuals were increasingly reducing alienation to a personal matter, southern intellectuals were, however inconsistently, experiencing alienation as social and ideological estrangement from a dominant culture the premises of which they did not accept and against which they had a socially grounded alternative. That they drew so heavily on the language developed by their bourgeois opponents confuses but should not be allowed to obscure the issue.

That was another sense, invoked by Faust and Simpson, in which the southern intellectuals felt alienated: however much they supported the southern social system, as professional intellectuals—or as those who wished they could afford to sustain themselves as professionals—they lived uncomfortably in the South. The intellectuals or men of letters of whom Faust and Simpson speak were primarily literary men. The southern intellectual stratum was dominated by ministers, lawyers, physicians, and others who commanded considerable prestige. Men from these professions published widely on scientific, political, philosophical, economic, and even literary subjects. An occasional Edmund Ruffin aside, those who suffered from neglect were primarily poets, novelists, and literary critics who would have liked to earn a living from their chosen work. They complained bitterly of being unappreciated at home and of having to support themselves from plantations only few knew how to operate or from the practice of law or medicine. Augustus Baldwin Longstreet is best known for his writing, but he was also a planter, a Methodist preacher, a college president, and a financially successful lawyer and jurist.

There is no evidence that they felt guilty about defending slavery and personally owning slaves, but there is much evidence that they felt uneasy about having to protest against their unfair treatment by a society they deeply believed in—as if their protest constituted an act of moral weakness, if not of treason. They knew that the very nature of their society precluded recognition of an autonomous intelligentsia and, to the contrary, demanded subordination of its intellectuals to social and ideological discipline. The South had abundant room for those who thought freely about politics, religion, art, and science, but only if they stood within the moral consensus that slavery promoted and required. The South had little room for those who stood outside that moral consensus and questioned the social relations upon which the slaveholders' civilization rested.

Thomas Roderick Dew, perhaps, with George Frederick Holmes, one of the most erudite southerners of his generation and, with John C. Calhoun and George Tucker, one of its most acute thinkers, unwittingly exposed the dilemma. He denounced the ancien régime for stifling criticism of its social and political relations. Notwithstanding the monarchy's patronage of the arts, he argued, it dared not permit the freedom of thought that alone could engender material and moral progress and that must ossify when not allowed to focus on the social and political relations at the heart of any society. So strongly did he feel on this subject that he pronounced the French Revolution epoch-making and defended it as necessary and good despite the horrors of the Terror and Jacobinism. Yet, while reiterating these views in the 1840s, Dew applauded the suppression of antislavery views in the South as a necessary and proper defense of the social order. He never did explain how the South could progress under such conditions; nor did he explicitly abandon his lifelong commitment to freedom of thought as the mainspring of the progress of civilization.[20]

The constraints upon the intellectual life of the South came not only from the coercion of the state, the civil institutions, and a readily mobilized public opinion. They also came from the irresistible tendency toward self-censorship among intellectuals who had honorable reasons for supporting the regime. More ominously, they came from those intellectuals whose commitment to the regime led them to take for granted both the prevailing social relations and their role as defenders of the faith. The proslavery intellectuals as a group fell prey to that tendency, which manifested itself with varying intensity from person to person. And to the extent that intellectuals (both men and women) fell prey, they separated themselves from the Republic of Letters and surrendered their claims to autonomy.

In seeking to establish a tradition, the southern writers recognized their world as a product of history and, as such, as dynamic, changing, and internally rent. Immersed in the bourgeois culture of their epoch, they also recognized it as a product of Mind. Torn between the internal logic of a culture they admired and the claims of a social order to which they committed themselves, they sought to affirm their world's continuity with a valued and living past and yet to reject and

reverse the frightening consequences of modernity's assimilation of God to Self and Mind. Their project, notwithstanding its ultimate impossibility, drew plausibility from the
side of the contradictory southern social relations that they
viewed as positive—the organic, paternalistic side, which
offered a vision of continuity with a premodern world ostensibly unassailed by the separation of Self from society. But
their literary imagination crumbled before their inability,
not to mention unwillingness, to purge Mind, specifically
their own minds, of the historical consciousness that had irreversibly transformed it.

Although as a group they fell short of assuming the primacy of Mind, castigating the abolitionists' willingness to
place individual conscience even above the Bible if need be,
they also fell short of repudiating its power. They sought a
contradictory and unrealizable status: ideally, they would
have enjoyed the inflated status of artist or genius that bourgeois culture was conferring on those whom T. S. Eliot would
claim should be understood only as craftsmen and whom
some twentieth-century Marxists would try to call specialized producers. Yet, beneath the nimbus of glory, those bourgeois custodians of Mind owed their status to the values of a
marketplace society, and frequently anguished cries of neglect notwithstanding, to its material rewards as well. The
southerners could not readily see that the status could not
be divorced from the bourgeois society and culture that engendered it. And the southerners did not want that society
and culture. The contradiction between their personal desires and their social commitments accurately reflects their
specific historical condition.

In "The Sexuality of History," Simpson analyzes the novels of Elizabeth Madox Roberts and the condition of the
modern writer in general, but he might well also have been
thinking particularly about the writers of the Old South.

A Buried Treasure ends with an almost medieval delight in
the garden of the world. The more complex Black Is My True
Love's Hair poses the nostalgic possibility of recovering the bal-
ladic world. But even these novels turn on the sense of what
intervenes between the self of the modern artist and a sacramental connection with "the simple and uncomplicated earth":
the terrible intimacy with history. In this intimacy both metaphysical and physical reality have disappeared. They are illu-

sions generated by the self-consciousness that is history and the history that is self-consciousness. Having modeled our society—a society of science and history—on mind, we believe in the idea but not in the fact: in the idea of the heart but not in the heart; in the idea of the flesh but not in the flesh; in the ideal of the community but not in community; in the idea of responsibility for one another but not in the responsive, and thus responsible, act of sympathy; in the ideal of love but not in the act of love. We believe in togetherness, or in "interaction"; but are alienated from each other.[21]

Antebellum southerners could fasten upon the genuinely organic aspect of the master-slave relation as the cure for the ills, but they could not escape the negation of that aspect imposed by the realities of the marketplace in which their society was embedded.

The history that engendered southern slave society—the living history that no heroic myth-making could overcome—was the history of an expanding world market that intruded deep into the southern household itself. It should be enough to recall that those black members of "our family, white and black," could be and often were peddled like so many cattle. Proslavery apologists indignantly argued that no southern gentleman would do such a thing unless, of course, compelled by stern economic necessity. They failed to notice, as Mrs. Stowe did notice, that that stern economic necessity was an ever present threat in their daily lives and that it betrayed all visions of a garden, of a plantation on a hill, when it did not expose them as palpable fraud. Southerners often wrote as if they could only espouse the master-slave relation as superior to its bourgeois alternative by demonstrating that it had all the features of the lord-peasant relation in a medieval village world that probably never had existed.

Simpson expresses more clearly than any other scholar the sound reasons for rejecting as misleading the attribution of a prebourgeois traditionalism to the Old South, but he does so too starkly and invites an alternate misunderstanding: "The struggle of the Old South was not between a traditionalism rooted in European forms of feeling and emotion and an outside (or an inside) insurgent modernism. Under the historical circumstances that it faced—under the historical nature of its existence—the South's struggle was between the rise of a unique slave society and the forces of modernism."[22] Those antebellum southern writers, while self-consciously modern men, had a noticeably conflicted attitude toward the Middle Ages. They deplored the material and intellectual backwardness of the Middle Ages and, in any case, knew that plantation slavery departed from the ideal as well as the practice of medieval feudalism. But they also knew that slavery shared with seigneurialism a firm repudiation of marketplace values, and they aspired to a resurrection of the spirit of premodern social relations. It is no argument that the organic relations of the slave plantations were often brutal and subverted to greed. So were the organic relations of the medieval villages and manors. They were each, albeit in radically different ways, based on a political economy in which men faced men unmediated by the market and the consequent ravages of what Marx called the fetishism of commodities.

On this matter Simpson writes: "The Old South sought not to root the rationale of its difference from the modern world in the deep places of the mind; but, to the contrary, to found its existence and establish its difference from modernity on a new mind."[23] We agree, but do not accept the implication that the southern struggle for a new mind precluded a legitimate quest for continuity with European civilization. The deepening religious consciousness in evidence during the nineteenth century deserves more attention than Simpson has so far given it. That consciousness encouraged a sense of continuity with premodern Europe as necessary to its sense of a southern slave society that could claim to be the rightful heir of the Christian tradition. And the theologians of the 1840s and 1850s left no doubt that they regarded the subjugation of labor in a stratified society as God-ordained. Simpson is right to insist that the southerners knew that slavery was not feudalism and that they, as slaveholders, were very different people from medieval lords. But he is in danger of obscuring their sense of a strong link to medieval feudalism in the organic—that is, noncommodity—relation between the classes and thereby of obscuring what they themselves recognized as a measure of shared sensibility.

Simpson may also be too rough on Simms and Timrod in his generally illuminating discussion of their tortured relation to modernity. Their commitment to the politics of slavery, he argues, made them incapable of conceptualizing "the ironic drama of their careers or to grasp the ironic meaning of the South as a modern slave society."[24] Simpson assumes that if they had glimpsed the irony, they would have been plunged into a crisis of conscience, rent by their loyalty to the regime and their dedication to the world of letters. We would suggest, as an alternative, that they may well have glimpsed, and more than glimpsed, the dilemma of trying to reconcile the irreconcilable and, in the end, bravely made their choice.

Simpson's treatment of the southern alienation of Self from Self and therefore from society—of the extent to which southerners, too, succumbed to the lure of the Third Realm—displays some disquieting ambiguity as well as considerable strength. Step by step in his essay "The Ferocity of Self: History and Consciousness in Southern Literature" he modifies his earlier formulation by moving toward a judgment of southern society as psychically rent. We have no quarrel with the judgment but confess to being uneasy at the extent to which it appears to fold the southern experience into the broadly American. Gently parting company with Allen Tate, he writes that the Old South "in its inmost nature was centered less in family than in self." Simpson is no longer at home with Tate's insistence that the Old South was "a society of manners and custom" with "the family at the heart."[25]

In this essay Simpson effectively challenges the southern Agrarians' notion that a modern writer could, as an act of will, reject the world of isolated and fragmented selves and identify, in Simpson's words, "with the old corporate, hierarchical society of manners and custom, in which the problem of being a self never arose."[26] As a critique of the Agrarians' utopianism and of Tate's—and he might have added the no less formidable Richard Weaver's—curious interpretation of the Old South as a feudal society, the essay scores heavily. Here and elsewhere Simpson demonstrates that the genie of self-consciousness and its assimilation of history to Mind cannot be put back into the bottle and could not have been in the Old South. Put another way, antebellum southerners, whatever their protests and aspirations, were products of the cultural revolution unleashed by the Renaissance and Enlightenment and could not escape knowledge of the fundamental antagonism between Self and society.

Simpson here invokes Hegel, who introduced the concept of alienation into Western thought, and he might profitably have invoked the fate of that concept at the hands of Karl Marx, who set about to abolish the alienation of Self from society by treating it as a historically specific atribute of capitalism. The great social and political movement that he founded has made enormous conquests and has had historic accomplishments to its credit, but it has signally failed even to approximate Marx's dream. Despite pretenses and ritual bows, it no longer even believes in that dream. That much has been widely noticed. What has largely gone unnoticed is Marx's own failure to assimilate his dream of a liberated communist New Man and New Woman to the profound interpretation of history that marked the height of his genius.[27]

The experience of Marx, of Marxism as theory and practice, and of the socialist world, like the experience of the slave society of the Old South, suggests that the liberation of Mind effected since Petrarch has been irreversible. Marx and Engels opened the *Communist Manifesto* by praising the bourgeoisie as the most revolutionary class in world history. They did not expect it to remain so, but in this respect it has, bequeathing to the classes it has overthrown, and to those which have overthrown it, an inescapable cultural legacy.

Slave and socialist societies are not thereby reduced to variations on bourgeois society, much less to variations on each other. It may be useful, even necessary, to elaborate the ways in which all modern societies correspond, but not at the expense of careful attention to essential differences. And as with societies in their political-economic aspect, so in their cultural. Simpson, we fear, is once more in danger of conceding too much to that "middle-class" interpretation of the Old South which he has so long and brilliantly contributed to demolishing.

Skillfully invoking two celebrated essays on the phenomenology of slavery—Jefferson's "Eighteenth Query" in *Notes on the State of Virginia* and Hegel's "Lordship and Bondage" in *The Phenomenology of Mind*—Simpson makes slavery the expression of the dark side of the Self, on which southern society presumably centered. But the burden of his decades of interpretation of the Old South as a slave society compels stern modification of his own modification. Tate was not entirely wrong in seeing that society as family-centered, in contrast to the bourgeois society of the North and the Atlantic world generally. Nor was he entirely wrong in seeing that society as heir to Europe's prerevolutionary Christian civilization. As first approximations of a complex and internally rent reality, these judgments serve well. But Tate was wrong to pretend, in his more flamboyant passages, that the Old South could be understood wholly in such terms and that its spiritual life and ethos largely escaped contamination. He knew better, as his private correspondence makes clear, but he was interested in remaking the modern world, not in historical precision. The price he paid for his liberties with history, and the price paid by Weaver and the Agrarians generally, was to reduce slavery to a blemish on southern society, a problem, an unfortunate accident, and thereby to obscure slaveholding as the essence of the society they revered.

Simpson's determination to unearth the ideological and psychic contradictions in what he clearly affirms as a novel slave society leads him to the brink of uncharacteristic polemical excess. The southern assertion of Self, with its attempt to establish slavery as a possible foundation for Mind, had a special character that marked it off from its bourgeois rivals in ways that Simpson reveals throughout his work. But those ways were not disembodied creations of Mind nor even solely direct projections of an attempted assimilation of slavery to Mind. They were also products of a political economy based on the master-slave relation that created a world of material reality as well as of social ideal. Tate, Weaver, and the remarkable southern conservatives whose thought has been a jewel of twentieth-century American letters—even if not yet recognized as such in New York and its colonies—paid dearly for their contempt for the materialist interpretation of history, and their historical judgment remained suspended among ideal constructs. Simpson has transcended their performance as historians and has established himself as our greatest cultural historian of the South by focusing his clear eye on the social relations that shaped political, economic, and cultural life. But he will, we trust, not cavil at our saying that he remains heir to the thought of those whose historical performance he has transcended. If he has built on their impressive accomplishments, he has also clung to their essential idealism. He notes that the intellectuals assimilated slavery to Mind, with fateful consequences.

No doubt. But they did so only after their own assimilation to a master class for which slavery was, above all, the decisive form of its power.

The temptation of idealism haunts Simpson much as the temptation of Mind haunted the antebellum southerners. For Simpson's subject is Mind and its products. The bourgeois culture that shapes us all has ensconced Mind as its centerpiece and standard. Under such conditions, how can mere mind resist that lure? Under such conditions, how do we resist the compelling insight that history itself reduces to Mind's fabrication? The problem lies less in that recognition of the fundamental subjectivity and, hence, ultimate isolation of the individual mind than in its own kind of totalitarian pretensions. Systematic idealism has built prisons that rival those of mere material life. For Mind, in assimilating history and the world to itself, denies not merely the countervailing force of material reality, but the consciousness of other minds. Simpson at his customary best grasps that danger and the tensions it pretends to obliterate or transcend. History, whether of social relations, which are the historical form of material conditions, or of intellectual relations, which are the historical form of the relations among minds, will not down. The illusion of history as the mere product of Mind constitutes the great deception that consists in taking Mind at its false word that it has subsumed all minds to itself. In the end, the deception lies in labeling interpretation as Truth. As the most skilled of interpreters, Simpson in particular should recognize the temptation of Mind as precisely temptation. Only on condition that we find the language with which to restore history to its proper role as the whetstone of Mind—or perhaps as its opposing magnetic pole—can we harness the revolutionary implications of the bourgeois dream of Mind to the service of a society capable of anchoring it.

Antebellum southern culture, as a distinct strand in bourgeois culture, wrestled with the angel—or demon—of Mind. Yet, its sense of its own history survived Mind's reductionism through its explicit and extreme subordination of some to others. Confusion persists among those who fear that to justify this history's role in the life of the culture means to justify slavery. Simpson unambiguously says no. Perhaps that no has strained his empathy for those who in pressing the claims of history have also implicitly defended oppression or, perhaps worse, abstracted from it completely. Yet again, his understandable admiration for the heights of Western culture may have led him to accept somewhat uncritically its own terms. Simpson, more than any other critic, has penetrated the nature of southern society. The clarity of his gaze, more even than any of his discrete judgments, testifies to the unique power of a mind in contest with other minds—with the history that never totally succumbs to its particular vision.

Notes

1. The development of Simpson's interpretation of the Old South may be traced most conveniently through three of his books: *The Man of Letters in New England and the South: Essays on the Literary Vocation in America* (Baton Rouge, 1973); *The Dispossessed Garden: Pastoral and History in Southern Literature* (Athens, 1975); and *The Brazen Face of History: Studies in the Literary Consciousness in America* (Baton Rouge, 1980).

2. Simpson, *Man of Letters*, 83.

3. For an elaboration of this view see Elizabeth Fox-Genovese and Eugene D. Genovese, *Fruits of Merchant Capital: Slavery and Bourgeois Property in the Rise and Expansion of Capitalism* (New York, 1983), and especially Elizabeth Fox-Genovese, "Antebellum Southern Households: A New Perspective on a Familiar Question," *Review* [Fernand Braudel Center, SUNY-Binghamton], VII (1984), 215–53. A much-expanded version of this essay will appear in Elizabeth Fox-Genovese, *Within the Plantation Household* (Chapel Hill, forthcoming).

4. Simpson, *Man of Letters*, 83.

5. This emergent communitarianism is analyzed with respect to legal theory and practice in Mark V. Tushnet, *The American Law of Slavery, 1810–1860: Considerations of Humanity and Interest* (Princeton, 1981).

6. Simpson, *Man of Letters*, 239.

7. George Tucker's contributions to economic analysis were among the very few by antebellum Americans praised or even noticed in Joseph A. Schumpeter's magisterial *History of Economic Analysis* (New York, 1954), 519, 521–22, 714. For divergent interpretations of Tucker's attitude toward slavery see Robert Colin McLean, *George Tucker: Moral Philosopher and Man of Letters* (Chapel Hill, 1961), and Tipton R. Snavely, *George Tucker as Political Economist* (Charlottesville, 1964).

8. For an elaboration see Eugene D. Genovese and Elizabeth Fox-Genovese, "Slavery, Economic Development, and the Law: The Dilemma of Southern Political Economists, 1800–1860," *Washington and Lee Law Review*, XLI (1984), 1–29.

9. Simpson, *Man of Letters*, 215.

10. *Ibid.*, 240.

11. Our view of the structural constraints on economic and social reform is elaborated in Eugene D. Genovese, *The Political Economy of Slavery: Studies in the Economy and Society of the Slave South* (New York, 1965).

12. Simpson, *Man of Letters*, 220.

13. See especially Henry Hughes, *Treatise on Sociology: Theoretical and Practical* (1854; rpr. New York, 1968).

14. Frederick A. Ross, *Slavery Ordained of God* (1857; rpr. Miami, Fla., 1969). For an elaboration of our views on these and related matters see Eugene D. Genovese and Elizabeth Fox-Genovese, "The Religious Ideals of Southern Slave Society," *Georgia Historical Quarterly*, LXX (1986), 1–16; and Eugene D. Genovese, *"Slavery Ordained of God": The Southern Slaveholders' View of Biblical History and Modern Politics* (Gettysburg, 1985).

15. Lewis P. Simpson, "The South's Reaction to Modernism: A Problem in the Study of Southern Letters," in Louis D. Rubin, Jr., and C. Hugh Holman (eds.), *Southern Literary Study: Problems and Possibilities* (Chapel Hill, 1975), 48–68.

16. Drew Gilpin Faust, *A Sacred Circle: The Dilemma of the Intellectual in the Old South, 1840–1860* (Baltimore, 1977). But see also her subsequent work, which, we believe, substantially modifies her interpretation—especially her fine Introduction to her anthology, *The Ideology of Slavery: Proslavery Thought in the Antebellum South, 1830–1860* (Baton Rouge, 1981).

17. The intellectual history of the Old South in relation to that of the Atlantic world has made great strides in recent years, thanks in no small part to the pioneering efforts of Michael O'Brien. See especially O'Brien, *A Character of Hugh Legaré* (Knoxville, 1985); O'Brien (ed.), *All Clever Men, Who Make Their Way: Critical Discourse in the Old South* (Fayetteville, Ark., 1982); and O'Brien and David Moltke-Hansen (eds.), *Intellectual Life in Antebellum Charleston* (Knoxville, 1986).

18. Fox-Genovese, *Southern Women*, Chapter 2.

19. For an elaboration of our interpretation of the southerners' conflicted attitude toward the Middle Ages and feudalism see Eugene D. Genovese, "The Southern Slaveholders' View of the Middle Ages," *Proceedings* of the Center for Medieval and Early Renaissance Studies, SUNY-Binghamton, forthcoming.

20. For an elaboration see Eugene D. Genovese, *Western Civilization Through Slaveholding Eyes: The Social and Historical Thought of Thomas Roderick Dew* (New Orleans, 1986).

21. Lewis P. Simpson, "The Sexuality of History," *Southern Review*, n.s., XX (1984), 802.

22. Simpson, *Brazen Face of History*, 71–72.

23. Simpson, "The South's Reaction to Modernism," in Rubin and Holman (eds.), *Southern Literary Study*, 55.

24. Simpson, *Brazen Face of History*, 265.

25. Lewis P. Simpson, "The Ferocity of Self: History and Consciousness in Southern Literature," *South-Central Review*, Nos. 1–2 (1984), 67.

26. *Ibid.*, 69.

27. For an elaboration see Elizabeth Fox-Genovese and Eugene D. Genovese, "Illusions of Liberation: The Psychology of Colonialism and Revolution in the Work of Octave Mannoni and Frantz Fanon," Chapter 9 of

Stephen Resnick and Richard Wolff (eds.), *Rethinking Marxism: Struggles in Marxist Theory: Essays for Harry Magdoff and Paul Sweezy* (Brooklyn, 1985); and Eugene D. Genovese, Introduction to *In Red and Black: Marxian Explorations of Southern and Afro-American History* (Rev. ed.; Knoxville, 1984), esp. xxvii–xliii.

SACVAN BERCOVITCH

The Modernity of American
Puritan Rhetoric

In his classic study of the mythology of the American South, Lewis Simpson describes the early-seventeenth-century immigrants to Virginia and Massachusetts as "small bands of reactionaries to modernity. The settlements they made in a 'new world' were in one way or another responses to the dispossession of the integral and authoritative community of an 'old world' by modern history. If they sowed the New World gardens with the seeds of modernity, the initial makers of these gardens did so unwittingly." Unwittingly, however, they did, at least in Massachusetts. Simpson finds that "the New England religious thrust" underwent a "significant metamorphosis" by the time of the Revolution, as in the writings of Timothy Dwight.

> In Dwight the image of the gardener in the garden as the man of God, the minister, in reaction against modernity, merges with that of the man of letters confronting modernity. Dwight combines the functions of poet and preacher, or more broadly, of religion and literature; in poems like *Greenfield Hill* and *The Triumph of Fidelity*, he becomes a transitional figure in the New England garden—herald, although not by his conscious design, of a shift in the concept of this garden. No longer will it exist in the New England imagination under a religious covenant but more nearly, if more loosely, under a literary one.[1]

My own sense of the New England imagination is a different one, and I take this opportunity to clarify the difference, in tribute to Simpson's sustained, enriching, and fortifying

influence on my work and that of a whole generation of
Americanists. What I want to argue is the profound modernity of Puritan New England from the start. The argument
might be made from a historical point of view. The English
Puritans helped establish the forms of a nascent capitalism
that transformed seventeeth-century England, as Christopher
Hill has shown, and the Massachusetts Bay Company, Incor-
porated, represented that modernist thrust *in extremis*.[2] Far
from seeking to escape the process of transformation, the
settlers of the 1630s—largely members of the middle classes
(lawyers, literate yeomen and artisans, merchants, craftsmen, and university-trained clergy)—imported wholesale
the emergent forces of what was to become American free-
enterprise society. I have discussed this elsewhere in general
cultural terms.[3] Here I want to address the issues of rhetoric
and vision, which Simpson has so richly elaborated with regard to both northern and southern writing. My own view,
centering on the literature of early New England, has long
been nourished by my engagement with his work, and it begins in a qualification of his distinction between the religious
and the literary imagination. Literary though Dwight's poems
are, they are grounded in religious language and concepts.
And religious though Dwight's Puritan predecessors were,
their vision of New England and the New World was quintessentially literary, a product of the myth-making imagination.
Dwight's poems express the Puritan aspect of a rather loose
association of colonies seeking to establish themselves as a
nation; the early New England writings express the effort of
a voluntary association of dissenters seeking to establish a
church-state modeled on the examples of Israel and early
Christianity. What links the two very different ventures—and
what makes both part of the modern world—is the literary-
religious vision of America.

The basic terms of that connection are set out in Dwight's
Greenfield Hill and, some twenty years earlier, in his poem
"America," which adapts Puritan typology to make the voyage of Columbus a foreshadowing of the New England migration and which ends with a millennial paean to the forces of
progress.[4] Almost a century before *Greenfield Hill*, a similar
design was set out by another, equally important "transitional figure in the New England garden." Looking back in
the autumn of 1692, the bicentennial of Columbus' transatlantic passage, to the "antiquities" of New England, Cotton

Mather recognized that those "twin migrations" were the key to a great design. To begin with, the voyage of 1492 was one of three shaping events of his "epocha," all of which occurred in rapid succession at the turn of the sixteenth century: "the *Resurrection of Literature,*" which had been made possible by the invention of the printing press (1456) and which in turn made the Bible accessible for the first time to the entire community of believers; the discovery of America, which opened a New World, hitherto shrouded in "heathen darkness," to the light of the gospel; and the Protestant Reformation, which signaled the dawn of a new era "after the long night of Catholic persecution." And in turn all three beginnings—textual, geographical, and spiritual— pointed forward to something grander still: the immanent renovation of all things in "a new heaven and new earth." A new beginning, then, and a newly urgent sense of an ending; and intermediate between these, at once linking them in time and confirming the overall design, like an apocalyptic play-within-a-play, was the story of New England. That, too, had its providential beginnings, culminating in 1630 when the *Arbella* fleet set sail for Massachusetts Bay. Mather describes the journey in language appropriate to its momentous spiritual-geographical-textual significance: "The *Church* of our Lord Jesus Christ, well compared unto a *Ship,* is now *victoriously* sailing round the Globe . . . [carrying] some thousands of *Reformers* into the Retirements of an *American Desart,* on purpose that . . . He might there, *To* them first, and then *By* them, give a *Specimen* of many Good Things, which He would have His Churches elsewhere aspire and arise unto. . . . *Geography* must now find work for a *Christiano-graphy* in . . . the HISTORY OF A NEW-ENGLISH ISRAEL . . . to anticipate the state of the *New Jerusalem.*"[5]

By the 1690s all this was cultural commonplace. Mather's recognition was a summing up of local tradition, the *re*cognition of a long-nurtured view of the colony's origin and mission. One reason for its persistence, from John Cotton to Cotton Mather, and from Mather to Dwight, was the power of the vision itself. Another reason was that on some basic level it told the truth. I mean not only the truth as rhetoric, the growth of New England as the Puritans perceived it, but historical truth, as the facts bore out their perception. For as Simpson has taught us, what we call history is rhetoric and fact entwined, inseparably the event interpreted and the interpretation become event. To deny the significance of the one in favor of a "factual" account is as misleading as to deny the other in favor of a spiritual "deeper meaning." History is not different from vision, but the dialectic between the two primary meanings of vision, what is seen out there and how we see it, the dynamic interaction between what forces itself into our view and the view by which we force it to conform to our habits of perception. So understood, Mather's re-cognition is interchangeably the past seen under the aspect of prophecy and prophecy redefined through what historians now consider to be three central factors in the making of the modern world: the invention of the printing press, the discovery of America, and the growth of Protestantism.

Of the three, the invention of the printing press, along with "the resurrection of literature," is most obviously an example of the connection between rhetoric and fact. "Gutenberg's galaxy," as Marshall McLuhan termed it, marks a turning point as decisive in cultural history as the Copernican revolution in the history of science.[6] It has particular relevance to the New England Puritans because of their extraordinary reliance on texts. They were not only, like all Puritans, a self-declared people of the Book. They were a community that invented its identity *ex verbo*, by the word, and continued to assert that identity throughout the seventeenth century, expanding, modifying, and revising it in a procession of sermons, exhortations, and declarations, histories and hagiographies, covenants and controversies, statements and restatements of purpose—a stream of rhetorical self-definition unequaled by any other community of its kind (and proportionately, perhaps of any kind). That mode of identity they bequeathed to the nation that was to usurp the symbol of America for itself. Dwight's "America" (1771) and Joel Barlow's *Vision of Columbus* (1787) were landmarks in that process, but their antecedents include Nathaniel Ward's *Humble Cobler of Aggawam in America* (1647) and, above all, Mather's *Magnalia Christi Americana* (1693–1702). Not accidentally, it was the New England Puritans who first used the name *American* to refer to European immigrants, rather than (like other immigrants) to the continent's native inhabitants. The legacy of the Puritan vision, as the first-begotten corporate offspring of the printing press, was a rationale, a technique, and (in the material sense of the word) a *process* whereby a community could constitute itself by publication, declare itself a nation by verbal fiat, define its past, present, and future by proclamation, and justify its definition in epic histories, like Mather's *Magnalia* and Dwight's *Conquest of Canaan*, which in one form or another translated geography into Christianography.

I mean Christianography in a broader literary sense than Mather intended, but his religious meaning applies as well. The Puritan vision was also the offspring of the two other germinal events he refers to: the discovery of America and the growth of Protestantism. It was an unlikely mixed marriage at the start. The discovery of America was preeminently a secular venture, a process of exploration and appropriation empowered by what scholars have come to call the forces of modernization: capitalist enterprise, state nationalism, and the expansion of Western European forms of society and culture throughout the world. So considered, "America" meant the triumph of European imperialism. It was an act of naming that doubly certified the invaders' control of the continent: it meant control by brute power (land-grabbing, enslavement, genocide) and control by symbol and trope. "America" denoted far more than the Italian con-man entrepreneur whose falsified sightings, once published, claimed the terra incognita for the Spanish throne. "America" entitled a carnival of European fantasies. It meant the fabled land of gold, the enchanted Isles of the West, springs of eternal youth, and "lubberlands" of ease and plenty. It verified theories of "natural man" and "the state of nature." It promised opportunities for realizing utopia, for unlimited riches and mass conversions, for the return to pastoral arcadia, for implementing schemes for moral and social perfection. Columbus thought that this new continent, providentially set between the cultured West and ancient East, had been the actual site of Eden. Later explorers and settlers, translating the myths of biblical geography into the landmarks of Renaissance geomythology, spoke of America as a second Eden, inhabited by pagan primitives (or perhaps the ten lost Hebrew tribes) awaiting the advent of civilization.

History and rhetoric: conquest by arms and conquest by the word—the "discovery of America" is the modern instance par excellence of how these two kinds of violence are entwined; how metaphor becomes fact, and fact, metaphor; how the realms of power and myth can be reciprocally sustaining; and how that reciprocity can encompass widely disparate outlooks. The same thing may be said about the rise of Protestantism, though from a wholly different perspective. Protestantism was from its origins a spiritual movement. It began as a protest against the worldliness of the Roman Catholic church—against the Catholic emphasis on temporal authority (as in the papacy), geographic locale (the Holy Roman Empire), and mercenary practices, from the selling of indulgences to political alliances. According to the early Reformers, Catholicism had set itself, historically and rhetorically, as a mediator between God and his people, whereas Christianity demanded a leap from history to the timeless and a faith free of merely rhetorical devices (scholasticism, church ritual, institutional dogma). It demanded, above all, an unmediated relation between the believer and Christ, the one true Mediator—which was to say, between the believer, on one hand, and, on the other, Christ as he manifested himself (through grace) in the believer's soul, and as he was manifest for all to see in the Bible (both the Old Testament, prophetically, and the New). *Sola fides* and *sola scriptura*, the primacy of personal faith and the supreme authority of scripture: upon these twin principles Protestantism was established. But once established, it, too, like every other venture in transcending human limitations, found itself entangled in the webs of history and rhetoric.

Scholars have discussed that process of entanglement from various angles, including those of virtually every term associated with the discovery of America: capitalist enterprise, nationalism, and the expansion of Western forms of culture. Indeed, in this case as in others, the very impulse toward transcendence may be traced to the needs of a certain historic moment and the logic of certain rhetorical modes. For my present purpose, I limit myself to one aspect of the process: the Protestant view of history. For in spite of their emphasis on the individual (*sola fides*), the Protestants identified themselves collectively, as a church or association of churches, in opposition to Roman Catholicism. And through their emphasis on the Bible (*sola scriptura*), they identified themselves temporally, as part of the gradual progress of God's people, from the chosen Israelites to the New Christian Israel to the "latter-day" Israel that would usher in the millennium. The main text for that divine plan, the Book of Revelation, spoke in figures or types of an "elect nation" that in the "last days" would defeat "Antichrist, the Beast of

Rome," and so prepare the way for the Second Coming. That in any case was Martin Luther's view of Reformation history. For a time he identified Germany as the elect nation, and though he later abandoned that particular hope, he and the other founding Reformers retained the basic tenets of his historiography. Protestantism, they declared, was the true church; Catholicism, the Antichrist; and the conflict between these was the central action of this final period of time, attended by all the long-awaited "signs and wonders" (political and natural as well as ecclesiastical) of the Apocalypse.[7]

After its initial spiritual protest, then, Protestantism returned to history with a vengeance. But it was a special kind of history, sacred as distinct from secular. It was the story not of mankind but of God's "peculiar people," the covenanted saints who constituted the real subject of the unfolding drama of redemption. Basically, that is, Protestant rhetoric retained its traditional Christian roots—remained grounded in the belief that Christ's kingdom was not of this world—and so could break free, if necessary, of any national specificity. Thus, Luther could reject the concept of national calling without qualifying his vision of universal progress. Thus, too, English Protestants of the late sixteenth century could abandon their revision of Luther's concept—their chauvinist rhetoric of England as elect nation—without in any way modifying their allegiance to the Reformation. It should be added that the rhetoric itself remained a force in the development of modern nationalisms. It would surface again in England under the Puritan Commonwealth (1642–1660) and later in the imperial claims of Victoria's "British Israel." In Germany it informs Hegel's encomia to the Prussian state and (in our century) the millennialist *Sturm und Drang* of the Third Reich. But in all cases the concept of national mission retains the imprint of its universalist origins. Prussia's decline did no basic damage to Hegelians' faith in the progress of the World-Spirit (just as, a century later, a failed communist revolution in any single nation would not basically contravene Marx's inverted-Hegelian dialectics of the classless society). Milton could abandon the dreams of Cromwell's Revolution—as the English Romantics later turned from *their* political millenarianism—without forgoing his faith that New Jerusalem would one day renovate England's green and pleasant land.

The immigrant Puritans of 1630 shared this ambiguous universalist-nationalist outlook. Broadly speaking, they represented one of three Puritan groups of the time. The largest, most eclectic of these groups were the Presbyterians, who sought to purify the country at large to a state worthy of its special calling. The smallest of the three groups, the Separatists, took the opposite course. They purified their faith to the point where they refused allegiance to any institutional authority, including that of the English Protestant church, whether Anglican or Presbyterian. Instead, they hoped to join the progress of the "universal invisible church" in small congregations, composed exclusively of "visible saints." Some remained in England; others fled persecution to Amsterdam and then, in the case of the Plymouth Pilgrims, to the New World. The Massachusetts Bay immigrants of 1630 sought a "middle way" between these extremes. In doing so, they meant not to compromise but to perfect. They set out to combine what seemed to them in each case a partial gesture at reformation, in church and in state. Accordingly, they proclaimed their "purified church-state" a model for all Christendom. They were congregationalists in a "federal" or "national" covenant; a community of "visible saints" gathered for a venture in history; de facto Separatists who insisted not only on their vital connection to English Protestantism but (through this) on their central role in the worldwide struggle against the Antichrist.[8]

The European connection thus opened to the connection, through New England's mission, between the Old World and the New. And that connection in turn opened up the meaning (again, mediated by the concept of New England's mission) of the New World as "America." It seems a logical sequence in retrospect, but it was neither natural nor inevitable. The Puritan vision was not brought to New England aboard the *Arbella*; nor was it a flower of the New World wilderness. Rather, it was the product of certain unforeseen historical exigencies and certain possibilities for interpretation inherent in Puritan rhetoric.

The immigrants of the 1630s do not seem to have had a distinct vision of the continent at large. Their focus was on the Reformation already under way: New England was to be a "model of Christian charity" for Protestants abroad, "a city set upon a hill" as a beacon to Europe. These phrases come from John Winthrop's justly famous lay sermon aboard the *Arbella*, and when he added that "the eyes of all people are upon us," he was thinking mainly of the peoples of England, Germany, Holland, and other Protestant countries.[9] His vision was transatlantic, rather than American; it tended toward the universalist aspect of the immigrants' ambiguously universalist-nationalist outlook. By placing New England at the apex of history, Winthrop was admitting its dependency on the Old World. It was not enough to set up "a specimen of the New Jerusalem"; *their* eyes had to be on it, and their hearts and minds ready to follow. So it was that Cromwell's revolution lured back a considerable number of immigrants. So it was, too, that after the failure of the English Puritan Commonwealth—and with it the waning of apocalyptic fervor throughout Protestant Europe—New Englanders found themselves trapped in an embarrassing paradox. They had declared themselves the advance guard of the Reformation, committed themselves to a worldwide mission, and invested their credentials of authority in scriptural prophecy. In 1660 the vision was intact, the community prospering, and their authority still dominant; but to all appearances history had betrayed them. They were a beacon unheeded by the world, a city on a hill that no one noticed, or noticed only to scorn. In Perry Miller's words, they "were left alone with America."[10]

Not entirely alone, however; for the rhetoric they carried with them offered a ready means of compensation. It allowed them by scriptural precedent to consecrate their "outcast," "exiled," "wilderness condition." If they could not compel the Old World to yield to their vision, they could interpret the New in their own image. That interpretation was implicit from the start. I said above that Winthrop emphasized the universalist aspect of the Protestant outlook, but the "national" or "federal" aspect—the sense of the importance of *this* people in *this* locale—was there as well. New England was to be an example for others by providing a model in its own right. From the opening reference to the immigrants as "Christian Tribes" to his concluding comparison of himself with Moses, exhorting Israel into Canaan, Winthrop was subtly redefining the immigrants' identity. Genealogically, of course, they were *English* Puritans, but as a *New* English community, he implied, they were a new chosen people, "knit together as one man in Christ" and together

"commissioned by the God of Israel" to secure a new promised land, there to progress toward a better state "in wisdom,
power, goodness, and truth than formerly" existed.[11]

Progress and *New Canaan:* these terms, though relatively muted in Winthrop's address, were nonetheless organic to his vision. They became increasingly prominent as
the first-generation leaders consolidated the enterprise and
defended its claims against an increasingly indifferent or
hostile world. Gradually, in promotional tracts and apologias
for the church-state, in evangelical treatises, sermons on Indian conversion, guides to the saint's preparation for salvation, and exegeses on Bible prophecy, in histories, "prog-
nostics," poetry, and polemics against sectarians at home
and opponents abroad, from the Separatists to the Anglicans,
the colonists drew out the implications of their New England Way.[12]

In doing so, they laid the ground for the great rhetorical
shift that once and for all resolved the paradox of vanguard
isolation. Having been left alone with America, the second-
and third-generation Puritans felt free to incorporate Renaissance geomythology, as it suited their purposes, into their
own vision. Explicitly and implicitly, they adapted the European images of America (land of gold, second paradise, utopia, "primitivism" as moral regeneration) to fit the Protestant view of progress. And having thus taken possession of
the rhetoric of America, they proceeded one crucial step further. Recasting the relational aspect of their vision, changing
it from a transatlantic to a transcontinental direction, they
situated the Protestant apocalypse—or what amounted to
the same thing, the Protestant road to the apocalypse—in
the New World.

We can hardly overestimate the importance of that astonishing westward leap of the imagination. It was an achievement comparable in its way to the two great rhetorical shifts
on which it built: the Hebrews' redefinition (by verbal fiat)
of Canaan—territory, name, "antiquities," and all—as *their*
country; and the imperialism of the *figura* or type, by which
the Church Fathers declared that the Old Testament, the
story of Israel in its entirety, from Adam through Abraham
and David to the Messiah, heir of David, really belonged
to Christ.

The Hebrews' triumph was nationalist, the self-assertion
of a scattered community in exile; the triumph of early

Christianity was universalist, the self-assertion of marginal groups of believers. The universalist-nationalist vision of New England arose out of similar circumstances. Having been left behind by Europe, the Puritans proceeded to recapture it for themselves, rhetorically, as part of all that was not-America—the benighted "Old World," awaiting its redemption by the "mighty works of Christ in America." Confronted with the uncertain meaning of their locale, the Puritans discovered the New World in scripture—not literally (like Columbus) as the lost Eden, but figurally (in the manner of the Church Fathers discovering Noah in Moses and both in Jesus) as the second paradise foreseen by all the prophets. New Canaan was not a metaphor for them, as it was for other colonists. It was the New World reserved from eternity for God's latter-day elect nation, which he would gather as choice grain from the chaff of Europe-Babylon-Egypt, so that "He might there, to them first, and then by them, give a specimen of many good things" to come. In short, driven back by history upon the resources of language, the second- and third-generation New Englanders united geography, textuality, and the spirit in what amounted to a new symbology, centered on the vision of America.

The decisive decades in this development were the 1660s and 1670s, when a series of crises threatened to put an end to the enterprise altogether. First, the restoration of King Charles endangered not only the colonial charter but Puritan rule. Next, the apparent decline of religion among the immigrants' children—what the clergy bewailed as the "degeneracy of the rising generation"—forced important modifications in the New England Way. In the course of this turmoil, the last of the immigrant leaders died, and anxieties of succession became a main theme of pulpit and press. Then in the mid-1670s the several Indian nations in the region allied to reclaim their land, in a sudden attack that threatened to decimate New England from Stockbridge to Boston.

The literary result of these "Wars of the Lord" (as the ministry termed all the various events) was the first native flowering of New England mythology, through the first English-language genre developed in the New World, the American Puritan jeremiad. The immigrants had imported the jeremiad as an immemorial mode of lament over the corrupt ways of the world. Their heirs transformed it into a vehicle of social continuity. The lament continued, but here it served to celebrate the trials of a people in covenant. Here as nowhere else, the clergy explained, God's afflictions were like a "refining fire," intended to purify and strengthen, or like the punishment meted out by a loving father, the token of his special care. "God's controversy with New England," wrote the poet Michael Wigglesworth in 1662, *ensured* the colony's success. In the words of the Reverend Arthur Dimmesdale in *The Scarlet Letter*, it signaled "a high and glorious destiny for this newly chosen people of the Lord."[13]

Dimmesdale is an immigrant minister, of course, here delivering the election-day sermon of 1649. This was not inaccurate on Hawthorne's part: there were ample first-generation foreshadowings of the American Puritan jeremiad, from John Cotton's *God's Promise to His Plantations* (1630) through Edward Johnson's apocalyptic *Wonder-Working Providence of Sion's Savior in New England* (1649–1654). But as a distinctive New World genre, the jeremiad was essentially a ritual of continuity through generational rededication. It required a set of *local* precedents, a pride of tribal heroes to whom the community could look back in reverence and from whom, therefore, it could inherit its mission. The immigrants had imported the rhetoric; their children and grandchildren supplied the antiquities needed to make the rhetoric American. They enshrined their forebears in scriptural types, re-cognized them as giants of a golden age, like Virgil's legendary Trojans entering upon the future site of Rome. Winthrop could compare himself with Moses only by implication; Cotton had only the story of the pre-American Israel to illustrate the terms of "God's promise to His New World plantations." The next generations felt neither of these restrictions, personal or historical. They could sanctify Winthrop as the New England Moses—or the American Nehemiah (after the prophet who rebuilt the walls of Jerusalem)—and Cotton as the American Abraham, Joshua, and John the Divine combined. These and other immigrant leaders they canonized as founding fathers, translated their Atlantic crossing as the Great Migration, antitype of the Hebrew exodus, and consecrated their church-state as a venture that, *because* it fulfilled Old World prophecy, was wholly an event of this New World. It led by promise from New England *then* to New England as it *would be*, when the "American desert" would reveal itself to all people as the "Theopolis Americana, the Holy City, the streets whereof are pure gold."[14] It was a mission into America, by the American Israel, for America first and then the world.

So it was that the second- and third-generation colonists completed the founders' errand into rhetoric: they gave the Puritan vision a local habitation and a name. What they achieved has become something so familiar by now, so much a matter of common historical sense, that it is difficult to convey its sheer audacity and sweep. Only once afterward was there anything at all comparable with it in the culture. That was the consecration of the "nation's founding fathers" by the generation following the Revolution—a myth that relegated the colonial immigrants, by figural rite, to the role of *Ur*-fathers, like Noah to Moses and both to Jesus—and clearly the rhetoric of this second founding was much indebted to that of the first. The Puritans made three lasting contributions to the American Way. First, they justified the New World in its own right. Other colonists and explorers brought utopian dreams to the New World, but in doing so, they claimed the land (New Spain, New France, Nova Scotia) as European Christians, by virtue of the superiority of Christian European culture. They justified their invasion of America either through European concepts of progress or else (as in Virginia) through European dreams of agrarian harmony, which constituted a reaction against progress. The Puritans denied the very fact of invasion by investing "America" with the meanings both of progress and of "primitive" harmony and then identifying themselves as the people peculiarly destined to bring those meanings to life. "Other peoples," John Cotton pointed out in 1630, "have their land by providence; we have it by promise."[15] The next generation of New Englanders drew out the full import of his distinction. They were not claiming America by conquest, they explained; they were reclaiming what by promise belonged to them, as the Israelites had once reclaimed Canaan or (in spiritual terms) as the church had reclaimed the name of Israel.

By that literal-prophetic act of reclamation the Puritans raised the New World into the realm of *figura*. "America" for them was neither an outpost nor a backwater of Europe. Nor was it simply an open stage for Europeans to experiment on in models of church-state, quick ways to get rich, or schemes for social and moral perfection. All of these things might well happen in the New World, but only because the continent itself had a unique meaning involving a special kind of

identity—rooted not so much in the past as in the future—
an identity *in process.* Beginning with New England, continuing into the wilderness, and culminating as the New
World Jerusalem, America was *"pulchèrrima inter mulieres,*
the youngest and loveliest of Christ's brides."[16] It was the
last, best hope of mankind, whether mankind knew it or not.

That vision of the New World was the harvest of the Renaissance rhetoric of discovery. It marked the Puritans' first
contribution to American identity; the second was inextric-
ably bound up with it. I refer to the corporate ideal through
which they resolved the ambiguities of their universalist-
nationalist venture. For as their opponents were quick to
point out, this self-proclaimed latter-day Israel was unlike
any other community, sacred or secular. It was not limited
by genealogy, like Israel of old. Nor was it circumscribed by
territory, tradition, and custom, like modern England or Germany. Nor was it a wandering congregation of Christians
seeking a haven in the world's wilderness, like the Plymouth
Pilgrims or the Pennsylvania Quakers. And yet, the Puritans
insisted on incorporating all of these elements: the tribal
sense of Israel, the designation "national," the importance of
place, and the Separatist emphasis on the voluntarist, personal, and spiritual bond of "Christian brotherhood." Their
key to incorporation, I have suggested, was the Protestant
concept of national election. But the concept itself was by
definition uncharted. It signified an entity that had never before existed: a community designed for (and confined to) the
"end-time." That lack of specificity, that absence of precedence or principle of delimitation—of *frontiers,* in the European sense of the term—left the colonists open to attack
from all quarters. But the same conceptual vagueness that
made them vulnerable to historical analysis also freed them,
rhetorically, to bring together what tradition and common
sense had declared fundamentally separate: church and state;
sacred and secular; a community gathered by voluntarist,
spiritual commitment, and a community defined by locale,
local origins, and territorial errand.

In retrospect, we can see how these ambiguities were latent in the idea of national election, inherent in the Reformers' historical re-cognition of their spiritual protest. But the
ambiguities presented themselves as a problem to European
Protestant nationalists. Elect nationhood was an interpretation, after all. As a textual abstraction it stood apart from

whatever historically formed nationality it was meant to identify; as a national designation it was preempted by more deeply rooted, pre-Reformation, even pre-Christian bonds of community. The Reformers tried to solve the problem by a rhetorical ambiguity. They spoke of the covenant of national election as being interchangeably national or federal. I stress the federal alternative to convey its distinctively Protestant character. National identity antedated Protestantism, but federal identity was a sort of wild seed of the Reformation, a by-blow of regional pride and apocalyptic hope that never found a stable home in the Old World. Despite its reappearance in various guises of chauvinism, it remained a suspect and disputed foster child in the ancient European family of nations, wandering uneasily from Luther's Germany to Calvin's Geneva to John Foxe's England—an identity in search of a community—until, in the westward course of empire, it found its proper home in Puritan New England.

For as Cotton Mather or Timothy Dwight might have put it, the dream of national election was heaven-sent for the Massachusetts Bay colonists. As nonseparating congregationalists they had effectually dehistoricized their venture. Their effort at intellectual synthesis ("visible saints," "church-state") deprived them of their concrete connections with the past—all their English antiquities, except those inscribed in Protestant historiography, just as the past they invented for America deprived the continent's native inhabitants of *their* antiquities. They were a community in search of an identity commensurate with their New World mission. When they adopted the rhetoric of federalism as their "peculiar" social bond, the covenant of national election flowered, and the elect nation of Jeremiah, Isaiah, and John became incarnate in the first wholly Protestant contribution to modern nationalism, the American Israel.

Nationalism is not the accurate term for the colonial Puritans, of course, except as a figure of speech, a metaphor for the federal model of community. But then, the same may be said about the designation *American*. The federal metaphor was designed to replace the communal past with a visionary history of the future. It signified a community in process and therefore released from the usual restrictions of genealogy, territory, and tradition—a "nation born at once," "in a day," as the Bible put it, for the express purpose of making "the desert blossom as the rose" (Isaiah 66:8, 35:1).

Thus, New England came to signify a "Way," an "errand *into* the [indefinite American] wilderness." It denoted a people that was neither purely religious nor merely national, but that nonetheless combined both these terms in a voluntary sacred-secular contract that merged the principles of *sola fides* and *sola scriptura*, the inward spiritual road to salvation and the communal road in time and space to the millennium. Thus, too, the ritual I mentioned of generational rededication focused on the past in order to elicit the anxieties of progress. To recognize the meaning of New England, as John Danforth explained in his great election-day address of 1670, was to understand the colony *now* in terms of its cause and end, in relation to its New World antiquities and to the New World Jerusalem, of which those antiquities were a specimen. Inevitably, this was to realize (through an inward sight of sin) "how far we have fallen" and at the same time to realize (through prophetic insight) "how far we must rise to make ourselves worthy of our errand."[17] And that double sense of shortcoming implied its own remedy: an *act* both personal and public, through which the inward turning to the spirit issued in a social commitment to progress.

It has been argued that the rhetorical assertions of the immigrants betray feelings of nostalgia and guilt. If so, it may be said of their successors that they managed to redirect such feelings into a positive anxiety about the future. Turning nostalgia into a commemoration of the fathers' "pristine wilderness," and guilt into an incentive toward what still remained to be done, their rituals celebrate a federal identity expanding, in a movable symbolic-territorial feast, from regional myth to continental prophecy.

Danforth's *Brief Recognition of New England's Errand into the Wilderness* is characteristic in this regard. It echoes and is echoed in turn by a long procession of exhortations, which together constitute a triumph of the colonial Puritan imagination.[18] To some extent they persisted as a literary genre, through intertextual connections from one ritual occasion to the next—on fast and thanksgiving days, days of humiliation, election days, and days of covenant renewal. But above all, they persisted for functional reasons, as an organic expression of the community. They were the *cultural* issue of a venture dedicated to the proposition that prophecy is history antedated, and history, postdated prophecy. They represented a community in crisis and therefore using crisis as a strategy of social revitalization; a settlement in peril and therefore drawing strength from adversity, transition, and flux; a company-in-covenant deprived by history of their identity and therefore using their self-declared newness to create a vision of America that reconceived history at large (including that of the Old World) as hinging on their failure or success.

The legacy of this ritual mode may be traced through virtually every major event in the culture, from the Great Awakening through the Revolution and the westward movement to the Civil War, and from that Armageddon of the Republic to the Cold War and the Star Wars of our latter days. At every point, the rituals of generational rededication build on the distance between fact and promise; at every point they interpret that distance in terms of "errand" or its various equivalents ("manifest destiny," "continuing revolution," "new frontiers"); and at every point the errand is defined as the special obligation of the "Israel of our time," federally covenanted as "the nation of futurity" to be "the heir of the ages" and "the haven for God's outcasts and exiles"—"a new breed of humans called an American," destined "to begin the world over again" and "to build a land here that will be for all mankind a shining city on a hill." [19]

These phrases come from a variety of Americans, as distant in time from each other as John Adams and Ronald Reagan, and as different in mind and imagination as Herman Melville, the manifest destinarian John L. O'Sullivan, and that forerunner of the Moral Majority, Charles Grandison Finney. My purpose in running their words together is not to blur the differences. On the contrary, it is to highlight the disparate uses to which the Puritan vision lent itself. These include religious as well as literary uses, and as a rule both simultaneously, such as in the rationalist-evangelical (or libertarian-millennialist) poetry of the Revolution. Perhaps the best-known example is Philip Freneau's "Rising Glory of America":

> Here independent power shall hold her sway,
> And public virtue warm the patriot breast:
> No traces shall remain of tyranny,
> And laws, a pattern to the world beside,
> Be here enacted first. . . .

. . . .

A new Jerusalem, sent down from heaven,
Shall grace our happy earth—perhaps this land,
Whose ample bosom shall then receive, tho' late,
Myriads of saints, with their immortal King,
To live and reign on earth a thousand years,
Thence call'd *Millennium*. . . .
. . . .
. . . A Canaan here,
Another Canaan shall excel the old. . . .
. . . .
Such days the world,
And such AMERICA, thou first shalt have,
When ages yet to come have run their round,
And future years of bliss alone remain.

Freneau's poem was written in 1771; six years later, during the War of Independence, his friend Timothy Dwight wrote what was to become the unofficial national anthem through the Revolutionary and Federalist periods:

Columbia, Columbia, to glory arise,
The queen of the world, and the child of the skies!
Thy genius commends thee; with rapture behold,
While ages on ages, thy splendors unfold.
Thy reign is the last, and the noblest of time.

He amplified this figural vision in his pastoral *Greenfield Hill*.

Yet there, even there, Columbia's bliss shall spring
Rous'd from dull sleep, astonish'd Europe sing,
O'er Asia burst the renovating morn,
And startled Afric in a day be born;
As, from the tomb, when great *Messiah* rose,
Heaven bloom'd with joy, and Earth forgot her woes,
His saints, thro' nature, truth and virtue spread,
And light, and life, the *Sacred Spirit* shed;
Thus, thro' all climes, shall Freedom's bliss extend,
The world renew, and death, and bondage, end;
All nations quicken with th' ecstatic power,
And one redemption reach to every shore.[20]

Hence the provocative implications in Simpson's distinction between sacred and secular imagining. What he shows eloquently to have been a decisive shift in the development of Virginia is precisely what did *not* happen in Massachusetts. Here it was a main function of the rhetoric of America, from its colonial origins, to blur or conflate the religious and the literary—to subsume the Old World scripture in the New World dream. And the persistence of that strategy, *mutatis mutandis,* across three centuries and more of turbulence and change is a remarkable testament to the modernizing impulse of the Puritan vision. Indeed, the Virginia contrast (if I may call it so) makes the Puritan achievement all the more remarkable. I think it is fair to say that while southerners were evolving their "vision of Virginia as a paradise, in contrast to a wilderness"—enclosing themselves in their paradoxical "pastoral garden of the chattel"—the colonial New Englander launched an errand *into* the wilderness that was the first and, as it turned out, the most successful effort in the West to consecrate the theory and practice of modern capitalism. Socially and economically, the Puritan vision issued in a federal nation "under God," committed to progress as prophecy, contract as covenant, expansion as destiny, and (through the primacy of personal faith) the divine right of self-possessive individualism. That is one reason, surely, why, when the southern "community would be destroyed as apostate to modern history . . . this destruction would be owing to the apostatic imagination of New England, the concentrated, most intense and furious expression of this imagination stemming from its power to summon back the Lord God of Hosts as the leader of a mission to purify the American garden of chattel slavery."[21]

Simpson's vivid image of the war between the apostates speaks directly to the qualification I would make. The apostasy of the South, he shows, occurred the moment Virginia abandoned its religious rhetoric of mission, "entered into modernity," and "began to evolve into a uniquely reactionary community." The apostasy of the North, I would argue, occurred the moment the spokesmen for Massachusetts *refused* to abandon their religious rhetoric, decided to shape it instead to the realities of a new economic world (so as to be able to turn or shape those realities to their purposes), and began to evolve into a self-declared "Israel of our time." By the 1860s, with "an unrivaled unanimity and fervor," this modern community could present its "struggle for the Union as a decisive religious battle."[22]

There is an important sense, however, in which this northern rhetoric, grounded though it was in a fusion of the literary and religious spheres, does conform to Simpson's distinction. I refer to the aesthetic "flowering of New England" in the mid-nineteenth century, and I think in particular of the internalized, adversarial, absolute "America" that inspired Emerson and his heirs—"the only true America," as Thoreau called it, which the major figures of the American Renaissance drew upon (or withdrew into) as an alternative to the dominant American Way. That alternative America is the third aspect I referred to of the Puritan legacy, and it has its roots in the last phase of the development of the New England Puritan vision. By the autumn of 1692, when Cotton Mather undertook his *Magnalia Christi Americana,* the church-state was defunct, and in his view New England had tragically abandoned its calling. The *Magnalia* affirms the vision *in spite of* social continuities; it reconstitutes the entire errand, from its antiquities in the Great Migration to its fulfillment in the millennium, *as rhetoric.* "I write the *Wonders* of the CHRISTIAN RELIGION, flying from the Depravations of *Europe,* to the *American Strand"*: with this double allusion to what he considered the main epics of classical and Reformation history, Virgil's *Aeneid,* the myth of Rome's founding, and Foxe's *Book of Martyrs,* the founding myth of England's national election, Mather began his would-be greater New World epic. Then he added, in a justly famous one-line paragraph of the General Introduction: "But whether *New England* may *Live* anywhere else or no, it must *Live* in our *History."* [23]

This poignant but defiant transvaluation of fact into trope may be seen as the logical end of the Puritan vision. The second-generation colonists had turned to rhetoric to compensate for the betrayal of the Old World. Mather took their strategy one step further: he transformed the rhetoric into compensation for the betrayal of New England. For him, too, "New England" was a conjunction of geography, scripture, and the spirit; he also created his symbology out of the rhetoric of discovery, the authority of the word, and the primacy of personal faith. But his aim in all this was not to clothe local history in myth. It was to preserve the myth from history. This was the aim, too, of many of his later works, as well as those of other Old Guard visionaries, all of which might have been titled, like Samuel Sewall's tract of 1697, *Phaenomena Quedam Apocalyptica; or, A Description of the New Heavens as It Makes to Those Who Stand upon the New Earth.*[24] It would seem an apt finale to what

I termed the apocalyptic play-within-a-play of "the history of New English Israel." With this anachronistic procession of cloud-capped America's passing unheeded into Yankee New England, the Puritan vision seems to come full circle. "Elect nation," "New World," "the wilderness," "peculiar people," "federal covenant," "New Canaan," "latter-day Israel"— all the foundations of the New England Way were literary-religious figures of speech. Conceived in rhetoric, they sprang to life for a season—a nation born *ex verbo* in a day—and then returned in due time to the realm of rhetoric.

There is a satisfying sense of closure in this view and a certain poetic justice as well. But it happens to be historically inaccurate. The fact is that the Puritan vision survived the demise of the church-state. Like Hawthorne's anachronistic Gray Champion, it returned as an agent of social cohesion, with "a gesture at once of encouragement and warning,"[25] at every stage of cultural transition—including, ironically, the transition from Puritan colony to Yankee province and, climactically, the transition from antebellum America to the Gilded Age of reconstruction, industrialization, incorporation, and the Dynamo. The fact is, too, that New England retained its mythic status as the origin of American identity (long after the region had lost its national importance), just as the telos it claimed to prefigure remained in one form or another (and quintessentially in scriptural form) inherent in the cloud-capped American dream. And the fact is, finally, that the strategy of Mather's *Magnalia*, his determination to make "history" of *his* Theopolis Americana—to bring interpretation to "life," whether it lived historically anywhere else or not—became a ritual mode of our literary tradition. What distinguishes our classic writers in this respect is what I called the distinguishing mark of the latter-day New England Puritans: unlike their European contemporaries and predecessors, they did not abandon the vision even when they were persuaded that the country had. Of course, the New Englanders of 1850 re-cognized the vision for their own literary-religious purposes: the wilderness became for them the expanding "open territories," the Great Desert or Garden of the West; they made the spirit consonant with Romantic consciousness; and they reconceived the text as a vaguer expression, at once more general and more subjective, of the principle of *sola scriptura*.

But here as elsewhere, re-cognition suggests the way a vision persists; it attests to the process of imaginative continuity *through* change, the dialectic between imaginative response and cultural reflex. Intrinsic to that process, from the Romantic period onward, was the spiritual use of geography as *American* nature, the geographic specificity of consciousness as *American* self-realization, and the sustained use of scripture as pre-text of *America*'s promise. That symbology our classic New England writers never disavowed. However universalist their outlook, however fixed they were on transcendence and the self, they invested the meaning of those concepts in the same federal vision. In their optative moods they spoke as unacknowledged representatives of America. In their despairing moods they interpreted the betrayal of the vision as the betrayal of all human aspirations—inverted millennium into doomsday, and mankind's best hope into its last. And more than that: the "America" that the Puritans bequeathed took on a sort of protean utopian force in our major writers—became variously a symbolic battleground; a visionary community "struggling against dispossession by modern history";[26] an ideal to which "true Americans," North and South, could always aspire in word because it could never be realized in fact; and an alternative *cultural* authority through which they could denounce (or even renounce) the United States. But here, too, rhetoric and history are inextricable. The Puritan vision of New England was the child of Protestantism, Renaissance exploration, and the printing press. But "America," as the single most potent cultural symbol of the modern world and also (in its various aesthetic-religious forms) as a symbolic center of our modernist literary tradition, was the discovery of Puritan New England.

Notes

1. Lewis P. Simpson, *The Dispossessed Garden: Pastoral and History in Southern Literature* (Athens, 1975), 1–2, 10, 13.

2. See, for example, Christopher Hill, *Puritanism and Revolution: Studies in the Interpretation of the English Revolution in the 17th Century* (London, 1958), 236.

3. See, for example, my "The Rites of Assent: Rhetoric, Ritual, and the Ideology of American Consensus," in Sam B. Girgus (ed.), *The American Self: Myth, Ideology, and Popular Culture* (Albuquerque, 1981), 5–42.

4. Timothy Dwight, *America; or, A Poem on the Settlement of the British Colonies* (New Haven, [1780?]).

5. Cotton Mather, *Magnalia Christi Americana; or, The Ecclesiastical History of New England, Books I and II*, ed. Kenneth B. Murdock (Cambridge, Mass., 1977), 118, 119, 93, 121, 123.

6. Marshall McLuhan, *The Gutenberg Galaxy: The Making of Typographic Man* (London, 1962), 6.

7. The biblical texts come from Rev. 2, 5, 11, 13, 15, 16, and 19; also from Old Testament prophecy (*e.g.*, Dan. 2, 10, and Hos. 3) and New Testament apocalyptica (*e.g.*, Luke 3:19 and 1 Tim. 4:1). The Protestant identification of Antichrist is standard after the mid-sixteenth century, *e.g.*, "ANTICHRIST, S. An Enemy to Christ. The papists" (John Butterworth, *A New Concordance to the Holy Scriptures . . . in Which . . . the Signification Is Given of All Proper Names* [Boston, 1848], 25). On the concept of the elect nation, see William Haller, *Foxe's Book of Martyrs and the Elect Nation* (London, 1963), and on Reformation historiography in general, see Constantinos A. Patrides, *The Phoenix and the Ladder: The Rise and Decline of the Christian View of History* (Berkeley, 1964).

8. For background on these specialized terms, see Edmund S. Morgan, *Visible Saints: The History of a Puritan Idea* (New York, 1963).

9. John Winthrop, "A Model of Christian Charity" (1630), in Edmund S. Morgan (ed.), *Puritan Political Ideas, 1558–1794* (New York, 1965), 90–95.

10. Perry Miller, *Errand into the Wilderness* (Cambridge, Mass., 1958), 16.

11. Winthrop, "Model of Christian Charity," in Morgan (ed.), *Puritan Political Ideas*, 84–91.

12. Some representative works (in the order of the genres listed in the text): Francis Higginson, *New England's Plantation* (London, 1630); Edward Winslow, *Good News from New England,* ed. E. Arber (1633; rpr. London, 1897); John Norton, *The Orthodox Evangelist* (London, 1654); Richard Mather, *Church Government and Church Covenant* (London, 1643); John Eliot, *The Christian Commonwealth* (London, 1659); Thomas Hooker, *The Soules Preparation for Christ* (London, 1638); Peter Bulkeley, *The Gospel-Covenant* (London, 1651); John Cotton, *The Churches Resurrection* (London, 1642) and *An Exposition upon the Thirteenth Chapter of the Revelation* (London, 1655); Ephraim Huit, *The Whole Prophecies of Daniel Explained* (London, 1644); William Aspinwall, *A Brief Description of the Fifth Monarchy* (London, 1653); Anne Bradstreet, "Dialogue Between Old England and New" (1642), in *The Works of Anne Bradstreet,* ed. J. Hensley (Cambrige, Mass., 1967), 185–87; John Cotton, *A Letter to Mr. [Roger] Williams,* ed. R. A. Guild (1634; rpr. Providence, R.I., 1866). Here and elsewhere I use short titles for Puritan materials.

13. Cotton Mather, *Magnalia Christi Americana,* ed. Thomas Robbins (2 vols.; Hartford, 1853–55), II, 487–579; Michael Wigglesworth, "God's Controversy with New England," in Alan Heimert and Andrew Delbanco (eds.), *The Puritans in America: A Narrative Anthology* (Cambridge, Mass., 1985), 231–36; Nathaniel Hawthorne, *The Scarlet Letter,* ed. Millicent Bell (New York, 1983), 332–33. In this section of the essay I make use of materials in my *American Jeremiad* (Madison, 1978), though I have altered my interpretation of them.

14. Cotton Mather, *Theopolis Americana: An Essay on the Golden Street of the Holy City* (Boston, 1710), 9. In this section of the essay I make use of materials in my *Puritan Origins of the American Self* (New Haven, 1975), again with a revised view of those materials.

15. John Cotton, *God's Promise to His Plantations* (London, 1630), reprinted in *Old South Leaflets* (8 vols.; Boston, [1896]), III, no. 53, p. 17.

16. Mather, *Theopolis Americana,* 16.

17. John Danforth, *A Brief Recognition of New England's Errand into the Wilderness,* in A. William Plumstead (ed.), *The Wall and the Garden: Selected Massachusetts Election Sermons* (Minneapolis, 1968), 57–62.

18. For example: John Higginson, *The Cause of God and His People* (Cambridge, Mass., 1663); William Stoughton, *New England's True Interest* (Cambridge, Mass., 1670); Urian Oakes, *New England Pleaded With* (Cambridge, Mass., 1673); James Allen, *New England's Choicest Blessing* (Boston, 1679); William Adams, *The Necessity of the Pouring Out of the Spirit* (Boston, 1679); Samuel Torrey, *A Plea* (Boston, 1683); John Whiting, *The Way of Israel's Welfare* (Boston, 1686); and a procession of sermons by Increase Mather from, say, *The Day of Trouble Is Near* (Cambridge, Mass., 1674) to *The Surest Way* (Boston, 1699).

19. Melville, *White-Jacket; or, The World in a Man-of-War,* ed. G. Thomas Tanselle (New York, 1983), 506; Charles Grandison Finney, *Lectures on Revivals of Religion* (Boston, 1835), 66–70; John Adams to Thomas Jefferson, October 9, 1878, in Lester J. Cappon (ed.), *The Adams-Jefferson Correspondence* (New York, 1971), xliv; Thomas Paine, *Representative Selections,* ed. Harry H. Clark (New York, 1961), 61; John L. O'Sullivan, "The Great Nation of Futurity," *United States Magazine and Democratic Review,* VI (1839), 427, 430; Daniel Webster, "The Bunker Hill Monument," in

The Works of Daniel Webster (Boston, 1857), I, 61; Lyman Beecher, *A Plea for the West* (Cincinnati, 1835), 177; Francis Wayland, "Encouragement to Religious Efforts," *American National Preacher,* V (1830), 44; Ronald Reagan, "Closing Statement [to televised presidential debate]," New York *Times,* September 22, 1980, p. B7.

20. Philip Freneau, "Rising Glory," in Freneau, *Poems on Various Subjects* (London, 1861), 50–51; Timothy Dwight, *Columbia: A Song* (New Haven, 1940), unpaginated; and Dwight, *Greenfield Hill* (New York 1794), 158.

21. Simpson, *Dispossessed Garden,* 14, 15, 32.

22. *Ibid.,* 14; James H. Moorhead, *American Apocalypse: Yankee Protestants and the Civil War* (New Haven, 1978), 81.

23. Henry David Thoreau, *Walden; or, Life in the Woods,* ed. Robert F. Sayre (New York, 1985), 486; Mather, *Magnalia Christi Americana,* ed. Murdock, 89, 94.

24. For example: Mather, *Shaking Dispensations* (Boston, 1715), *The Stone Cut out of the Mountain* (Boston, 1717), *The World Alarm'd* (Boston, 1721), and *Terra Beata* (Boston, 1726); Joshua Scottow, *A Narrative of the Planting of Massachusetts Colony* (Boston, 1694); Nicholas Noyes, *New England's Duty* (Boston, 1698); Joseph Morgan, *The History of the Kingdom of Basaruah* ([New York], 1715).

25. Nathaniel Hawthorne, "The Gray Champion," in Hawthorne, *Tales and Sketches,* ed. Roy Harvey Pearce (New York, 1982), 240.

26. Simpson, *Dispossessed Garden,* 14.

J. A. LEO LEMAY

Robert Beverley's *History and Present State of Virginia* and the Emerging American Political Ideology

The dominant recent explanation of the American Revolution has been that the patriot leaders adopted the ideology and characteristic diction of the seventeenth-century commonwealthmen and of the eighteenth-century opposition writers.[1] Caroline Robbins, Bernard Bailyn, Gordon Wood, and J. G. A. Pocock proved that the American pamphleteers often used the same terms as the earlier English writers, frequently quoted them, and appealed to their writings as sources of authority.[2] Intellectually, the American Revolution directly descends from English opposition thought.

Another important contribution to early American historiography complements this tradition. John M. Murrin has argued that America was anglicized throughout the period from the Glorious Revolution through the eighteenth century. Murrin maintains that no other influence upon the eighteenth-century colonial Americans was as strong as the English example.[3] The thesis adds indirect support to the Robbins-Bailyn-Wood-Pocock interpretation. Of course, theories of the origin of the Revolution stressing imperial, social, demographic, economic, military, religious, and other forces all have validity; though I am here focusing upon the intellectual and the emotional background of the Revolution, all the causes are necessarily interconnected.

But the current historiography largely ignores the most important influences upon the American revolutionaries. The English writers were not so important to the Americans as their experiences in the various colonial assemblies, as the local essays and speeches in their newspapers,[4] as their histories and political traditions, or as the influence of their friends, contemporaries, and role models from either a present or previous generation.[5] One might challenge this commonsensical statement with the objection that the local influences cannot be the most important ones, for the earlier English (rather than the American) writers are the authors primarily cited by the revolutionaries in their newspaper essays, pamphlets, and books. But that objection ignores the provincial circumstances of early America. In arguing against the English imperial authorities, the Americans had to use a common language—and a common group of past authors— if they were to communicate successfully. Colonial Americans had to cite English parliamentary history and English writers in order to make a telling point to an English audience. It was not wise for them to cite (though they nevertheless sometimes did) their own experiences in the colonial assemblies, for that opened them to the charge of provinciality. What had happened in the colonial assemblies was, to the English, intellectually and historically unimportant and irrelevant. The patriots could not refer to earlier American writers (though during the Revolution some writings by earlier Americans were republished in the colonies as propaganda), for the English writers had not read them and did not care what they said. Whenever the American revolutionaries cited their American predecessors, it allowed their English (and some of their supercilious American) contemporaries one more occasion to sneer at the Americans' provincial culture.

If any single colony provided more leaders for the American Revolution than any of the others, it was Virginia. The inspiration for the protests against the Stamp Act came from Patrick Henry in the Virginia House of Burgesses. The first president of the Continental Congress, Peyton Randolph, was the Speaker of Virginia's House of Burgesses. The author of the Declaration of Independence, the commanding general during the Revolution, and the father of the Constitution are only three leading figures among a host of dominant Virginians of the Revolutionary period.

No one would doubt that the Virginians' immediate past political experience influenced them. Bernard Knollenberg, in his *Origin of the American Revolution*, includes a chapter on Virginia's Twopenny Act (or Parsons' Cause) controversy, and Bernard Bailyn, in *The Pamphlets of the American Revolution*, discusses the Twopenny Act pamphlets in his introduction and edits one in the text.[6] I have recently traced the influence of Richard Bland's arguments concerning the Twopenny Act upon the Virginia burgesses' protest of 1764 over the proposed Stamp Act and subsequently upon the sentiments and even, in some details, the diction of Patrick Henry's Stamp Act Resolves.[7] Further, Edmund S. Morgan points out that Governor Robert Dinwiddie believed the Virginians in the 1750s who attempted to oppose the pistole fee were "very much in a Republican way of thinking."[8] He adds that "the governor's diagnosis gains credence by the fact that many who stood against him in the pistole-fee dispute also stood against the British Parliament a dozen years later when the colonies' ultimate quarrel with England began." Morgan then states, "Who taught them" a republican way of thinking, "besides Parks and Stith, will remain something of a mystery."[9] But William Parks, who began printing in Virginia in 1730, and the Reverend William Stith, who in 1747 wrote his scholarly, detailed *History of the First Discovery and Settlement of Virginia* covering the period 1606–1624, had a distinguished predecessor in Robert Beverley (1678?–1722), who wrote an entertaining and popular history of Virginia in 1705.[10]

Beverley's *History and Present State of Virginia* was certainly known and read by all the dominant Virginia leaders of the Revolutionary period, as it had been by many educated Americans between 1705 and 1765. William Byrd of Westover, for example, evidently had a copy.[11] Cotton Mather copied from it (without giving credit) in his *Christian Philosopher*. And a writer in the Boston *Gazette* cited the Smith-Pocahontas story from Beverley to prove that America was not a poor subject for literature. William Stith knew the book and used it in his *History*. The "History of Virginia" for which John Mercer paid 2 shillings, 6 pence was almost surely Beverley's *History*, and Richard Bland evidently had a copy. Benjamin Franklin had a copy of the 1722 edition, for he reprinted excerpts from it in his *General Magazine*. George Washington paid 5 shillings in 1769 for a copy of the 1722 edition. Thomas Jefferson's 1705 edition, listed in the manuscript catalog of his library, was reported missing from the books shipped to the Library of Congress in 1815. Jefferson's copy of the French translation published at Amsterdam in 1707 survives. Jefferson recommended the book as part of necessary learning in a letter to Peter Carr in 1787, and he categorized and cited it in his *Notes on the State of Virginia.*[12]

Beverley's *History* has frequently been celebrated as an important work in American literature.[13] Recently I examined it for its deistic propaganda.[14] But its extraordinary value as a document revealing the emerging American political ideology has never been set forth. Indeed, because of Beverley's errors, the *History* has often been maligned by later historians, though Wesley Frank Craven and Wilcomb E. Washburn have praised him for his insights and explanations.[15] Beverley's errors, deliberate falsehoods, and plagiarisms should be exposed, of course, but his achievements should be recognized.

The Virginia patriots knew Robert Beverley's *History* as well as, or better than, any work by an English commonwealth or radical Whig writer. In addition, Beverley, who "thoroughly reflected the mores and perspectives of his time and class," expressed a vision of Virginia and of Virginia's politics familiar to all of the Virginia patriots through their own experience in Virginia assemblies.[16] Like the English opposition writers, Beverley believed in the legislative supremacy of government. Therefore, he maintained, only Virginians in the House of Burgesses had the right to impose taxes on Virginians. Like the opposition writers, he believed that the authorities, especially the Virginia governors, were avaricious and power-mad tyrants who plotted against the people's best interest. And like the opposition writers, he believed in the ancient rights and privileges of the English and Americans, going back to their semimythical foundation in the Magna Charta.

But unlike the English opposition writers, Beverley was an American patriot, who identified with Virginia and America—not with England and London. Beverley resented the English, scorned their pretensions to superiority, and despised many of the English governors and officials whom he knew personally. He objected to the Trade and Navigation Acts and to the general English policy of mercantilism. He protested against England's ever-increasing role in the governance of Virginia. Finally, like many other Americans, he espoused comparatively egalitarian principles, whereas most commonwealth and English opposition writers believed in social hierarchy and excluded the poor from their thinking.[17]

Beverley's attitudes are, I submit, similar to those that we associate with the patriots of the American Revolutionary period. But they differ in the latter points from the attitudes of the English opposition writers. And I believe that the American revolutionaries learned even the first set of attitudes as much from previous Americans like Beverley as from the English opposition writers that the patriots cited. I do not mean to imply that the English opposition writers were not important intellectual influences upon the American patriots. The eighteenth-century English opposition writers were undoubtedly important. But Beverley's values are ones that all the Virginia revolutionaries were familiar with from earlier American writings as well as from personal acquaintances among their predecessors and contemporaries in the Virginia House of Burgesses.

Bailyn himself approaches this position. Revising the introduction to his edition of the *Pamphlets*, he wrote in *The Ideological Origins of the American Revolution* that he had since "discovered that the configuration of ideas and attitudes . . . described in the General Introduction as the Revolutionary ideology could be found intact as far back as the 1730's; in partial form it could be found even farther back, at the turn of the seventeenth century." And Bailyn identified the "prototypical American treatise . . . indistinguishable from any number of publications that would appear in the Revolutionary crisis fifty years later" as Daniel Dulany's *Right of the Inhabitants of Maryland to the Benefit of English Laws* (1728).[18]

Bailyn is right. Dulany does anticipate the patriots of the 1770s. But Dulany (1685–1763) is not original. In fact, all his Maryland contemporaries would have recognized his *Right of the Inhabitants of Maryland* as an echo of and tribute to the opinions of Thomas Bordley (1683/4–1726), the Great Commoner of early-eighteenth-century Maryland politics. (I do not anachronistically borrow the epithet from William Pitt, for Bordley used it—and evidently created it— in 1725.[19]) And before Bordley, Robert Beverley expressed these attitudes—though, to be sure, not as legalistically as Bordley or Dulany. But Beverley's quick pace, shocking statements, daring *ex cathedra* opinions, amusing anecdotes, and psychological interest made his *History* more interesting and popular than the writings of Bordley or Dulany.

Among the important attitudes Beverley shared both with patriots of the Revolution and with the opposition writers, I shall discuss three. First, Beverley believed in legislative supremacy and scorned the "prerogatives" of the authorities. A famous clause in the *History* is: "and so the form of Government became perfect." The clause refers to the creation of a House of Burgesses, "chosen by the People." Beverley's sentence reads, "That in the year 1620 [actually 1619], an Assembly of Burgesses was first call'd, from all the inhabited parts of the Country, who sat in consultation with the Governor and Council, for setling the Publick Affairs of the Plantation; and so the form of Government became perfect."[20]

The key ingredient in legislative supremacy is control of finances. When describing the "Burgesses of Assembly," Beverley emphasizes that they control the taxes—and therefore the money raised—in the colony: "There are no appointed times for their Convention, but the Custom hitherto has been once in a year, or once in two years; and indeed, seldom two intire years pass without an Assembly; *They wisely keeping the power that is left them, in their own Hands, by the short continuation of the Imposition Acts*" (242; italics added). "The power that is left them": according to Beverley, Virginia's late-seventeenth-century governors usurped a series of powers that had belonged to the Assembly during the previous decades—but not the key authority to raise taxes (87–113).

Indeed, insofar as Book One, "The HISTORY of the First Settlement of *Virginia*, and the Government thereof, to the present Time," chronicles the changing government of Virginia, it may be divided into three parts: the rise to perfection; an edenic period when Virginians enjoyed their "old Constitution"; and then a Fall in 1680, followed by a postlapsarian world. The early history tells of the progressive advances of government under the London Company, climaxing at the triumphal creation of an Assembly and county courts in 1619 (26–47). The Crown confirmed the existing structure of government when Virginia became a royal colony in 1624, thereby sealing the "perfect" government structure (57). Virginia's edenic period of government lasted from 1624 to 1680 (58–87).[21]

One "arbitrary . . . unjust, . . . haughty [and] furious" governor, Sir John Harvey, disturbed the edenic scene, but "in the Year 1639, the Council sent him a Prisoner to *London*, and with him two of their Number to maintain the Articles against him" (60). According to Beverley, this first Virginia rebellion was bloodless and minor, involving no fundamental threat to Virginia's constitution. Although Cromwell introduced a navigation act in 1651, frequently changed governors, and put other "strange Arbitrary Curbs . . . upon the Plantations" (64), he did not change the basic structure of Virginia's government. That remained sound until "King *Charles* the Second, to gratifie some Nobles about him, made Two great Grants out of that Country," thereby calling into question the ownership of Virginia lands (75). The former status—except for the irritation caused by the Acts of Trade and Navigation—was supposedly confirmed by a new charter in 1676 (85).[22] But Virginia's happy days ended with the coming of Thomas Lord Culpepper to Virginia in 1680. The third part of the history of Virginia's government describes those postlapsarian "submissive Times" from 1680 to 1705, when various governors wrested concessions and powers from the assembly (88–113).[23]

Jon Kukla has pointed out Beverley's mistake in saying that the Council and the House sat in the same room until 1680.[24] Although the mistake exemplifies Beverley's carelessness with facts (since he worked with the colony's official records for years and since he preserved and arranged the surviving records after the disastrous fire of 1698, he should have known better), he may have made it deliberately.[25] In Beverley's history of the government, Lord Culpepper introduces arbitrary and rapacious proceedings, violates the old constitution of Virginia, and repeatedly strikes at the traditional rights of the House of Burgesses. Beverley believed that the House was more powerful when it met with the Council. He also implies that the House and the Council were more cooperative when they met in the same chamber. Describing the first assembly of 1619, he said, "These Burgesses met the Governour and Council at *James-Town* . . . and sate in Consultation in the same House with them, as the Method of the *Scots* Parliament is, debating Matters for the Improvement and good Government of the Country." The portrait is idyllic. He adds: "This was the First General Assembly that ever was held there. I heartily wish, tho' they did not unite their Houses again, they wou'd however unite their Endeavours and Affections for the Good of the Country" (48; see also 238). Their meeting together symbolizes the edenic portrait of government that Beverley believes (or pretends to believe) existed under the old Virginia constitution. On the other hand, the separation of the Council from the House symbolizes "Disputes" between the two. In the mythic underlying structure of the history of government relations, the rending asunder of the House and the Council belongs in the postlapsarian world introduced by Culpepper's arrival as Virginia's governor.

A second attitude that Beverley shared with both the patriots and the opposition writers was a contempt for "Rapacious, and Arbitrary Governours" (6). Bernard Bailyn has argued, "American resistance in the 1760s and 1770s was a response to acts of power deemed arbitrary, degrading, and uncontrollable—a response, in itself objectively reasonable, that was inflamed to the point of explosion by ideological currents generating fears everywhere in America that irresponsible and self-seeking adventurers—what the twentieth century would call political gangsters—had gained the power of the English government and were turning first, for reasons that were variously explained, to that Rhineland of their aggressions, the colonies." Although Bailyn is here partially describing the attitudes of the English opposition writers to the ministers and other English authorities, he is especially portraying the patriots' feelings about the colonial governors.[26]

The standard stereotype of the colonial governor was of a necessitous, money-grasping, hypocritical Englishman, scornful of America and Americans, who was ready to lie and steal to feather his own nest and who was only visiting America to earn a fortune before returning home to England. A host of such governors disgusted Americans during the seventeenth century. Although numerous complaints about the character of English governors appeared in the records, Beverley wrote the first sweeping, memorable, published indictment of a series of English governors. In this way he created the stereotype. Benjamin Franklin later put it in definitive form.[27] Beverley said of Thomas Lord Culpepper, "This Noble Lord was skilful in all the Ways of getting Money, and never let slip any Opportunity of doing it" (89). Beverley backed the statement with a series of proofs, including the outrageous claim that Culpepper raised and lowered the value of Virginia's money by proclamation for his own private gain (90).[28] Culpepper's successor, Francis Lord Howard of Effingham, "had as great an Affection for Money as his Predecessor, and made it his Business to equip himself with as much of it as he could, without Respect either to the Laws of the Plantation, or the Dignity of his Office" (95). Effingham's most dastardly scheme for illegally raising money was his charge for an official seal (a precursor of both Governor Robert Dinwiddie's pistole fee in the 1750s and the Stamp Act in the 1760s): "he imposed the Charge of a License under Seal, on all School-masters for teaching of Children, and on all Practitioners at the Bar, for Pleading. He also extorted an excessive Fee for putting the Seal, to all Probates of Wills, and Letters of Administration, even where the Estates of the Deceased were of the meanest Value. Neither could any be favour'd with such Administration, or Probate, without paying that Extortion" (96).

Evidently Beverley could not accuse either Edmund Andros or Francis Nicholson of being rapacious, but he does portray Nicholson as a complete hypocrite. The governor managed to win the queen's approval for a grant from the Virginia Assembly by saying that if he were allowed to accept it, he would give half to the newly proposed College of William and Mary, "and so he secured at once both the Money, and the Character of being a generous Person" (99). Later he supposedly gave nine hundred pounds toward New York's expenses in building forts, publicly boasting "that he gave this Money out of his own Pocket." But "at the same time that he pass'd the Bills, he prudently took a Defeasance from the Gentleman, to whom they were given, specifying, *That till Her Majesty shou'd be graciously pleased, to remit him the Money out of the Quit Rents, those Bills shou'd never be made use of.*" Beverley points out that Nicholson even had the effrontery to boast of this supposed generosity in the memorial that he and "his Creature" Richard Quary submitted to the Lords of Trade (104, 112).[29]

Beverley claims that the governors and other English authorities in America undercut the colonials by advising the English government of the best ways to oppress them. He quotes the most outrageous memorials: "In one of these, he [Nicholson] remonstrates, *That the Tobacco of that Country often bears so low a Price, that it will not yield Cloaths to the People that make it;* and yet presently after, in the same Memorial, he recommends it to the Parliament, *to pass an Act forbidding the Plantations to make their own Cloathing;* which, in other Words, *is desiring a charitable Law, that the Planters shall go naked"* (104).

Here Beverley is echoing William Byrd, who as agent of the colony protested that Nicholson's suggested law against the production of clothing would force the Virginians to become "Adamites and go naked." Byrd further complained that even if Virginians "were able to purchase 'em, they must be forc'd to take up with what the merchant pleases, and at what exorbitant Rate he pleases, without the naturall liberty of supplying himself by his honest Labour an other way; which will be a Bondage worse than ever was known in Egypt or Algiers, and not sutable to the naturall liberty of English men." Beverley had probably also seen Nicholson's letter to the Board of Trade of March 13, 1702/3, in which the governor commented on the lack of clothing and said: "If these are not supplied by shipping from England, the people may be forced to go upon woollen and cotton manufactures as they endeavoured to do last war . . . and here are discontented and designing people in these parts of the world, and great pretenders for liberty and property, who will be ready enough to invent ways and means to live by themselves."[30]

Beverley even manages to twist one of Nicholson's memorials into a proposal for a unified America. In telling of the memorial, Beverley arouses English and American fears of a standing army—and then suggests that a unified America with an oppressive standing army must result in a revolution for an independent America: "In a late Memorial concerted between him and his Creature Col. *Quarrey,* tis most humbly proposed, *That all the* English *Colonies on the Continent of North* America, *be reduced under one Government, and under one Vice-Roy; and that a standing Army be there kept on foot, to subdue the Queen's Enemies;* which in plain *English,* is imploring Her Majesty, to put the Plantations under Martial Law, and in the Consequence, to give the Vice-Roy a fair Opportunity of shaking off his Dependance upon *England"* (104).[31]

Although this is the only time Beverley predicts a unified American revolution, he discusses several past rebellions (as

I shall observe below) and claims that Culpepper nearly drove the Virginians to rebel by despotically repealing several laws by proclamation (90).

> This Arbitrary Method of doing Business, had like to have had a very unhappy Effect; insomuch, that if the late Misfortunes of *Bacon*, had not been so fresh in Memory, it might, perhaps, have occasion'd a new Commotion. For, at this rate of proceeding, People look'd upon their Acts of Assembly, to be of no more Force, than the Laws of an *Ottoman* Province, which are liable to be suspended or repeal'd, at the Pleasure of the *Bashaw*. In short, it bred such a Mutiny in the Country, that the succeeding Assembly was forced to make a particular Law, to provide against the ill Consequences of it. (91)

Another Virginia rebellion occurred in 1682. Between the overabundance of tobacco and the hard practices of the English merchants, the planters became desperate and "resolved a total Destruction of the Tobacco" in Virginia, "especially of the Sweet-scented; because that was planted no where else." The planters "contrived that all the Plants should be destroy'd, while they were yet in the Beds, and after it was too late to sow more." The ringleaders burned their own plants and "such of their Neighbours as were not willing to do it themselves," but they lacked the resolution to finish the work of destruction. "This was adjudged Sedition and Felony. Several People were committed upon it, and some condemn'd to be hanged" (92). As Beverley well knew, his father, Major Robert Beverley, led the plant-cutter rebellion.

Nicholson's crimes exceeded those of any former governor. (All contemporaries would have recognized Beverley's *History* as propaganda in the struggle to depose Governor Nicholson.) Nicholson not only represents "*Virginia* as Republican, and Rebellious" (112), but even gets "his Creature" Colonial Richard Quary to say so in his memorial to the Board of Trade (112). Beverley attributes the memorial to both Nicholson and Quary and quotes a passage characterizing Virginians as a group of rich radicals whose republican notions are undermining imperial authority. The memorial calls for harsher measures against the Americans: "they take upon them to describe the People of *Virginia, to be both numerous and rich, of Republican Notions and Principles, such as ought to be corrected, and lower'd in time; and that now or never is the only Time to maintain the Queen's Pre-*

rogative, and put a Stop to those wrong pernicious Notions, which are improving daily, not only in Virginia, *but in all Her Majesty's other Governments"* (113).

While in London writing his *History,* Beverley surreptitiously obtained copies of Quary's letters and memorials to the Board of Trade. Judging them mischievous, he sent copies back to the House of Burgesses together with a covering letter. When the burgesses next met, Beverley's letter and Quary's papers were read to the House (April 19, 1705). On April 24, the House passed a series of resolutions condemning Quary, charging him with a "false and Scandalous Reflection upon the Assembly" that "greatly" tended to destroy "the Liberty & priviledges of the said Assembly and other her Majestys good Subjects here." The House concluded by thanking Beverley for the "Service he has Done the Country in Sending his Letters & Papers Therewith." The burgesses addressed Queen Anne, saying that Quary "falsly Insinuates that nothing Less than your Majestys Displeasure backed with an Armed fforce will be Sufficient to Restrain us from Disobedience." The queen, however, replied on January 31, 1705/6, with praise for her faithful servant Quary and condemnation of Beverley's misrepresentation and the burgesses' groundless address.[32]

Despite his own evidence that Virginia frequently rebelled against its governors and despite his repeated threats of rebellion, Beverley nevertheless asserts in his *History* that Virginia is loyal to Queen Anne (such cant was necessary and has nothing to do with Beverley's actual opinions), should not be taxed, and should be allowed to continue to govern itself. He concludes Book One with the following declaration: "Thus are that loyal People privately, and basely misrepresented; because they struggle against the Oppression, which this Governour practices, in Contempt of Her Majesty's Instructions, and the Laws of the Country. But I challenge the Authors of that Memorial, to give one single Instance, wherein the Inhabitants of *Virginia,* have shown the least Want of Loyalty to the Queen, or the least Disaffection to *England"* (113).

Like other Americans before and after him, Beverley appeals to the tradition of rights and *"Liberties of* English *Subjects"* (107). This is the third attitude he shares with the patriots and the English opposition writers. The reasons the evil governors plot with a few cronies and some English authorities seem almost incomprehensible, though Beverley sometimes blames it upon their avariciousness. Although his frequent sarcasm and irony partially cover his outrage, a surprisingly violent language repeatedly breaks through: for example, "this Despotick way of Government," "this Arbitrary Method of doing Business," "the many Arbitrary Proceedings which he [Nicholson] boasts to have learn'd formerly in the Kingdom of *Morocco*," "the *French* method of governing by Edicts" (90, 91).

Beverley tells shocking stories of Governors Culpepper, Effingham, and Nicholson violating common rights. The loyalty oath that accompanied the Act of General Pardon and Oblivion especially drew Beverley's ire. A clause added to the act by Culpepper "imposes a Penalty of Five Hundred Pounds, and a Year's Imprisonment, upon any Man that shall presume to speak disrespectfully of the Governor."[33] Beverley sarcastically claims, "This is such a Safeguard to Tyranny, that, let a Governour commit never so many Abuses, no Person, while he is there, dare say a Word against him; nor so much as go about to represent it to the Throne of *England* for Redress, for fear of incurring this severe Penalty" (88). Beverley also tells an anecdote concerning Governor Nicholson that evidently remained popular in Virginia oral lore down to the time of the Revolution. When the Virginians dared to remind him of the constitutional restrictions upon his power and of their traditional rights, Governor Nicholson replied, "*That they had no Right at all to the Liberties of* English *Subjects, and that he wou'd hang up those that should presume to oppose him, with* Magna Charta *about their Necks*" (107).[34]

Although Beverley appeals to the rights and privileges of Englishmen, he bases his argument and his outrage mainly upon the governors' disregard and scorn for the "old Constitution" (93) of Virginia. He would like to pretend to believe that the individual governors ("neither Her Majesty's Instructions, nor the Laws of that Country can restrain him" [107]) are responsible for the loss of some traditional rights and privileges of Virginians, but he knows that the imperial government shares in the blame. In one foolish early instruction, "The King had commanded, that all Ships trading to *Virginia*, should go to *James-Town*, and there enter before they broke Bulk: But the Assembly, from the Impraticableness of that Command, excused all, except the *James-River*

Ships, from that Order" (67). Lord Culpepper brought over "with him some Laws, which had been drawn up in *England*, to be enacted in their Assembly" (87). These included an "Act for raising a publick Revenue for the better Support of the Government" that made the duties "perpetual" and allocated the monies raised ("which before used to be accounted for to the Assembly") to "his Majesty's sole Direction, for the Support of the Government" (89). As a reward, the king raised Culpepper's salary (which was taken from these funds) to "Two Thousand Pounds *per Annum*, instead of One Thousand, which was formerly allow'd" (89). Throughout the eighteenth century, when Virginians read the intercolonial news of vain attempts by Jonathan Belcher and other colonial governors to achieve a fixed salary, they must have felt rancor and frustration at their own situation.

Although Beverley generally identifies the House of Burgesses as the legislative group especially concerned with the "Liberty and Privilege" of "their Country-men" (93), he also expresses approval of the Council because it was "a restraint upon" the governor, "if he should attempt to exceed the bounds of his Commission" (240). But Beverley obviously felt that the Council had failed to do its job.[35]

Beverley's myth of degeneration from a perfect form of government was a Virginia version of the English myth surrounding the Magna Charta and of the Lockean myth concerning the state of nature and the origin of civil government. (New England's jeremiad version of the myth saw a decline in spirituality and an increase in materialism as being responsible for the supposed degeneration of the "present" time.) Virginia's popular politicians (like Beverley's father, Major Robert Beverley, and William Fitzhugh) were, in Beverley's Virginia myth, merely trying to recapture the ancient liberties implied in the first-contract theory of government and to recapture the ancient liberties rewon during feudal times. These positions were popularized by John Locke's *Two Treatises of Government* (1689/90), by numerous legal treatises, and by Henry Care's popular collection *English Liberties* (1680). Although John Dunn has argued that Locke's *Two Treatises* were comparatively unknown in colonial America before 1750, I have elsewhere proven its influence upon Cadwallader Colden's *History of the Five Indian Nations* (1727) and mentioned Locke's pervasive presence in the colonial newspapers.[36]

No catalog of Beverley's library exists, but his nephew and namesake, Robert Beverley of Newlands (1701–1733), probably inherited or bought items from it. Among the books that John Mercer purchased from Robert Beverley of Newlands on March 4, 1730, was a copy of Care's *English Liberties.* Care's book was a popular one, common in the colonies. Further, William Penn reproduced part of it in *The Excellent Privilege of Liberty and Property Being the Birth Right of Free-Born Subjects of England* (1687), and James Franklin reprinted the entire work in Boston in 1719. John Carter reprinted it in Rhode Island as revolutionary propaganda in 1774.[37]

The idea of ancient English liberties was commonplace in seventeenth-century England and America. (It can be seen as a version of the Renaissance and seventeenth-century general historiography of degeneration—an idea indebted, of course, to the Christian myth of the Fall of Man.) Nicholson's arbitrary actions had earlier caused the inhabitants of New York City to complain in 1689 that he was the most recent of a series of governors "who had in a most arbitrary way subverted our *ancient priviledges* making us in effect slaves to their will contrary to the laws of England."[38]

There were significant attitudes Beverley shared with the patriots of the Revolution that he did not share with the opposition writers. Four of those are especially important. The first is his affirmation of American identity. In the preface to the *History* he makes the notable assertion "I am an *Indian*" (9).

The development of American identity during the colonial period is still a comparatively little-studied and less-understood phenomenon. Most studies of American patriotism focus on the mid-eighteenth century and the following years. The only book devoted to the developing American patriotism throughout the colonial period is Carl Bridenbaugh's brief *Spirit of '76,* though a few essays bear upon the subject. But in a discussion of America's first folk song, I have recently shown that a full portrait of distinctive American identity existed in New England by 1643 and that this identity resulted in great part from English attitudes concerning America and Americans.[39]

Evidence of southern identity in the seventeenth century also exists. One aspect of a region's identity is a sense of difference from other places. Southerners generally had contempt for New Englanders—as "puritan calvinists" (1642/3), as "Roundheads" (1705), as "Saints of New England" (1736), and as "Yankees" (before 1776).[40] Virginians often drew a distinction between native Americans and "strangers" from England. Francis Nicholson wrote the Board of Trade in 1701 that "formerly . . . there were widows [who] had pretty good fortunes . . . but now if there be any widows or maids of fortune, the Natives for the most part get them; for they begin to have a sort of aversion to others, calling them strangers." Nicholson had contempt for Americans and presumed that the Board of Trade would agree with him in automatically favoring "an old Englander."[41] A snippet survives from a folk song celebrating the way of life in the colonial Chesapeake. Of course, the seventeenth-century promotional writers also celebrated America—and some, like John Hammond in *Leah and Rachel* (1656), proclaimed their love for it. But the most telling manifestation of southern identity was the rise of a native-born planter elite to positions of power in the Virginia Assembly and the Council, which was a major reason for a changing relationship between the leadership and constituents in late-seventeenth-century Virginia.[42]

Like other members of the planter elite, Beverley was patriotic. The very act of writing a history of Virginia exhibits patriotism. The 1705 title page proclaims that the book is *"By a Native and Inhabitant of the Place."* As Robert D. Arner has pointed out, Beverley contrasts the French ornamental style with the English "less Ornamental" and "more Sincere" prose—and then claims that American prose style is even plainer and blunter than the English. It is perhaps the first native southern claim that Americans have a different style from the English.[43]

But why does Beverley claim to be an Indian rather than an American? After all, a fellow Virginian, in a work that Beverley occasionally echoes (*An Essay upon the Government of the English Plantations,* 1701), had signed his book, "by An American." Most authorities credit Cotton Mather in the *Magnalia Christi Americana* (1702, written *ca.* 1697) with first using the word *American* in its common late-eighteenth-century meaning of a nonaborigine born in the English colonies. But at the time the primary meaning of *American* was an American Indian. One cannot be sure that Mather, too, was not claiming to be an Indian. Even if the usage had, among Americans, become known, the meaning of *American* for an English audience would necessarily be associated with an aborigine, *i.e.*, a natural man, rude and uncultivated—even, perhaps, a savage.[44] After all, the Indian queen—that common sixteenth- and seventeenth-century symbol for America—appears at the top of the engraved title page of Beverley's *History* as part of the arms of Virginia. The American identity was synonymous with the Indian, and Beverley chose to flaunt that association.

Beverley's main persona in the book is not a Virginian but a man with a more inclusive American identity. Even though he identifies New Englanders as "Roundheads" and Virginians as "Cavaliers" (287), he pretends the various colonies have a joint identity. Beverley's identification with all the mainland English colonies arises from his resentment of their shared mistreatment by English authorities. He knows that the "very great Duties . . . laid on the Fisheries of the Plantations" (76) mainly affect New England. And the duties "laid on the Trade from one Plantation to another" (76) oppress them all. Although he refers to Virginia ("the ancientest, as well as most profitable Colony, depending on the Crown of *England*" [5]) in the dedication to Robert Harley, he appeals to Harley as "the Patron of the *Plantations*" (5). Beverley says he is speaking for "we of the *Plantations*" (6). According to Beverley, Harley has a view of the true relationship between England and the colonies—mutual interest: "How happy therefore ought we of the *Plantations* to think our selves, in the Favour of a Gentleman, whose Thoughts are directed by unbiass'd Reason, and the real Advantages of *England*" (6). English attitudes drive Beverley (and later the pre-Revolutionary patriots) into an American (or Indian) identity. He wants to make it clear that, though his primary subject is "my Country," *i.e.*, Virginia (11), he is also speaking for all the mainland English colonies of America.

Beverley admires patriotism. Significantly, when he dedicates the book to Harley, he singles out Harley's patriotism as especially praiseworthy. Harley has "all along signalized a constant Love to" his country (7). But Beverley's is an American rather than an English patriotism. He repeatedly celebrates Virginia. Of course, such praise characterizes most promotion tracts, and Beverley's book is, in part, a promotion tract. As Lewis P. Simpson has pointed out, the book offers "an ecstatic and sensuous vision of the paradisical garden of

Virginia." Judy Jo Small has subsequently argued that the book contains "so many negative details that it hardly succeeds as promotion literature," but successful promotion literature had to deal with the widely known negative reports about America. Simpson correctly claims that Beverley's Book Two "is virtually a fertility hymn in praise of Virginia's waters and fish, and of its soils, native fruits, herbs, and grains." Beverley actually reports that all the standard English vegetables grow "in far greater perfection" in Virginia than in England (292).[45]

Beverley knows the anti-American rumors and the writings saying that men and nature degenerate in the New World—and he denies them (292–93).[46] He first asserts that American nature is really superior to Old World nature—a claim that America's best Augustan poet, Richard Lewis, elaborated, borrowing also the celebration of such specific details of American nature as the mockingbird and the hummingbird.[47] Beverley celebrates Oppechancanough's advanced age as "an Instance of the Healthiness and long Life of the Natives of that Country" (62). He even makes up a tall tale to prove the fertility and longevity of Americans. A poor old couple who lived in Stafford County had a son when the woman was seventy-six and her husband about ninety. Twelve years later they were still alive and well, though the man, "then above 100 Years old . . . notwithstanding his great Age, was strong in his Limbs, and Voice; but had lost his Sight" (103).

Beverley chafed at English prejudice against America. In his 1722 preface to the History, he said that he originally wrote the book because of the "prodigious Phantasms" that the English believed concerning America, for example, that "the Servants in Virginia are made to draw in Cart and Plow, as Horses and Oxen do in England, and . . . the Country turns all People black who go to live there" (1722 ed., sig. A2v.). In one of the book's many deliberate reversals, Beverley calls the Virginians true cosmopolitans and says that the English are really provincials. Beverley is resentfully replying to the usual English characterization of America as a wilderness and Americans as a rude, uncultivated people. Beverley's contemporaries, the Virginia planter Colonel John Bolling (1676–1729) and the New England minister John Barnard (1681–1770), both testified that the English commonly thought of Americans as black Indians who did not speak English.[48] Although Beverley attacked this common English stereotype, he may also have been directly refuting specific slurs on Virginians by English officials present in the colony. In their account of the "present state" of Virginia in 1697, Hartwell, Blair, and Chilton said that Englishmen who immigrated to Virginia had "Knowledge of the World" but that native Virginians "have had generally no Opportunity of Improvement by good Education" and that a majority of the House of Burgesses consisted of natives who had never seen a town.[49] Nicholson agreed. In a letter of 1701 to the Board of Trade, he said that "the Country consists now most of Natives, few of which have read much or been abroad in the world."[50]

Since Beverley knew the manuscript by Hartwell, Blair, and Chilton, and since he bribed the clerks of the Board of Trade to let him read the dispatches from Nicholson and Quary, he certainly read and resented these statements. He replied (echoing Nicholson's diction) that the Americans were actually the cosmopolitans.

> Here is the most Good-nature, and Hospitality practis'd in the World, both towards Friends and Strangers: but the worst of it is, this Generosity is attended now and then, with a little too much Intemperance. The Neighbourhood is at much the same distance, as in the Country in *England:* but with this Advantage, that all the better sort of People have been abroad, and seen the World, by which means they are free from that stiffness and formality, which discover more Civility, than Kindness: And besides, the goodness of the Roads, and the fairness of the Weather, bring People oftener together. (308)

Beverley even resented America's dependence upon England in material culture. He found it irritating that Americans "have their Cloathing of all sorts from *England.*" He charged that "the very Furrs" that Virginians' hats "are made of, perhaps go first from thence." The hides of cattle, deer, and sheep "lie and rot" instead of being tanned and used, though "sometimes perhaps a better manager than ordinary, will vouchsafe to make a pair of Breeches of a Deer-Skin" (295). Beverley further charged that Virginians "are such abominable Ill-husbands, that tho' their Country be overrun with Wood, yet they have all their Wooden Ware from *England;* their Cabinets, Tables, Stools, Chests, Boxes, Cart-Wheels, and all other things, even so much as their Bowls, and Birchen Brooms, to the Eternal Reproach of their Laziness" (295). Here Beverley may again be echoing Byrd, who argued that a planter "will certainly not give himself the trouble, to make" clothing, "for they are there [in Virginia] too much favourers of Idleness, not to prefer the easiest way of supplying their necessitys."[51]

Happily, we do have one account of Beverley's home. It shows that in his own life he did his best to achieve independence from England in material culture. In 1716 the Reverend John Fontaine visited Beverley and enjoyed his hospitality. Fontaine, however, expressed surprise at Beverley's style of life: "This man lives well, but has nothing in or about his house but just what is necessary, tho' rich. He hath good beds in his house but no curtains and instead of cane chairs he hath stools made of wood, and lives upon the product of his land." Beverley's wine-making may be interpreted as an effort to achieve American cultural independence in drink—an independence that would complement the common American diet of native foods.[52]

Beverley helped create the great legends of colonial Virginia by the attention he gave these topics in his history. Indeed, in retrospect, Beverley showed an extraordinary flair for fastening upon the very ideas of early Virginia that were to become of greatest interest both to the myth-makers (the creative writers and artists) and to the historians: he features the story of the Lost Colony (21–23), the birth of Virginia Dare (21), the story of Pocahontas saving Captain John Smith (39, 40), the "Starving Time" after Smith left (35), the first representative assembly in America (47–48), the arrival of the first Afro-Americans in Virginia (48), the Indian massacres of the whites in 1622 and 1644 (51–54, 60–63), Virginia as the colony of Cavaliers (64, 287), an especially long discussion of Bacon's Rebellion, complete with a series of explanations concerning its causes (74–86), the dramatic incident of Governor Berkeley baring "his naked Breast against the presented Arms" of Bacon's men (80), and, of course, the anecdote of the tyrannical Governor Nicholson threatening to hang those who opposed him "*with* Magna Charta *about their necks*" (107).

Not only is Beverley extraordinarily sensitive both to the legends and events of Virginia's history; he is a major creator of later visions of the South—including portrayals of edenic nature, noble Indians, and degenerate, lazy southerners. Although he writes as an "Indian" rather than as a Virginian, the southern identity is among Beverley's major themes.

A second attitude Beverley shared with the patriots but not with the opposition writers is the belief that the British were "Loading those Countries [the American colonies] with heavy Impositions" (6). In the *History*, the English oppression of America begins with the Navigation Act of 1651. Cromwell "had no sooner subdued the Plantations; but he began to contrive how to keep them under. . . . To this End . . . he contrived a severe Act of Parliament, whereby he prohibited the Plantations from receiving or exporting any *European* Commodities, but what should be carried to them by *English* Men, and in *English* built Ships." Beverley even tries to undercut the first Navigation Act by suggesting that it was part of Cromwell's attack on royalism. He points out that Virginia "was the last of all the King's Dominions that submitted to the Usurpation." It was therefore necessary for Cromwell to make sure the plantations would give him no trouble. "To this End he thought it necessary to break off their Correspondence with all other Nations; thereby to prevent their being furnish'd with Arms, Ammunition, and other Warlike Provisions" (64). The implication is that Cromwell feared the Americans would take up arms to defend the monarch. Beverley presents the first Navigation Act as one way that Cromwell attacked loyal, Royalist Englishmen. One wonders if Beverley believed his own suggestion. I suspect he just regarded it as good propaganda. He may, however, have known from the records that the Royalist Governor Sir William Berkeley in March, 1651, had claimed that Virginians should oppose Cromwell and Parliament because they "would take away . . . our right of giving and selling our goods to whom we please."[53]

Beverley declared that the Trade and Navigation Acts repeatedly drove Virginians to rebellion. "The strange Arbitrary Curbs" of Cromwell "made the People desperate, and inspired them with a Desire to use the last Remedy, to relieve themselves from his Lawless Usurpation" (64–65). Cromwell's taxes made the Virginians illegally choose Sir William Berkeley (the former royal governor) as governor. Fortunately, this rebellion against the official English government did not bring any retaliation. Beverley explains that the Virginia Cavaliers

were ready to hazard all for the King. Now, this was actually before the King's Return for *England*, and proceeded from a brave
Principle of Loyalty, for which they had no Example. Sir *William
Berkeley* embraced their Choice, and forthwith proclaim'd
Charles the Second King of *England, Scotland, France, Ireland*
and *Virginia*, and caused all Process to be issued in his Name.
Thus his Majesty was actually King in *Virginia*, before he was
so in *England*. But it pleased God to restore him soon after to
the Throne of his Ancestors; and so that Country escaped being
chastised for throwing off the Usurpation. (65)

And so the second Virginia rebellion ended happily.

Beverley ironically and resentfully reports that after the
Restoration "the Parliament was pleased to renew the Act
contrived by the Usurper for discouraging the Plantations,"
but the 1660 act had "severer Restraints and Prohibitions by
Bonds, Securities &c." (66). He further complains that a
"new Act of Parliament," the Staple Act of 1663, laid "a severer Restraint upon their Supplies than formerly" (70). The
law forbade Americans to purchase foreign goods that "were
not first landed in England . . . the former Restraint of importing them only by *English* Men, in *English* built Shipping, not being thought sufficient." The law was a double
blow: it reduced "their Staple Tobacco to a very low Price"
and raised "the Value of *European* Goods, to what the Merchants pleased to put upon them." The law "exasperated the
People, because now they found themselves under a Necessity, of exchanging their Commodities with the Merchants
of *England* at their own Terms" (70–71).

Just as the 1651 Navigation Act caused the second Virginia
rebellion, so these additional acts caused, Beverley says, the
third and most famous Virginia revolt of the seventeenth
century, Bacon's Rebellion. "The heavy Restraints and Burdens laid upon their Trade by Act of Parliament in *England*"
made the people desperate (75). And the English Parliament
in 1673 remorselessly added another act, laying duties on
the trade between plantations. "This was a new Hardship,
and the rather, because the Revenue arising by this Act, was
not applied to the Use of the Plantation wherein it was
raised: But given clear away." It seems almost surprising that
Beverley objected to a provision in the act that mainly affected New England.[54] "By the same Act also very great Duties were laid on the Fisheries of the Plantations, if manufactured by the *English* inhabitants there; while the People of

England were absolutely free from all Customs." He resents the unfair treatment of Americans: "Nay, tho' the Oil, Blubber, and Whale-Bone, which were made by the Inhabitants of the Plantations, were carried to *England* by *English* men, and in *English* built Ships, yet it was held to a considerable Duty" (76).

Virginians could get "nothing . . . by Tobacco; neither could they turn any other Manufacture to Advantage," and so they might as well "go Voluntiers against the *Indians*" (78). Beverley's explanations of the underlying causes of Bacon's Rebellion have been disputed, but recent historians, especially, have followed his lead. He probably influenced Edward Bancroft's arguments against the Navigation Acts before the Revolution. In 1769 Bancroft called them "the principal if not only Cause" of Bacon's Rebellion. And he repeated his charge in a letter to the London *Morning Chronicle* of May 19, 1774, which was reprinted in Rind's *Virginia Gazette.*[55]

Beverley anticipated Benjamin Franklin, Adam Smith, and the patriots of the American Revolution in believing that England's mercantilism benefited only a few British merchants and manufacturers, while unfairly oppressing the colonists. W. A. Speck writes: "Ever since Adam Smith attacked these restrictions [the Navigation Acts] upon free trade it has been commonplace to criticize them on the grounds that they favored the distributors rather than the consumers of goods. Smith attributed the policy behind them to the political influence of merchants." But in these opinions Smith reflected more than a century of American condemnation of the acts as primarily benefiting the English merchants. John Bland, for example, complained in 1661 that the Navigation Act of 1660 was created by "a few covetous ignorant, self-seeking men," that the merchants behind the act sought only "their own profit and interests," and that the colonists were "left to the mercy of a few Tobacconists . . . [who] make a prey of them." And Smith could hardly have been unaware of Benjamin Franklin's repeated attacks on the acts.[56]

Although Beverley knows that overproduction of tobacco was primarily responsible for its low price, he nevertheless resentfully writes that "the Merchants would hardly allow the Planter any thing for it" (92). He also blames the "Merchants of London" for selfishly opposing a Virginia law (written by his father, Major Robert Beverley) encouraging "Trade and Manufactures; whereby a certain Place in each County was appointed for a Town" (88), because the merchants feared that Virginians might thereby become less dependent upon them.

As I have shown elsewhere, "planter" is the earliest name for the American colonists. Beverley uses the word *planter* as synonymous with an American (*e.g.*, 92, 306); *merchant* is synonymous with an Englishman (*e.g.*, 92, 297). In this usage the age-old resentment of the farmer against the middleman is nascent. Beverley even once opposes "the Merchants of *England*" to "the People" (70–71), thereby dehumanizing the merchants and the English. Beverley's attitude did not change in the 1722 edition. There he noted that the assembly of 1706 passed a port act, but "the *Virginia* Merchants in *England* . . . complained against it to the Crown, and so it was also suspended" (1722 ed., 98).[57] Although John Rainbolt is undoubtedly right in downplaying agrarianism's role in early America, it was not altogether absent from seventeenth-century Virginia.[58] Beverley dedicates the *History* to Harley because Harley supposedly believes (as Franklin later did) that the proper attitude should be to consider the good of the entire British empire, not just England: "No Body is better instructed in the true Interest of *England*, than Your Self; No Body is more convinced, how much the *Plantations* advance that Interest; and consequently, no Body knows how to set a juster Value upon them. While some People, upon very mistaken Principles of Policy, are for loading those Countries with heavy Impositions, and oppressing them with Rapacious, and Arbitrary Governors; You, *Sir*, who are a better Judge of their Importance, are for milder Methods, and for extending the Blessings of Justice, and Property, to all the *English* Dominions" (5–6).

Whether mercantilism was really harmful or unfair to the Americans is, in this context, largely irrelevant. It is important that Beverley—like all the American revolutionaries (and even some Loyalists)—smarted under the system.[59] Like other colonials, he believed that Britain was unjustly taxing the Americans. Britain was acting selfishly and shortsightedly. British authorities, in the Navigation Acts, officially treated Americans as second-rate citizens. To Beverley, the Navigation Acts were a cancer eating at the pancreas, kidneys, liver, spleen, and nerves of British-American relations. As John Seelye has said, Beverley was delivering "a carefully couched warning to England concerning the incendiary possibilities of bad laws and worse governors" and was implying that Virginia's rebels "may be counted upon to repeat the performance under similar circumstances."[60]

Beverley describes and celebrates many local Virginia customs and institutions, but his praise of Virginia's legal system is especially striking. His affection for Virginia law is the third significant attitude he shares with the patriots but not the opposition writers. Despite portraying the history of Virginia since Culpepper's time as one of continuous degeneration from an "old Constitution" (93) that protected the rights and liberties of the individual, Beverley believed in progress and mocked English and European glorification of primitivism. He was, however, somewhat inconsistent. Although he satirized the seventeenth-century sailors for following the old route to Virginia (22), he celebrated the edenic abundance of nature and the happy condition of the Indians before the coming of the white men (17, 233). And yet, he portrayed the Indians as fierce, vengeful, and superstitious (18, 211, 226).[61]

Beverley wrote that Virginia had gradually been building a complete and distinctive body of common law based upon detailed legal opinions that were being used as precedents. In this contention he may have been deliberately refuting *An Essay upon the Government of the English Plantations*, in which the Virginia author claims that "no one of these Colonies on the Continent, have any tolerable Body of Laws." He also may be echoing William Fitzhugh, who praised the Virginia traditions in a speech to the House of Burgesses on April 24, 1682. Fitzhugh compiled a brief history of Virginia and a digest of its laws in the 1690s, which unfortunately dropped out of sight just after his death in 1701.[62]

According to the *History*, Governor Culpepper, however, "found fault with" this common-law approach and "caused the Judgments to be enter'd up short, without the Reasons, alledging, that their Courts were not of so great Experience, as to be able to make Precedents to Posterity" and should therefore make decisions speedily and without reasons, "according to the Innocence of former Times" (95). Although Stanley Katz argues that the "separation of adjudication from legislation marks a critically important point in the political development" of the colonies, I wonder if it might not also be regarded in some cases as a regression rather than a step forward in political development.[63] Beverley knew that the English authorities would generally side with the governors against the wishes of the colonists, and he condemned the change of jurisdiction of 1683 whereby legal appeals were taken away to be judged in England. Formerly, appeals from the General Court (*i.e.*, the governor and the Council) were made to the General Assembly (*i.e.*, both the House of Burgesses and the Council). Culpepper, who had been granted the Northern Neck of Virginia by Charles II, knew that the House would vote against his claims: "He fear'd the Burgesses would be too much in the Interest of their Country-men, and adjudge the Inhabitants of the Northern Neck, to have an equal Liberty and Privilege in their Estates, with the rest of *Virginia*, as being settled upon the same Foot. In order therefore to make a better Pennyworth of those poor People, he studied to overturn this odious Method of Appealing, and to fix the last Resort in another Court, that might judge more favourably of his unrighteous Patents" (93). Therefore, Culpepper "contrived to blow up a Difference in the Assembly, between the Council and the Burgesses, privately encouraging the Burgesses, to insist upon the Privilege of determining all Appeals by themselves, exclusive of the Council." He then reported the quarrel to the English authorities "with so many Aggravations that he got an Instruction from the King, to take away all Appeals from the General Court to the Assembly, and cause them to be made to himself in Council" (93; see also 255).[64]

Certainly the change lessened the Virginians' control over their own affairs. H. R. McIlwaine has observed that the Council may not have pressed charges against Major Robert Beverley in 1682 because the case would have been appealed to the General Assembly, where the burgesses would have found their favorite innocent. He also notes that the cases appealed generally involved the planters' debts to English merchants and that the burgesses especially wanted to keep these appeals in Virginia. In their address to the king of May 16, 1684, the burgesses called the change "Grievous and Ruinous."[65]

Under the old Virginia court system, cases were tried in the Assembly "by the Standard of Equity and good Conscience." The Assembly "us'd to come to the merits of the cause, as soon as they could without Injustice, never admitting such impertinences of Form and Nicety, as were not absolutely necessary: and when the substance of the case was sufficiently debated, they us'd directly to bring the Suit to a Decision" (255). Obviously, Beverley found the old system superior. It worked "with the least expense of Money and Time" and avoided "all the tricking, and foppery of the Law" that he thought typical of English courts.

In Book One of his history, Beverley condemns Culpepper for making "great Innovations in their Courts, pretending to follow the *English* Forms" (97). Contradicting himself in Book Four, Beverley actually praises Culpepper as "a Man of admirable Sense, and well Skilled in the Laws of *England*," who "admired the constitution of" the Virginia courts "and kept them close to this plain Method . . . although, at the same time, he was the occasion, of taking away the liberty of Appeals to the Assembly" (255).

Unlike Culpepper, Effingham was "absolutely unskill'd in the legal proceedings of *England*" but nevertheless "endeavour'd to introduce as many of the *English* Forms as he could."[66] For Beverley, it is with the law as it is with prose style. The American traditions and forms are praised as plain, fair, and efficient, whereas the English laws and lawyers are ornate and given to "tricking" and "foppery." Beverley censures Governor Andros for making "all the Statutes of *England* . . . to be Law in their Courts," thereby causing such confusion "that they knew not what was Law" (101; see also 256).[67] Interestingly, he does not comment on Andros' knowledge of English law—which was probably excellent. And as usual, Beverley especially lambasts Governor Nicholson, "a Man unacquainted with all Law, except that of *Morocco*, where he learnt the way of governing by force." Nicholson "has endeavour'd to introduce all the quirks of the *English* Proceedings" and supports "wretched Pettifoggers" as the source of his innovations (256). Beverley certainly knew and perhaps had in mind the exchange between Benjamin Harrison and Nicholson on April 17, 1703, when Nicholson passionately exclaimed, "Sir, are you the Queen's Council and pretend to set up a precedent in Virginia contrary to the practice of England?"[68]

Beverley respected the body of native Virginia law rather than the English traditions. He celebrated the persons responsible for codifying and compiling Virginia's past laws

(66, for example). Beverley's expertise in Virginia law and his respect for its traditions continued. Although he was removed as clerk of King and Queen County Court by Governor Nicholson on December 20, 1705, he was a leading lawyer of his day and acted as William Byrd's attorney throughout the early years of the eighteenth century. On December 8, 1715, Governor Spotswood's Council appointed him one of three legal experts (the other two were the attorney general and John Holloway) to prepare a "Scheme for the better Qualifying persons practising as Attorneys." Then, on May 21, 1718, he was appointed by Governor Spotswood's Council as presiding judge of King and Queen County. It was probably at this time that he compiled an abridgment of Virginia's laws featuring its precedents. He published it along with his revision of the *History* in the last year of his life.[69]

Another attitude Beverley has in common with the patriots of the Revolution but not the English opposition writers is an egalitarianism whose obverse side is a scorn for avaricious aristocrats. Expressions of this scorn repeatedly recur in the *History*. He makes the phrase "This Noble Lord" a synonym for *scoundrel* and *thief* (89, 90, 95, 239). In private correspondence, his epithet expressing sarcastic contempt for Governor Nicholson is "our Duke."[70] His scorn for nobility even spills over into an account of the Indians' preserving their dead princes: "So great an Honor and Veneration have these ignorant and unpolisht people for their Princes, even after they are dead" (216). Beverley practically defines "ignorant and unpolisht people" as those who honor and respect the nobility. When he tells of the grants made by Charles II, "to gratifie some Nobles about him," he suggests that the king will violate the law and oppress the people to please his cronies. "As soon as ever the Country came to know" about the grants "they remonstrated against them; and the Assembly drew up an humble Address to his Majesty, complaining of the said Grants, as derogatory to the previous Charters and Privileges granted to that Colony, by his Majesty and his Royal Progenitors" (75). The Virginia Assembly sent representatives to England to remonstrate against the grants and, if necessary, to buy the nobles out. The Assembly therefore had to raise funds. And so Beverley writes one of his many sympathetic portraits of the poor: these "Taxes and Amercements fell heaviest on the poor

People, the Effect of whose Labour wou'd not cloath their Wives and Children" (76).

Contradicting himself, Beverley later claims that Virginia really has no poor. The climate and soil are simply too good: "They live in so happy a Climate, and have so fertile a Soil, that no body is poor enough to beg, or want Food, though they have abundance of People that are lazy enough to deserve it" (275). He portrays American society as a happy medium: "as they have no body that is poor to beggary, so they have few that are rich" (275). The truth, as Beverley well knew, was quite different. He even talks of the different kinds of hospitality of the rich and the poor planter (313), and he describes the mansions that some wealthy planters were building in his own day (289–90).

An economic historian might portray Beverley, his brother-in-law William Byrd, and contemporaries like Robert "King" Carter as the robber barons of their time. In fact, Robert Quary, who succeeded Edward Randolph as surveyor general of the customs, viewed the great planters in just this way. In his memorial of 1703 to the Board of Trade, Quary says that the wealthy planters (who number "from ten to thirty" on each of Virginia's major rivers) oppress the poor and (like the nineteenth-century robber barons) run company towns. "These Gentlemen take care to supply the poorer sort with goods and necessaries, and are sure to keep them always in their debt, and consequently dependant on them."[71]

Unlike Quary, Beverley portrays Virginia as a comparatively egalitarian state for white men. "The Freeholders are the only Electors, and where-ever they have a Free-hold, (if they be not Women, or under Age) they have a Vote in the Election" (241). According to Beverley, everyone who wants a freehold can have one. He ignores slaves. He even ignores what he knows of Indian customs, seizing upon a misprint in Captain John Smith's *General History* to maintain that the Indians have "a sort of Servants among them . . . call'd Black Boys . . . [who] are attendant upon the Gentry, to do their servile Offices." Perhaps Beverley was simply mocking the ignorance of English readers who might believe this, but he may have meant to defend Virginia's increasingly common practice of slavery by suggesting that it existed even in a "state of Nature" (226). Beverley's only extended discussion of slaves occurs in Chapter 10 of Book Four, "*Of the Servants and Slaves in* Virginia," in which his major purpose is to re-fute the tales of "Cruelties and Severities imputed to that Country" regarding white indentured servants (274).[72]

Beverley states that every person has the right to fifty acres of land. Today's indentured servants are tomorrow's freeholders: "Each Servant at his Freedom, receives of his Master fifteen Bushels of Corn, (which is sufficient for a whole year) and two new Suits of Cloaths, both Linnen and Woollen; and then becomes as free in all respects, and as much entituled to the Liberties, and Priviledges of the Country, as any other of the Inhabitants or Natives are. Each servant has then also a Right to take up fifty Acres of Land, where he can find any unpatented: But that is no great Privi-lege, for any one may have as good a right for a piece of Eight" (274).

Celebrating Virginia as "the best poor Man's Country in the World,"[73] Beverley maintains that the poor are legally and in practice equal to "any other Inhabitants" (274). He claims that Virginia's servants and slaves are actually better off than the ordinary English farmer (272). Beverley reflects the omnipresent American Dream. Indeed, the whole idea of the American Dream (the major theme of all American pro-motion literature) posits that a poor person has the possibil-ity, the opportunity, to become rich and respected. More fun-damentally (as I have elsewhere pointed out), the American Dream is the idea of possibility, though its most common example is the material one expressed by the cliché of the rise from rags to riches.[74] According to Beverley, the Ameri-can Dream is frequently fulfilled in Virginia. Although Bev-erley must have known numerous poor people, he also must have known many wealthy contemporaries who were de-scended from former indentured servants.[75] Beverley presents the (supposedly typical) course of life of colonial Virginia's orphans as a paradigm of the rise of the disadvantaged. Or-phans "who are either without any Estate, or have very little" are well cared for as children, and at the age of eigh-teen (for girls) and twenty-one (for boys) are given their free-dom. "At which time, they who have taken any care to im-prove themselves, generally get well Married, and live in Plenty, tho they had not a farthing of paternal Estate" (260).

According to Beverley, the Virginia poor had the respect, commiseration, and charity of the rich. The ideal gentleman and the role model who appears in Beverley's *History* is William Byrd I, Beverley's father-in-law. It is Byrd who creates and takes pleasure in the garden that Beverley so celebrates (299), plans to mine for iron (55, 126), rationalistically mocks conjurations (204–205), and befriends the Huguenot poor (282–84). The Huguenots—"several hundred Families of Men, Women, and Children"—were shipwrecked and "set ashoar Naked and Hungry." Because they were numerous and foreign, some "Ill-natur'd People" fancied that the Huguenots came "to eat the Bread out of their Mouths." But Byrd, "Upon their first Arrival in that Country . . . receiv'd them with all the tenderness of a Father; and ever since has constantly given them the utmost Assistance" (283). The panegyric upon Byrd not only makes the usual Christian point that charity to the poor is a virtue but also suggests that the poor are innately equal to the rich. The Huguenots are all becoming freeholders. The *History*'s concluding praise for Byrd has an agrarian note. Beverley says that some of the Huguenots have begun "to shift for themselves." But the title to the land where they settled has not been officially conferred upon them, and so he urges Byrd to undertake an additional kindness: "However, they are not yet so far advanc'd, but that their Patron, may still have an opportunity, of shewing his Kindness towards them; which is to prevail with the Assembly, to bestow upon them a certain Title to the Land they now possess, to which as yet they have no other Right, but the bare sitting down upon unseated Land. This seems to be worthy of an early care, lest the Land which they have improv'd by their Industry from wild Woods, should hereafter unjustly be taken away from their Children" (284). Working the land gives one title to it. Beverley surely here implies a radical agrarianism. Like Captain John Smith before him and John Mercer and Benjamin Franklin after him, Beverley believed in comparatively egalitarian ideals (*i.e.*, an equal opportunity to achieve success) and believed that hard work would probably lead to success.[76]

Of course he elsewhere contradicts himself, and he ignores slaves, but it is a rare person who never violates his ideals. Beverley's tendency toward egalitarianism appears in his personal life. Although he was a dominant Virginia aristocrat and a leading lawyer, there are no records of him signing his name "Robert Beverley, gent." or "Robert Beverley, esq." (terms commonly used by his educational, social, and financial equals), but we do have one record of his signature as "Robert Beverley, yeoman."[77] Beverley anticipates Thomas Jefferson's yeoman ideal.[78]

In his *History and Present State of Virginia*, Beverley reflects his English and American predecessors and contemporaries. Robert D. Arner has pointed out his use of Locke's *Essay Concerning Human Understanding*, and Beverley seems to allude to Locke's tabula rasa when he says that the Indians, upon their first contact with the whites, "seem'd rather to be like soft Wax, ready to take any Impression" (16). Although Beverley cites Francis Bacon twice (178, 220), both passages are plagiarized from John Banister. He cites Charles Davenant (278) and Josiah Child (17), but I suspect these references are taken from *An Essay upon the Government of the English Plantations on the Continent of America*, which Beverley certainly knew and used. Learned references to such authors as Belon, Olearius, Piso, and Clusius (219, 220, 224) indicate his plagiarisms from Banister.[79]

Beverley's major sources, except for John Locke, are primarily in three literary traditions. First, he knows, quotes from, and sometimes plagiarizes the standard Americana—the literature of travel and exploration. Hakluyt, Purchas, Hariot, Smith, Hennepin, and Lahontan are favorites (though the passage citing "Heriot, De Bry, Smith, Purchass . . . [and] Parkinson" [218] is lifted from Banister).[80] Second, as a leading lawyer of his day, he was familiar with all the standard English legal literature.[81] His third and major source is Virginiana: the letters and memorials to the Board of Trade (not only those by Francis Nicholson and Robert Quary but also *The Present State of Virginia*, by Hartwell, Blair, and Chilton); the manuscripts and printed materials describing colonial Virginia; and the official records of Virginia. Of the manuscripts describing colonial Virginia it is certain that Beverley plagiarized extensively from John Banister. I believe he also used William Byrd's manuscript history of Virginia. He read its redaction by John Oldmixon, and he probably had a copy of the entire original. He certainly knew and used *An Essay upon the Government of the English Plantations on the Continent of America* (1701) "by An American." And he may have known William Fitzhugh's manuscript history of Virginia and description of its government.

Probably the Virginiana that Beverley knew best were the official proceedings of Virginia's government: the House of Burgesses, the General Court, and the county courts. At various times he served as clerk of King and Queen County Court, as clerk of the Sussex County Court, as clerk of the committee for public claims, as temporary clerk of the General Court, as clerk of the secretary of Virginia (*i.e.*, Ralph Wormeley, possible author of *An Essay upon the Government of the English Plantations*), as register of the court of admiralty, and as clerk of the House of Burgesses. He worked intensively with the various records of Virginia's legal and administrative history for at least ten years before writing the *History*.[82] Beverley himself confirms this impression. He opens the preface to the 1722 edition with the statement: "My first Business in the World being among the public Records of my Country, the active Thoughts of my Youth put me upon taking Notes of the general Administration of the Government" (1722 ed., sig. A2).

The records of Virginia in the immediate past would have had all the fascination for Beverley that the early records of Massachusetts had for Nathaniel Hawthorne. His father, Major Robert Beverley, was a chief actor in Virginia's history throughout the period from the mid-1660s to his death in 1686/7. Who could doubt that Beverley was greatly interested in the father who had died in Virginia when the young Beverley was a schoolboy of approximately fourteen in England? In the *History* his father's friends are generally the admirable figures in Virginia's immediate past, and his father's worst enemies are those contemptible "Noble Lords," Culpepper and Effingham. Since both Charles II and James II specifically attacked Major Robert Beverley, the historian son would have had some reason for resenting not only "Noble Lords" but also imperious kings. Beverley never mentions his father in the 1705 edition of the *History* (though in the 1722 edition he adds two allusions to his father's role as the most active commander in putting down Bacon's Rebellion [1722 edition, 72, 74]), and he often celebrates his own father-in-law, William Byrd I. But just as I believe the most important literary influence upon Beverley's attitudes were the manuscript records, journals, and laws of earlier Virginia, so too do I believe the most important role model and influence upon Beverley is that Great Commoner of Virginia politics of the 1670s and 1680s, Major Robert Beverley.[83]

William Fitzhugh (1651–1701) is generally regarded as the most studious and learned lawyer of late-seventeenth-century Virginia, but Fitzhugh judged Major Robert Beverley to be "the best acquainted with the practic part [of law] in Virginia." Besides being the most expert Virginia courtroom attorney of his day, Major Beverley famously defended the rights of the burgesses. In April, 1677, as clerk of the House of Burgesses, he refused to turn over the records of the House to the royal commissioners sent to investigate Bacon's Rebellion. After the commissioners seized them by force, the House of Burgesses protested that the seizure violated their rights and privileges. In reaction Charles II directed Culpepper to "find out . . . the authors and abettors" of the burgesses' defense of Beverley, "so they may receive the marks of our displeasure for this their great presumption." Again in 1682 Major Beverley protected the journals of the House— this time from the Council. He wrote the comprehensive bill for Virginia's economy in 1680 that his son disgustedly reported was defeated by the London merchants. In 1681 he organized the Middlesex County voters to call upon their burgesses for measures to limit the production of tobacco. He was responsible for calling the second session (April 18– 25, 1782) of the Assembly of 1680–1682; he had the burgesses' address to the deputy governor read aloud in every county (together with an abstract of the reasons for the address); and he evidently organized the plant-cutter rebellion in 1682.[84]

Imprisoned for his role in the plant-cutter rebellion, Major Robert Beverley hired his friend William Fitzhugh to defend him. Fitzhugh assured him on May 29, 1682, "Sir, Magna Charta, the Petition of Right and the divers Statutes made in Confirmation of the first, with the severall Commentarys and Expositions upon all, setting forth the liberty of the subject, together with the causes and occasions of this confinement, I am indifferently well furnished with, and assure your self shall not be wanting to one of the choicest of my friends."[85] Beverley was nevertheless held prisoner for over a year without being accused of a crime and without any recourse. He subsequently wrote a documentary narrative concerning the imprisonment. Since the manuscript remained in the family until the early nineteenth century, his historian son certainly read it.[86] As Major Beverley and his contemporaries knew, his imprisonment violated the traditional legal rights of Englishmen. Finally freed, reelected a burgess, and reelected clerk of the House of Burgesses, he caused the "unruly" procedures during the session of 1684. Therefore, James II, on August 1, 1686, wrote Effingham that Major Robert Beverley should "be declared uncapable of any office or public imployment within our collony of Virginia." Beverley was removed from his lucrative offices (and he died in 1686/7), and Virginians were evidently outraged by the directive against their leader. His lucrative position as surveyor was promptly awarded to his eldest son, Peter Beverley. Within a few years, the burgesses elected Peter to his father's major position of power, clerk of the House of Burgesses.[87]

In many ways Major Robert Beverley anticipates the attitudes and beliefs of his younger son, the historian Robert Beverley. Major Beverley not only repeatedly asserted the rights of the House of Burgesses and of the individual, but, in the opinion of John Rainbolt, he was also responsible for altering the style of leadership in colonial Virginia from patriarchical to popular and in shifting the colonial leaders away from a modified English mercantilism to a provincial mercantilism. Charles Campbell, the foremost mid-nineteenth-century Virginia historian, believed that Major Beverley greatly influenced his son, and so too does the contemporary historian Wilbur R. Jacobs.[88] No one can be certain of the degree of Major Beverley's influence, but there can be no doubt that his political attitudes prefigure his son's.

The historian Robert Beverley was an excellent writer, but he was not an especially original thinker. His political and emotional attitudes were common among his friends and older contemporaries. Indeed, key Virginia documents from the mid-seventeenth century to Beverley's day contain almost all the political attitudes expressed in *The History and Present State of Virginia*.[89] The *History* is all the more significant, however, for publicly representing the beliefs of Beverley and his contemporaries. It presents an early and relatively full portrait of the emerging American political ideology. The syndrome of attitudes in Beverley's *History* is the staple of colonial eighteenth-century political and historical writing, found frequently in the journals of the colonial legislatures, in speeches from the lower houses of assembly on such standard topics as the fixed salary for the governors, in the political essays appearing in the news-

papers, and even, commonly, in political sermons. One need
not look for eighteenth-century English origins of these attitudes when they are expressed by Benjamin Franklin, James
Otis, Patrick Henry, John Adams, Thomas Jefferson, and
others. They were a common American heritage.

The origins of the American Revolution are many and diverse. But the political ideology presented by Robert Beverley in his *History* in 1705 was, I claim, more important
and more familiar to more American revolutionaries than all
the English opposition writers whom the patriots felt free to
cite. One may then ask, If that is so, why did the American
Revolution not occur until 1775? Other necessary imperial,
social, economic, cultural, geographic, and demographic
changes were necessary before there could be a revolution.
Among the most important: Britain would have to outrage
all the colonies simultaneously by its actions and attitudes;
the mainland colonies would have to achieve a greater degree
of mutual communication and identification; the colonies
would have to attain a population and a geographical space
large enough and self-sufficient enough to sustain a protracted war; and the local institutions of colonial society
(legal, political, military, social, and religious) would have to
be well enough established to maintain order despite the
lack of a central authority. But Robert Beverley's *History and
Present State of Virginia* proves that by 1705 the emotional
and ideological bases for the American Revolution existed.

*Thanks are due Dr. John M. Hemphill of Colonial Williamsburg,
Inc., and Professor Raymond Wolters of the University of Delaware for reading and commenting upon an earlier version of this
essay.—J.A.L.L.*

Notes

1. Jack P. Greene, "The Reappraisal of the American Revolution in Recent Historical Literature," in Greene (ed.), *The Reinterpretation of the American Revolution, 1763–1789* (New York, 1968), 2–74; Robert E. Shalhope, "Toward a Republican Synthesis: The Emergence of an Understanding of Republicanism in American Historiography," *William and Mary Quarterly,* 3rd ser., XXIX (1972), 49–80 (hereafter cited as *WMQ*; series is 3rd unless otherwise specified); Shalhope, "Republicanism and Early American Historiography," *WMQ,* XXXIX (1982), 334–56; John M. Murrin, "The Great Inversion; or, Court Versus Country: A Comparison of the Revolution Settlements in England (1688–1721) and America (1776–1816)," in J. G. A. Pocock (ed.), *Three British Revolutions: 1641, 1688, 1776* (Princeton, 1980), 368–445, Pocock, "Political Development," in Jack P. Greene and J. R. Pole (eds.), *Colonial British America: Essays in the New History of the Early Modern Era* (Baltimore, 1984), 408–56.

2. Caroline Robbins, *The Eighteenth-Century Commonwealthman: Studies in the Transmission, Development and Circumstances of English Liberal Thought from the Restoration of Charles II Until the War with the Thirteen Colonies* (Cambridge, Mass., 1961); Bernard Bailyn, *The Ideological Origins of the American Revolution* (Cambridge, Mass., 1967); Gordon S. Wood, *The Creation of the American Republic, 1776–1787* (Chapel Hill, 1969); J. G. A. Pocock, *The Machiavellian Moment: Florentine Political Thought and the Atlantic Republican Tradition* (Princeton, 1975).

3. John M. Murrin, "Anglicizing an American Colony: The Transformation of Provincial Massachusetts" (Ph.D. dissertation, Yale University, 1966).

4. The newspapers and later the magazines often reprinted or reflected the dominant English writers. Although Stephen Botein, "'Meer Mechanics' and an Open Press," *Perspectives in American History* IX (1975), 197 n. 69, has called his conclusions too sweeping, Gary Huxford proves that John Trenchard and Thomas Gordon's writings (especially *Cato's Letters*) were well known and often reprinted in the colonial newspapers. Huxford, "The English Libertarian Tradition in the Colonial Newspaper," *Journalism Quarterly,* XLV (1968), 677–86.

5. For example, in his preface to *The History of the First Discovery and*

Settlement of Virginia (Williamsburg, 1747), iii, v, William Stith reveals the profound influence of two role models: Sir John Randolph and William Byrd of Westover. Jack P. Greene, "Search for Identity: An Interpretation of the Meaning of Selected Patterns of Social Response in Eighteenth-Century America," *Journal of Social History*, III (1970), 191–205, considers the influence of the colonial past upon the Revolutionary generation, but he slights the seventeenth-century Virginia past. T. H. Breen, ignoring abundant evidence to the contrary, actually maintains that Virginians had little interest in their own history. Breen, "Of Time and Nature: A Study of Persistent Values in Colonial Virginia," in Breen, *Puritans and Adventurers: Change and Persistence in Early America* (New York, 1980), 164–96, 262–70.

6. Bernard Knollenberg, *Origin of the American Revolution, 1759–1766* (Rev. ed.; New York, 1965), 57–66; Bernard Bailyn, *The Pamphlets of the American Revolution* (Cambridge, Mass., 1965), 292–354.

7. Bland and Landon Carter led the fight against the pistole fee (Governor Dinwiddie's charge of a pistole for a legal seal on new patents of land) and later against the parsons in the Twopenny Act controversy. J. A. Leo Lemay, "John Mercer and the Stamp Act in Virginia, 1764–1765," *Virginia Magazine of History and Biography* (hereafter cited as *VMHB*), XCI (1983), 3–38.

8. W. Paul Adams puts this passage in context in "Republicanism in Political Rhetoric Before 1776," *Political Science Quarterly*, LXXV (1970), 406.

9. Edmund S. Morgan, *American Slavery/American Freedom: The Ordeal of Colonial Virginia* (New York, 1975), 373.

10. On Parks, see J. A. Leo Lemay, *Men of Letters in Colonial Maryland* (Knoxville, 1972), 111–25. And see Darrett B. Rutman's introduction to Stith's *History of the First Discovery and Settlement of Virginia* (1747; rpr. New York, 1969), v–xix; and Thad W. Tate, "William Stith and the Virginia Tradition," in Lawrence H. Leder (ed.), *The Colonial Legacy: Volumes III and IV* (4 vols.; New York, 1971–73), 121–45.

11. Although the title in the manuscript catalog of Byrd's library is given only as "History of Virginia," it is an octavo, and "Smiths History of Virginia" is listed later in the catalog as a folio. Byrd also had two octavo volumes entitled "State of Virginia" and one simply called "Virginia" in the catalog. John Spencer Bassett (ed.), *The Writings of William Byrd* (New York, 1901), 415, 416, 439.

12. J. A. Leo Lemay, Review of Mitchell Robert Breitwieser, *Cotton Mather and Benjamin Franklin*, in *American Literature*, LVIII (1986), 128; Lawrence W. Towner, "*Ars Poetica et Sculptura:* Pocahontas on the Boston Common," *Journal of Southern History* XXVIII (1962), 482–85; William Stith, *History of the First Discovery and Settlement of Virginia* (1747; rpr. Spartanburg, S.C., 1965), 16, 154, 160, 182; C. Malcolm Watkins, *The Cultural History of Marlborough, Virginia: An Archeological and Historical Investigation* (Washington, D.C., 1968), 200; Richard Beale Davis, *Intellectual Life in the Colonial South, 1585 to 1763* (3 vols.; Knoxville, 1978), II, 544; *General Magazine* (February, March, and April, 1741), 83–88, 147–53, 217–18; Appleton P. C. Griffin and William Coolidge Lane, *A Catalogue of the Washington Collection in the Boston Athenaeum* (Boston, 1897), 23; E. Millicent Sowerby, *Catalogue of the Library of Thomas Jefferson* (5 vols.; Washington, D.C., 1952–59), no. 503; Thomas Jefferson to Peter Carr, Au-

gust 10, 1787, in Julian P. Boyd *et al.* (eds.), *The Papers of Thomas Jefferson,* (Princeton, 1955–), XII, 14–19; Jefferson, *Notes on the State of Virginia,* ed. William Peden (Chapel Hill, 1955), 177, 188, 297.

13. For the secondary bibliography see Jack D. Wages, *Seventy-Four Writers of the Colonial South* (Boston, 1979), 61–68; John Seelye, *Prophetic Waters: The River in Early American Life and Literature* (New York, 1977), 343–62; Davis, *Intellectual Life in the Colonial South,* I, 84–91; and Judy Jo Small, "Robert Beverley and the New World Garden," *American Literature,* LV (1983), 525–40.

14. J. A. Leo Lemay, "The Amerindian in the Early American Enlightenment: Deistic Satire in Robert Beverley's *History of Virginia* (1705)," in Lemay (ed.), *Deism, Masonry, and the Enlightenment: Essays Honoring Alfred Owen Aldridge* (Newark, 1987), 79–92.

15. Stith, *History of the First Discovery and Settlement of Virginia,* 154; Robert A. Brock, in Justin Winsor (ed.), *Narrative and Critical History of America* (8 vols.; Boston, 1884–89), III, 165; Jarvis M. Morse, *American Beginnings* (Washington, D.C., 1952), 216; and Richard L. Morton, *Colonial Virginia* (2 vols.; Chapel Hill, 1960), I, 172; Wesley Frank Craven, *Dissolution of the Virginia Company* (New York, 1932), 4; Wilcomb E. Washburn, *The Governor and the Rebel: A History of Bacon's Rebellion in Virginia* (Chapel Hill, 1957), 177.

16. Alden T. Vaughan, "The Evolution of Virginia History: Early Historians of the First Colony," in Vaughan and George A. Billias (eds.), *Perspectives on Early American History: Essays in Honor of Richard B. Morris* (New York, 1973), 31.

17. Morgan, *American Slavery/American Freedom,* 320–26, 381–84; Daniel A. Baugh, "Poverty, Protestantism, and Political Economy: English Attitudes Toward the Poor, 1660–1800," in Stephen B. Baxter (ed.), *England's Rise to Greatness, 1660–1763* (Berkeley, 1983), 63–108; Virginia Bernhard, "Poverty and the Social Order in Seventeenth-Century Virginia," *VMHB,* LXXXV (1977), 141–55.

18. Bailyn, *Ideological Origins,* xi, 43. See also A. E. Dick Howard, *The Road from Runnymede: Magna Carta and Constitutionalism in America* (Charlottesville, 1968), 58–65.

19. J. A. Leo Lemay, "The Great Commoner," *Notes and Queries,* n.s., XXVII (1980), 420. On Bordley's achievements and influence, see Lemay, *Men of Letters,* 74, 93–94, 112; and Lemay, "John Mercer," 26–29.

20. Robert Beverley, *The History and Present State of Virginia* (1705), ed. Louis B. Wright (Chapel Hill, 1947), 237. Hereafter page references to the *History* will be given in the text and are to this edition unless otherwise specified. See also Wesley Frank Craven, ". . . And So the Form of Government Became Perfect," *VMHB,* LXXVII (1969), 131–45.

21. Building upon Lewis P. Simpson's observation that Beverley uses the edenic motifs of promotion literature, Judy Jo Small finds that the Christian scheme of Eden, the Fall, and a postlapsarian world provides a recurring structural motif in Beverley's *History,* though she does not find such a structure within Book One. John Seelye noted that Beverley "posits a Golden Age and a Good Governor, the both identified with Sir William Berkeley." Simpson, *The Dispossessed Garden: Pastoral and History in Southern Literature* (Athens, 1975), 15–17; Small, "Robert Beverley and the New World Garden"; Seelye, *Prophetic Waters,* 346.

22. Beverley temporarily forgot that the charter of October 10, 1676, was not the one drafted by the Virginians that "contains that which we humbly conceive to be the right of Virginians, as well as all other Englishmen, which is, *not to be taxed but by their consent, expressed by their represen-tatives*"—but was instead "a poor, evasive, makeshift of a charter." William Waller Hening (ed.), *The Statutes at Large: Being a Collection of All the Laws of Virginia* (13 vols.; Richmond, 1809–23), II, 535; Morton, *Colonial Virginia*, I, 210. Thomas J. Wertenbaker prints this charter which did not pass the Great Seal, in "The Virginia Charter of 1676," *VMHB*, LVI (1948), 263–66. Beverley corrected his account in the 1722 edition, writing, "All those agents could obtain . . . was merely the Name of a new Charter."

23. A report to the Board of Trade written in 1697, though not published until 1727, singled out Culpepper for special censure. In his *History* Beverley sometimes echoes it and sometimes disagrees with it—though he never acknowledges it. For the report's strongest diatribe against Culpepper, see Henry Hartwell, James Blair, and Edward Chilton, *The Present State of Virginia, and the College*, ed. Hunter Dickinson Farish (Williamsburg, 1940), 57; *cf.* 26–27, 32, 42, 46.

24. Jon Kukla, "Robert Beverley Assailed: Appellate Jurisdiction and the Problem of Bicameralism in Seventeenth-Century Virginia," *VMHB*, LXXXVIII (1980), 415–29.

25. H. R. McIlwaine (ed.), *Executive Journals of the Council of Colonial Virginia* (6 vols.; Richmond, 1925–66), I, 392–93 (hereafter cited *Executive Journals*). In his introduction to the burgesses' journals, McIlwaine finds it "remarkable that so careful a writer as *Beverley*, the son of that *Robert Beverley* who was for a long time the distinguished clerk of the House of Burgesses, should make a mistake in reference to such an important question." H. R. McIlwaine and John Pendleton Kennedy (eds.), *Journals of the House of Burgesses of Virginia* (13 vols.; Richmond, 1905–15), II (1659/60–1693), xx (hereafter cited *JHB* with date).

26. Bernard Bailyn, "The Central Themes of the American Revolution: An Interpretation," in Stephen G. Kurtz and James H. Hutson (eds.), *Essays on the American Revolution* (Chapel Hill, 1973), 13.

27. See Leonard W. Labaree *et al.* (eds.), *The Papers of Benjamin Franklin* (24 vols. to date; New Haven, 1959–), XV, 8, *cf.* V, 444.

28. Hartwell, Blair, and Chilton, *The Present State of Virginia*, 14–16, explains why governors did not want fixed rates of exchange.

29. Quary's memorial of June 16, 1703, is printed in *Collections of the Massachusetts Historical Society*, 3rd ser., III (1838), 223–42. For his account of Nicholson's giving his own money, see 232. Beverley echoes James Blair's contention that Nicholson was partly responsible for Quary's letters and memorials. See Blair's affidavit of April 25, 1704, in William Stevens Perry (ed.), *Historical Collections Relating to the American Colonial Church, Vol. 1: Virginia* (Hartford, Conn., 1870), 104 (hereafter cited as *Historical Collections*).

30. Louis B. Wright, "William Byrd's Opposition to Governor Francis Nicholson," *Journal of Southern History*, XI (1945), 76–77; Nicholson to the Board of Trade, March 13, 1702/3, in W. N. Sainsbury *et al.* (eds.), *Calendar of State Papers, Colonial Series, America and West Indies* (42 vols.; London, 1860–1953), XXI, 259 (hereafter cited *CSP*).

31. Quary proposes a unified America, but I did not find his suggestion for a standing army. Quary, memorial of June 16, 1703, pp. 230, 231, 234. But James Blair charged Nicholson with this desire in his affidavit of April 25, 1704, in *Historical Collections*, 106–107. Beverley probably echoes Blair. Stephen Saunders Webb does not doubt that Nicholson and Quary did desire a standing army. Webb, "The Strange Career of Francis Nicholson," *WMQ,* XXIII (1966), 540–41.

32. *JHB,* 1702–12, pp. 49, 90, 93, 116; *CSP,* XXIII, 22, 28. A pseudonymous tract by a Virginian had censured "the mischievous contrivances of some Evil Ministers about the Court, whereby the Plantations have been very much injured and oppressed." An American, *An Essay on the Government of the English Plantations on the Continent of America* (1701), ed. Louis B. Wright (San Marino, Calif., 1945), 13. James Blair charged Nicholson and Quary with misrepresenting Virginia and Virginians. *Historical Collections,* 102, 106–107. Beverley's actions anticipate Franklin's in the affair of the Hutchinson and Oliver letters. Labaree *et al.* (eds.), *The Papers of Benjamin Franklin,* XX, 539–80.

33. Hening (ed.), *The Statutes at Large,* II, 463–64.

34. Again Beverley echoes Blair's affidavit. *Historical Collections,* 109. Blair and Beverley may both have known that Nicholson, earlier, in Maryland, had threatened to hang the first supporters of King William as rebels "with Magna Charta about their necks." Webb, "Strange Career of Francis Nicholson," 533n.

35. Beverley follows Hartwell, Blair, and Chilton, *The Present State of Virginia,* 22–26.

36. John Dunn, "The Politics of Locke in England and America in the Eighteenth Century," in John W. Yolton (ed.), *John Locke: Problems and Perspectives* (Cambridge, England, 1969), 45–80; J. A. Leo Lemay, "The Frontiersman from Lout to Hero: Notes on the Significance of the Comparative Method and the Stage Theory in Early American Literature and Culture," *Proceedings of the American Antiquarian Society,* LXXXVIII (1979), 204–206; Lemay, "The Amerindian in the Early American Enlightenment," note 3.

37. Watkins, *The Cultural History of Marlborough, Virginia,* 192; Howard, *The Road from Runnymeade,* 78–98.

38. Edmund B. O'Callaghan (ed.), *Documents Relative to the Colonial History of the State of New York* (15 vols.; Albany, 1853–87), III, 583 (italics added).

39. Carl Bridenbaugh, *The Spirit of '76: The Growth of American Patriotism Before Independence* (New York, 1975); Chester E. Eisinger, "Land and Loyalty: Literary Expressions of Agrarian Nationalism in the Seventeenth and Eighteenth Centuries," *American Literature,* XXI (1949–50), 160–78; Michael Zuckerman, "The Fabrication of Identity in Early America," *WMQ,* XXXIV (1977), 183–214; Carole Shammas, "English-Born and Creole Elites in Turn-of-the-Century Virginia," in Thad W. Tate and David L. Ammerman (eds.), *The Chesapeake in the Seventeenth Century: Essays on Anglo-American Society* (Chapel Hill, 1979), 274–96; J. A. Leo Lemay, *"New England's Annoyances": America's First Folk Song* (Newark, 1985), esp. 50–65.

40. Lemay, *Men of Letters,* 26; *An Essay on the Government of the En-*

glish Plantations, 3; Beverley, History (1705), 287; Marion Tinling (ed.), The Correspondence of the Three William Byrds of Westover, Virginia, 1684–1776 (2 vols.; Charlottesville, 1977), 474, 487.

41. Shammas, "English-Born and Creole Elites in Turn-of-the-Century Virginia," 274–96; Francis Nicholson to the Board of Trade, December 2, 1701, CSP, XIX, 641–42, 631.

42. Lemay, Men of Letters, vii, 39–42; Eisinger, "Land and Loyalty," 161–64; John C. Rainbolt, "The Alteration in the Relationship Between Leadership and Constituents in Virginia, 1660 to 1720," WMQ, XXVII (1970), 411–34, esp. 431.

43. Benjamin T. Spencer, The Quest for Nationality: An American Literary Campaign (Syracuse, 1957), 7–12, traces American (mainly New England) preference for a plain style from William Morrell's New England (1625) to Emerson and Thoreau. See also Robert A. Bain, "A Note on James Blair and the Southern Plain Style," Southern Literary Journal, IV (Fall, 1971), 68–73; and Theodore Hornberger, "A Note on Eighteenth-Century American Prose Style," American Literature, X (1938), 77–78. George Sandys commented that his translation of Ovid's Metamorphosis (1626) was "bred in the New-world, of the rudenesse whereof it cannot but participate." Richard Beale Davis, "America in George Sandys' 'Ovid,'" WMQ, IV, (1947), 297–304.

44. Calhoun Winton, "Jeremiah Dummer: The First American," WMQ, XXVI (1969), 105–108, points out that Dummer referred to himself as "Anglus Americanus" in 1703. His epithet is later than either Cotton Mather's or the Virginia author of An Essay on the Government of the English Plantations. If we include compound phrases, then Thomas Gage's best seller, The English-American: His Travail by Sea and Land (London, 1648) has priority. Lemay, "The Frontiersman," 219–21. The earliest usage of American that I am certain indicates a non-Indian born in the American colonies occurs in Benjamin Tompson's 1708 elegy on Fitz-John Winthrop: "The third of a Renowned line / Which wee Americans deemed next Divine." Peter White (ed.), Benjamin Tompson, Colonial Bard: A Critical Edition (University Park, Pa., 1980), 163.

45. Simpson, Dispossessed Garden, 16; Small, "Robert Beverley and the New World Garden," 526. Moses Coit Tyler, Leo Marx, and John Seelye have also emphasized the promotional aspect of Beverley's History.

46. Most seventeenth-century intellectuals believed in the old theories of the degeneration of nature and of man and associated it with the supposed degeneration of the American Indian. Anne Bradstreet, George Alsop, and John Josselyn are among the seventeenth-century Americans who found degeneration in American nature. Unfortunately, the exhaustive study by Antonello Gerbi, The Dispute of the New World: The History of a Polemic, 1750–1900, tr. Jeremy Moyle (Pittsburgh, 1973), deals only cursorily with the ideas before 1750 (35–45). Clarence J. Glacken, Traces on the Rhodian Shore: Nature and Culture in Western Thought from Ancient Times to the End of the Eighteenth Century (Berkeley, 1967), supplies the context.

47. Lemay, Men of Letters, 153–57.

48. Robert Bolling, A Memoir of a Portion of the Bolling Family (Richmond, 1868), 4, and Bolling's poem "The Blunt Reply" in his manuscript volume "Hilarodiana," on microfilm in Alderman Library, University of Vir-

ginia, Charlottesville, p. 21; "The Autobiography of the Rev. John Barnard," *Collections of the Massachusetts Historical Society*, XXV (1836), 199–200.

49. Hartwell, Blair, and Chilton, *The Present State of Virginia*, 45, 14; *cf.* 5.

50. Nicholson to the Board of Trade, December 2, 1701, in *CSP*, XIX, 631.

51. Wright, "William Byrd's Opposition to Governor Francis Nicholson," 78.

52. Edward Porter Alexander (ed.), *The Journal of John Fontaine: An Irish Huguenot Son in Spain and Virginia, 1710–1719* (Charlottesville, 1972), 86.

53. *JHB*, 1619–58/9, p. 76.

54. *Cf.* John C. Pearson, "The Fish and Fisheries of Colonial Virginia," *WMQ*, 2nd ser., XXII (1942), 213–20, 353–60, XXIII (1943), 1–7, 130–35, 278–84, 435–39, 3rd ser., I (1944), 179–83.

55. Edward Bancroft, *Remarks on the Review of the Controversy Between Great Britain and Her Colonies* (London, 1769), 67, cited in Washburn, *The Governor and the Rebel*, 8; John Kukla, "Order and Chaos in Early America: Political and Social Stability in Pre-Restoration Virginia," *American Historical Review*, XL (1985), 294.

56. W. A. Speck, "The International and Imperial Context," in Greene and Pole (eds.), *Colonial British America*, 386; Joyce Appleby, *Economic Thought and Ideology in Seventeenth-Century England* (Princeton, 1978); John Bland, *To the Kings Most Excellent Majesty, The Humble Remonstrance . . . on Behalf of the Inhabitants and Planters in Virginia and Mariland* [1661?], reprinted in *VMHB*, I (1893–94), 145, 153, 152; Lebaree *et al.* (eds.), *The Papers of Benjamin Franklin*, V, 441–47, 449–51.

57. Lemay, *"New England's Annoyances"*, 60–61; Hening (ed.), *The Statutes at Large*, III, 404–19. *Cf.* Morton, *Colonial Virginia*, I, 395–96.

58. John C. Rainbolt, "The Absence of Towns in Seventeenth-Century Virginia," *Journal of Southern History*, XXXV (1969), 344–45.

59. John J. McCusker and Russell R. Menard, *The Economy of British America* (Chapel Hill, 1985), 353–58. Although he ignores most printed sources, Thomas C. Barrow proves that Americans resented the Navigation Acts from the beginning. Barrow, *The British Customs Service in Colonial America, 1660–1775* (Cambridge, Mass., 1967).

60. Seelye, *Prophetic Waters*, 353.

61. For other American satires on primitivism see Lemay, *Men of Letters*, 225, 246–47.

62. *An Essay on the Government of the English Plantations*, 24; Richard Beale Davis (ed.), *William Fitzhugh and His Chesapeake World, 1676–1701* (Chapel Hill, 1963), 112, 224, 246, 318, 321, 326–27, 330, 345–49.

63. Stanley N. Katz, "The Problem of a Colonial Legal History," in Greene and Pole (eds.), *British Colonial America*, 482.

64. Hartwell, Blair, and Chilton, *The Present State of Virginia*, 22, 26–27, also views the end of appeals to the General Assembly as a step for the worse, since it thereby canceled one of the three checks on the governor's power.

65. *JHB*, 1659/60–1693, p. xxxviii, note 45, p. xlvi, note 61, p. 228.

66. Hartwell, Blair, and Chilton, *The Present State of Virginia*, 47, is

especially irritated by Virginia's forms of proceeding because they are "almost in every thing, disagreeable to the Laws of *England*."

67. Beverley echoes *An Essay on the Government of the English Plantations*, 23, which questions whether the statutes of England should be law in the colonies and complains that "no one can tell what is Law, and what is not, in the Plantations." Hartwell, Blair, and Chilton, *The Present State of Virginia*, 40, 42–44, also calls attention to the problem.

68. Samuel Clyde McCulloch (ed.), "The Fight to Depose Governor Francis Nicholson—James Blair's Affidavit of June 7, 1704," *Journal of Southern History*, XII (1946), 418–19. Nicholson wrote the Board of Trade on March 6, 1704/5, of "the ill consequence of having custome and common law in these parts." *CSP*, XXII, 436.

69. *Executive Journals*, III, 67, 420, 425, 487; Louis B. Wright and Marion Tinling (eds.), *The Secret Diary of William Byrd of Westover, 1709–1712* (Richmond, 1941), 269, 533; *An Abridgement of the Public Laws of Virginia . . . to Which Is Added . . . Precedents of All Matters . . . Peculiar to Those Laws; and Varying from the Precedents in England* (London, 1722). Although the *Abridgement* is anonymous, William H. Martin definitively attributes it to Beverley. Martin, "Some Virginia Law Books in a Virginia Law Office," *Virginia Law Register*, n.s., XII (1926), 194–98. Fairfax Harrison adds further evidence for the attribution in "Robert Beverley, the Historian of Virginia," *VMHB*, XXXVI (1928), 344. Sowerby, citing neither Martin nor Harrison, misattributes the book because Thomas Jefferson wrote on his copy of the 1728 edition that it was by "William Beverley," Beverley's son. Sowerby, *Catalogue of the Library of Thomas Jefferson*, no. 1870.

70. Beverley uses the nickname both in his letter to David Gwyn of February 12, 1703/4, and in the "Narrative" of the same date. *Executive Journals*, II, 391–92; *CSP*, XXII, 299–300.

71. Quary, memorial of June 16, 1703, p. 232.

72. On Smith's "Black-boys," see Philip L. Barbour (ed.), *The Complete Works of Captain John Smith*, (3 vols.; Chapel Hill, 1986), I, 171–72, II, 124–25.

73. Although James T. Lemon adopts this phrase for the title of his study and comments that it and variations on it were common in Pennsylvania's promotion literature, his earliest example dates from 1724. Lemon, *The Best Poor Man's Country: A Geographical Study of Early Southeastern Pennsylvania* (Baltimore, 1972), 229, note 1.

74. J. A. Leo Lemay, "Franklin's *Autobiography* and the American Dream," in Lemay and P. M. Zall (eds.), *Benjamin Franklin's Autobiography* (New York, 1986), 351.

75. Thomas Jefferson Wertenbaker, *The Planters of Colonial Virginia* (Princeton, 1922), 74, points out that one quarter of the Virginia burgesses in 1652 had emigrated as indentured servants. But Lois Green Carr and Russell R. Menard show that career opportunities for former indentured servants declined during the late seventeenth century. Carr and Menard, "Immigration and Opportunity: The Freedman in Early Colonial Maryland," in Thad W. Tate and David L. Ammerman (eds.), *The Chesapeake in the Seventeenth Century: Essays on Anglo-American Society* (Chapel Hill, 1979), 206–42. See also McCusker and Menard, *The Economy of British America*, 138.

76. Lemay, "John Mercer," 32; Lemay, *The Canon of Benjamin Franklin*,

esp. 130–32. On Smith, see my forthcoming study *The American Dream of Captain John Smith.* Beverley's attitudes toward work partly explain his views concerning his "lazy" contemporaries.

77. Philip Alexander Bruce, *Social Life of Virginia in the Seventeenth Century* (2nd ed.; Lynchburg, Va., 1927), 121. Negative evidence may also be significant. Although books from the libraries of his younger brother (Harry Beverley) and his nephew (Robert Beverley, 1701–1733) survive with an armorial bookplate, our subject, Robert Beverley II, evidently did not use such a bookplate. Thus, alas, we know nothing of his library.

78. Morgan, *American Slavery/American Freedom,* 370–80, presents several suggestive quotations concerning the comparative egalitarianism (relative to Britain) of Virginia society before the Revolution.

79. Joseph Ewan and Nesta Ewan, *John Banister and His Natural History of Virginia 1678—1692* (Urbana, 1970), 357, 379, 380, 382; *An Essay upon the Government of the English Plantations,* 33, 17.

80. Ewan and Ewan, *John Banister,* 378.

81. Bailyn has pointed out that the legal literature was of major importance to the patriots and that the Loyalists and English writers also made good use of it in their opposing arguments. Bailyn, *Ideological Origins,* 30–31. I might add, however, that the disproportionately large number of lawyers advocating "rights and liberties" in the seventeenth and eighteenth centuries identifies that position as an occupational ideology. See Howard, *The Road from Runnymede,* 113–32.

82. A convenient summary of Beverley's various official positions is in Jon Kukla, *Speakers and Clerks of the Virginia House of Burgesses, 1643–1776* (Richmond, 1981), 144–46.

83. Harrison, "Robert Beverley," 334, notes that "during the American Revolution Virginia looked back to the immigrant Beverley as a protomartyr of resistance to arbitrary government by the crown."

84. Davis (ed.), *Fitzhugh,* 93; JHB, 1659/60–1693, xxvii–xxviii, xxxiii, xxxvii–xxxviii.

85. Davis (ed.), *Fitzhugh,* 113–14. See also Howard, *The Road from Runnymede,* 33.

86. Hening (ed.), *The Statutes at Large,* III, 551–71; see also 541–43.

87. *Ibid.,* 41. On Peter Beverley (*ca.* 1668–1728), older brother of the historian, see Kukla, *Speakers and Clerks of the Virginia House of Burgesses,* 103–105.

88. Rainbolt, *From Persuasion,* 117–20, 122–25; Charles Campbell, introduction to Robert Beverley, *History and Present State of Virginia* (Richmond, 1855); Campbell, *History of the Colony and Ancient Dominion of Virginia* (Philadelphia, 1860), 359; Wilbur R. Jacobs, "Robert Beverley: Colonial Ecologist and Indian Lover," in J. A. Leo Lemay (ed.), *Essays in Early Virginia Literature Honoring Richard Beale Davis* (New York, 1977), 91–99.

89. For example: the articles of submission to the Puritan Commonwealth of March 12, 1651 (Hening [ed.], *The Statutes at Large,* I, 363–68); the proposed Virginia charter of 1675 (*ibid.,* II, 523–27, 534–37); the burgesses' address to the king of May 16, 1685 (JHB, 1659/60–1693, pp. 228–30); the burgesses' proceedings in November and December, 1685 (*ibid.,* xlix–1, 503–505; the burgesses' address to William and Mary of May 17, 1691 (*ibid.,* 351–52). Comparable statements can be found in all the existing colonies during the same period.

LOUIS D. RUBIN, JR.

The Romance of the Colonial Frontier: Simms, Cooper, the Indians, and the Wilderness

The first two American novelists to make important literary use of the frontier, the wilderness, and the Indians as shaping forces in the national history were James
Fenimore Cooper and William Gilmore Simms. The New
York–born Cooper, seventeen years older than his South
Carolina compatriot, got there initially with *The Pioneers*
(1823), but obviously it was the second of his five Leatherstocking Tales, *The Last of the Mohicans* (1825), that had
most to do with encouraging Simms to write his first tale of
early American frontier war. *The Yemassee* (1835), like *The
Last of the Mohicans,* was set in the New World forest, involved warfare with the Indians, and reenacted the death of
an Indian tribe. And just as *The Last of the Mohicans* was
the most popular of all of Cooper's novels, so *The Yemassee*
has lasted longest of all Simms's numerous books. It went
through three printings in its first year, appeared in new editions throughout the nineteenth century, and thereafter has
been resurrected from time to time.

As C. Hugh Holman has pointed out, Simms later learned
how to handle narratives in more skillful fashion, develop
more complex characters, and pay more attention to realistic
detail, but "never after *The Yemassee* was he to find again a
group of characters, a situation, an action, and a poetic vision of experience that would speak with as much directness
and force to as large a segment of the American public."[1] *The
Yemassee* may not be Simms's best-crafted work of fiction,
it may be written in slipshod, almost careless fashion at

times, but beyond question Simms's third novel is his most compelling.

Almost nobody today reads either Cooper or Simms without being instructed to do so in an American literature class. The New York novelist, however, wrote a series of books that enjoy a considerably higher reputation among scholars, not so much because he was a better technician of the art of fiction or even a more felicitous writer of prose, as because he was able to tap a vein of myth and meaning of more profound significance to the Western imagination than ever Simms managed. From that moment in *The Pioneers* when, having set out to create a novel of manners, he introduced a dilapidated old frontiersman, Natty Bumppo, and his aged Indian companion, Chingachgook ("pronounced Chicago, I think," according to Mark Twain), Cooper's imagination moved swiftly and decisively into the high romance of civilized man's arrival in the virgin forests of the New World. The Leatherstocking Tales are the saga of our bittersweet conquest of nature, a transaction that offered not only the clash of white versus red man, but the pathos inherent in the fall of timeless innocence in nature before human complicity in history.

However awkwardly handled—and as Mark Twain said, it can get pretty awkward—the characterization of Natty Bumppo, alias Deerslayer, Hawkeye, Leatherstocking, La Longue Carabine, etc., functions at a level of elementary magnificence worthy of the theme being reenacted.[2] The white hunter who puts Western civilization behind him to live in the woods, and in whose personality are joined the natural freedom of the wilderness and the moral conscience of civilization, embodies in his thought and actions the stirring possibility of human nature being reborn into purity through willed innocence, and the inevitable realization that the effort at regeneration must fail. The price of his personal survival is the doom of the circumstance that made the attempt possible: as mediator between wilderness and society he is the unwilling agent of the community from which he flees in its relentless encroachment upon the forest in which he seeks refuge.

So great a drama is not only a central fact of our nation's early history; it is also a symbolic representation of the commencement of that history. When in *The Last of the Mohicans* the chief of the Mohicans, Chingachgook, articulates his loneliness after the death of his son Uncas, the last warrior of a once mighty tribe, Leatherstocking's pledge that he remains as the Indian's friend and companion will not alter the outcome of what has happened. The North American continent is now open to conquest, and whether as friend or foe, the Indian must relinquish the forest to the civilization of the white race whose reluctant pathfinder Leatherstocking is.

Like *The Last of the Mohicans,* Simms's *The Yemassee* is set on the frontier and involves Indian warfare. It, too, recounts the death of a once mighty Indian tribe, and like Cooper's saga it deals, in C. Hugh Holman's words, "with one of the great matters of American tragic romance, the conflict of Indian and white cultures, the pain and injustice with which civilization hacks its path into the American wilderness, the suffering and the tragic grandeur of being one of a fated folk overwhelmed by the onrushing wave of history."[3] Much of the power of Simms's narrative comes from the starkness and finality with which he portrays the Yemassee Indians' desperate effort to drive the early white colonizers of coastal South Carolina back into the sea.

Set during a period early in the history of the Carolina colony, Simms's novel is based on an Indian uprising in the year 1715, when after a period of steady white encroachment on their lands and probably with the encouragement of the Spanish in Florida, the Yemassee Indians banded together with a number of other tribes to fall upon the English settlers, massacring hundreds of whites before they were halted and defeated. The subsequent fighting went on for almost two years, until the last hostile Indian tribe was subdued. The victory cleared the way for English settlers to move from the lands immediately adjacent to the coast into the Carolina backcountry and westward into what is now the state of Georgia.

It has often been pointed out that Simms actually knew considerably more about Indians than Cooper did. Not only had he observed them as a small boy growing up in Charleston, South Carolina, but as a young man, visiting his father in the Southwest, he had spent time among them. For neither Simms nor Cooper, however, did the presence of Indians ever constitute a threat to the communities they lived in. They were writing in a time when the Indians had been thoroughly and effectively eliminated as a menace to the Eastern Seaboard and were being removed to areas west of the Mississippi River. In their presentation of the Indian side of the clash of cultures, therefore, both novelists could write with detachment and could recognize the genuine pathos involved.

Undoubtedly much of the appeal of *The Yemassee* to its readers lay in the detail with which Simms depicted his Indians, as well as in the exciting, if melodramatic, tale. In the former instance he improves on Cooper by showing a great deal more about tribal organization, customs, and little details of Indian life, and by making the story of their defeat dramatically as well as symbolically central to the action of his story. The melodrama of the expulsion of the dissolute young Yemassee warrior Occonestoga from his tribe because he has been corrupted by the white man's gifts, in particular whiskey, and the dramatic action of his mother, Matiwan, in braining him with a hatchet before he can be disgraced for eternity by the removal of the sign of the Yemassee arrow, his tribal totem, from his shoulders, made for exciting reading for novel readers of the 1830s.

Cooper set *The Last of the Mohicans* in the time of the French and Indian War, and the good Indians—mainly Chingachgook, Uncas, and the friendly Delawares—take part on the side of the English, while the wicked Magua and his Hurons aid the French. The obligatory love story accompanying the historical action, with romantic hero and heroine, involves a Virginia-born British officer attempting to escort several young Englishwomen through the forest. Cooper hints at a little race mixing by setting up a secondary romance between Uncas and one of the English girls—who however turns out to be part Negro, so that no affront to the sensibilities of Cooper's audience is offered. Moreover, both are killed off before any permanent genetic damage can be done, and only the pureblood officer and his equally pureblood sweetheart survive to plight their troth.

Simms's love plot, which is even less relevant to the historical situation than Cooper's, has no hint of miscegenation about it. Lord Craven, operating under the alias of Captain Harrison, is in love with the virtuous Bess Matthews, daughter of a frontier dissenting minister. Craven/Harrison easily wins his suit, at the expense of a local swain, Hugh Grayson.

There is also a dastardly pirate, Henry Chorley, who improbably is from the same town as the Matthewses in England and is now on the scene with his ship to deliver Spanish arms to the Yemassees. Chorley attempts to make off with Bess Matthews, but Craven/Harrison, every bit as redoubtable a marksman as Natty Bumppo though considerably less talkative about it, dispatches the pirate with one well-aimed rifle shot.

No one except Craven/Harrison's faithful black slave Hector and one or two others knows that the masterful Captain Harrison, so skilled in Indian fighting that the Yemassees call him "the Coosaw-killer," is in reality the lord palatine and governor of the Carolina colony, though the reader is scarcely deceived; as Holman says, it is one of the most poorly maintained secrets in the history of the novel in America.[4] The historicity of Simms's novel does not extend to the love story; there was indeed a Governor Craven whose energetic leadership beat off the Yemassee attack in 1715, but he certainly had nothing in mind in the way of matrimony with any colonial lass known to historians. Simms's theory of the historical novel readily permitted such flagrant tampering with known historical fact—as did Cooper's on occasion, though fortunately not to the same degree. The South Carolinian's performance in this respect is not unlike that of certain contemporary writers such as E. L. Doctorow, but for very different reasons and to considerably different effect. Doctorow and others are deliberately toying with historical authenticity for purposes of undercutting the traditional authority of "objective reality," historical and otherwise, whereas Simms believes so strongly in the firmness of naked historical fact that he sees no danger whatever in taking pleasing artistic liberties and extensions in order to make it more interesting.

What is largely absent from Simms's version of the white man and the Indian in the forest is the vital dimension that makes the Leatherstocking Tales, for all their clumsiness, so deeply engaging a reenactment of the conquest of the New World wilderness: the tension betwen nature and society, the possibility of moral regeneration within nature, and the inevitability of failure in the attempt. It is this that in the Cooper fiction gives philosophical depth to what is otherwise a social confrontation between two competing races.

And it is important to try to understand *why* the theme is missing in Simms but present in Cooper.

That Simms saw the matter almost exclusively in terms of a social, historical confrontation is made clear in several quite specific passages in *The Yemassee*. Early in the novel the Indian chieftain Sanutee sets out for the forest, and Simms deposes as follows:

> He was one of those persons, fortunately for the species, to be found in every country, who are always in advance of the masses clustering around them. He was a philosopher not less than a patriot, and saw, while he deplored, the destiny which awaited his people. He well knew that the superior must necessarily be the ruin of the race which is inferior—that the one must either sink its existence in with that of the other, or it must perish. He was wise enough to see, that, in every case of a leading differ-ence betwixt classes of men, either in colour or organization, such difference must only and necessarily eventuate in the for-mation of castes; and the one conscious [*sic*] of any inferiority, whether of capacity or of attraction, so long as they remain in propinquity with the other, will tacitly become subjects if not bondmen.[5]

The comment is worded carelessly enough; surely Simms meant that it was the inferiority itself, and not the con-sciousness of it, that would doom the group. But what the passage indicates is that Simms was thinking of the Indian-white relationship of the early 1700s in terms of the slavery controversy that was beginning in the 1830s to attain such momentous proportions in American political life. The same motif is sounded in his handling of the relationship between Craven and his faithful slave Hector, who toward the close of the novel saves his master's life, after which Craven informs Hector that henceforth he is a free man. This produces one of the earliest examples of what in years to come would be-come almost a standard scene in southern fiction, in which a slave, upon being told he is free, indignantly declines to ac-cept his new status. In thus refusing his master's offer, Hec-tor is made by Simms to propose a frequently used proslav-ery argument against emancipation: "Ha! you make Hector free, he turn wuss more nor poor buckrah [*i.e.*, lower-class white]—he tief out of de shop—he git drunk and lie in de ditch—den, if sick come, he roll, he toss in de wet grass of de stable. You come in de morning, Hector dead—and, who know—he no take physic, he no hab parson—who know, I say, maussa, but de debble fine em 'fore anybody else?'"⁶ Left to his own devices in a society dominated by his racial superiors, that is, he will be unable to fend for himself. For a black man, freedom is thus no blessing; he is much better off under the philanthropic care of his master. If given his freedom, he will do just what the young Indian chieftain Occonestoga has done: become a prisoner to his baser instincts and lie about drunkenly in the streets.

Fenimore Cooper's views on the competence of Africans were much the same as Simms's, as any reader of *The Pioneers* knows. If anything they come across to a twentieth-century audience even more offensively because, not being on the defensive about the Peculiar Institution, Cooper feels no need to present it in a favorable light. In the first of the Leatherstocking novels, for example, he shows a slave terrified of his master's lash and clearly thinks it highly amusing. But that was in eighteenth-century New York State, and by Cooper's own day African slavery had all but disappeared north of the Mason-Dixon Line.

Cooper's views on racial superiority and inferiority, as expressed in *The Last of the Mohicans*, are about on a par with Simms's. At one juncture in that novel the wicked Huron chief Magua delivers an oration on race and skin color that, obviously with Cooper's approval, makes the point that the Great Spirit created black-skinned people to be slaves, white-skinned people to be clever owners of slaves, and red-skinned people to be brave, free children of the forest. But though both novelists could portray the Indian-white confrontation as pathetic and the extinction of the red man's hunting society by the more technologically advanced Europeans as tragically inevitable—the Indian was equally gone from Cooperstown as from Charleston—Cooper would identify the Indians *with* the forest, and their disappearance with the disappearance of primitive naturalness. There did not exist for him, in the countryside of rural New York State, another supposedly "inferior" race that not only had no ties whatever with the receding American wilderness, but also played a role in the regional economy that made its preservation— as a subordinate race— of great economic importance to the community he lived in. And of course there is the obvious difference that in Simms's South Carolina of the 1820s and

1830s much of the wilderness had by no means been replaced by farms and homes.

There is more to the matter than merely a question of physical propinquity. Later on we will return to such considerations, but for now I want to compare Simms's protagonist in *The Yemassee*, Lord Craven/Captain Harrison, with Cooper's great hero, Natty Bumppo. We have seen how Simms combines his love story with his adventure plot, in that the hero who directs the defense of the Carolina colony against the onslaught of the Yemassees is also the romantic lead, engaged in winning the hand of the beautiful Bess Matthews. Cooper by contrast builds his love story around a high-minded young Virginia major, Duncan Heyward, and an English girl who is the daughter of a colonel in command of Fort William Henry.

Although courageous and noble-spirited, the major is of little use in fighting off hostile Indians; it is the dauntless Leatherstocking (usually referred to as Hawkeye in this particular story) who takes the lead in forest warfare. But Simms's English-born Lord Craven, in his guise as Captain Harrison, is like Leatherstocking extremely adept at combating hostile red men on their own terms in the wilderness. Although not given to the kind of ingenious use of woodlore that Cooper's hero employs, such as turning streams out of their beds to discover footprints or determining the direction of a fort from the impact of cannonballs on the grass, Craven has long since earned the respect of friend and foe as a frontier fighter. He is an effective frontiersman because he pays attention to signs that others ignore, identifies and analyzes evidence carefully and dispassionately, and generally combines physical dexterity and strength with sharp reasoning and calculated audacity.

Craven/Harrison's gift for leadership is as fully developed as his fighting skills. A stranger among the settlers in the backcountry, he inspires trust and resolution through his demonstrated good judgment and bravery. Thus, when, the battle won, he reveals to the borderers he has led to victory that he is the governor of the Carolina colony, the lord palatine, Charles Craven himself, he only confirms a status that he has *already earned* through his accomplishments as a frontiersman. A century later, and instead of an English lord he might have been Andrew Jackson.

Although as skilled a fighting man as Craven/Harrison, Cooper's Leatherstocking does not himself customarily function as a commander of men so much as an expert in woodcraft and Indian behavior whose advice is very good to have when there is danger about. In *The Last of the Mohicans* he is able, from his long experience in the forest, to match the Hurons' cunning with similar cunning and to function in their milieu as effectively as they can, while also bringing to that milieu the superior knowledge, mental powers, and skill at using firearms of the white man. No Indian can hope to equal his exploits with his rifle, named Killdeer; well do the red men call him La Longue Carabine. But Leatherstocking would not think of presuming to assume the leadership of a beleaguered colony or of acting in any other than in his capacity as scout. And in any kind of complexity of social situation involving the workings of white society, he is out of his element, for he is a humble backwoodsman, scarcely educated, with no claims or pretensions whatever to rank or position.

The difference, then, between Simms's and Cooper's protagonists is in part one of class. The English-born aristocrat Charles Craven *disguises* himself as Gabriel Harrison, a man without public social status, in order to lead the borderers in the defense of the Carolina frontier, whereas Natty Bumppo *is* a member of what in pre-1776 rural New York State is incipiently a middle-class yeomanry, even though it has thus far not had opportunity to do much more than begin clearing the edges of the forest. In his strength of character and purity of morality Leatherstocking might be said to be "nature's nobleman," but insofar as any relationship to the community around him is concerned, his position is lowly. He cannot seriously think, for example, of forming a romantic attachment to Colonel Munro's daughter Alice.

Yet, it is interesting that Simms gives his protagonist a double identity. Whatever his dramatic reasons for so doing— one thinks of the Saxon-born Wilfred of Ivanhoe and his alter ego, the Disinherited Knight, in Simms's favorite Walter Scott novel—the social implications of the division are instructive. It was as if Simms could conceive of an aristocratic young governor, the lord palatine of the recently established colony, being associated with the ugly, catch-as-catch-can warfare of the frontier, but not *in* his role as aristocratic young governor. What might have been feasible in a Scott novel set in England or Scotland was not appropriate to the Carolina backcountry. (Had there been an organized military situation involving professionally trained armies, it might have been different.) To lead the settlers in forest fighting, to command the respect and trust of men who lived on the frontier and knew its ways, Craven's status as English-born aristocrat would not suffice; he must masquerade as Captain Harrison. When there is Indian fighting to be done, the attitudes and assumptions of a sophisticated, well-born gentleman are inappropriate qualifications, just as they are for Cooper's Major Duncan Heyward in *The Last of the Mohicans*. Yet, whereas the New York novelist cannot so much as conceive of the two separate sets of qualifications existing within a single characterization, Simms can imagine it happening, provided an alias is used.

We might note certain differences in the backgrounds of Cooper and Simms. The older novelist was the son of a distinguished judge and was on both his mother's and father's sides descended from colonial gentry. As is well known, his attitude toward democracy and the political role of the common man was ambivalent; a Jacksonian Democrat, he nevertheless believed strongly in social subordination, and his stance was always that of the assured patrician. In his social fiction he repeatedly rebuked his fellow countrymen for their vulgarity and their lack of respect for manners and tradition. Simms, by contrast, was self-made, without antecedents among the gentry, and as a young man enjoyed neither wealth nor social status. As a Jacksonian Democrat, he associated Old Hickory with his Irish-born father, who served under him in the Indian wars of the 1810s and 1820s. Like Jackson himself, though on a lesser scale, Simms forced his way, as it were, into the gentry of South Carolina through his literary distinction and his keen intelligence. When his first wife died and he later remarried, it was to the daughter of a plantation owner.

In respect to plot and to fictional plausibility, it would have been simple enough for Simms to have chosen to write his novel about the Yemassee War with a member of the plain folk as his warrior-hero, without undue violation of historical plausibility (indeed, from that standpoint one wishes that he had not decided to give Lord Craven a fictional frontier bride). His decision to make the aristocratic Craven his protagonist has been ascribed to his attachment, as a southerner, to the Cavalier ideal of the highborn leader.

We might, however, look at the matter the other way around. If, as we have noted, Simms could envision an aristocratic lord palatine as also an effective frontiersman and Indian fighter, albeit in disguise, then does it not also follow that he could envision a frontier figure as Lord Craven—*as an aristocrat?* As he saw it, in other words, it was possible for a man who was an effective leader of middle-class settlers, a vigorous fighter, intelligent and able to outthink his savage foes, and thus a person of proven practical virtues, to *be* the lord palatine, thus fulfilling the social assumptions of the romantic love story as well as those of the action plot.

Simms knew, of course, that historically the leader of the defense of the Carolina colony against the Yemassees in 1715 was Lord Craven, that he was not of the plain folk and did not come from a backwoods milieu. To portray Craven in that way would have been to stretch the creative embellishment of historical truth too far even for Simms. In early-eighteenth-century South Carolina, colonial governors and lords palatine were simply not drawn from the ranks of the plain folk. But later, in the nineteenth century, after the American Revolution had brought an end to British hegemony, similar careers *would* be open to talent. A citizen of humble circumstance, if his mettle were sufficient and his abilities superior, could aspire to lofty status and could gain it by virtue of his own merits—as witness Andrew Jackson, Sam Houston, and numerous others.

With a writer such as Simms it will not do to place too much significance upon what he *does* with a character for purposes of plot; not only was the convention of historical romance of his day, by Cooper out of Scott, an extremely loose affair, with what a modern audience might consider realistic probability subordinated to melodramatic possibility, but as a writer of fiction Simms was, especially at this early point in his career, more loose and more inventive than most. What *can* be legitimately and intensively scrutinized, I think, is *how* a particular characterization or plot development gets into a story in the first place. What does its presence represent, about and for Simms's imagination?

Consider the characterization of Craven/Harrison. Joseph V. Ridgely, in an excellent study of Simms, has noted how Simms's hero's views on religion correspond closely to those of Simms himself.[7] The hero of *The Yemassee* also possesses Simms's keen sense of humor, which sometimes gets him into trouble with the overly pious, just as it did Simms. Moreover, the qualities of leadership and practicality that enable Craven/Harrison to gain his ascendancy over the Carolina backwoodsmen and mobilize them for defense against the Indians are those of the "natural aristocrat," the born leader, rather than the titled nobleman who assumes command by virtue of birthright and decreed position. At no point does Craven/Harrison draw upon his privileged social status to gain his ends; he leads, he cajoles, he persuades the settlers to do what he wishes, and they follow his direction not because he possesses royal warrant but because he can perform better than they can in the woods against the Indians. He reveals his noble status only after he has achieved all that he sets out to do, including the winning of the fair Bess Matthews' hand.

What I am getting at is that in *The Yemassee* Simms took the historical figure of an English-born royal governor and made him what is essentially a *middle-class American* frontier hero, who shares many of the attitudes and opinions of Simms himself. Charles Craven *pretends* to be Gabriel Harrison; surely he does so in order to gain the confidence of the backwoods settlers. It is as if Simms felt that, whether in 1715 or in his own time, what was required to make middle-class American frontiersmen accept one's right to lead them was not hereditary aristocratic status but true leadership qualities, which meant demonstrated mastery of the frontier situation. To be Craven was not sufficient; it was necessary to be what Harrison exemplified. Only after proving his right to command by virtue of ability may Craven then assert his right to do so by virtue of his noble status.

There are numerous indications that in writing his first historical romance of Carolina, Simms brought into play powerful emotional involvements having to do with his own situation. There is in the novel a minor character, an Irishman named Teddy McNamara. Almost his sole plot function in the story is to be taken prisoner by the Indians, subjected to torture, and after defying it, in his flight involuntarily to reveal the hiding place of Craven/Harrison, so that the governor is himself captured. Why, however, an Irishman? It seems clear that he constitutes, in his defiance of his torturers and his willingness to fight back, a tribute to Simms's own Irish-born father, who had died not long before the novel was written, out in Mississippi.

As noted earlier, when Simms had visited his father there in the mid-1820s, he had spent much time among the Indians, and his father had earlier served under Andrew Jackson in the Indian campaigns. The elder Simms had urged his son to leave Charleston and live permanently in the West, where he could practice law and enter politics. In the newly settled territories Simms's lack of highborn social status would be no barrier to his advancement, his father had impressed upon him, whereas if he remained in Charleston he would never be able to overcome his lowly origins. Thereafter Simms recurrently expressed regret at not having followed his father's advice. The characterization of the gallant Teddy McNamara, and his presence there on the frontier in the novel, obviously bears a symbolic relationship, in the mind of the novelist, to the whole matter of leadership, authority, and the frontier. The very nature of his sudden appearance, arbitrarily and with no foreshadowing, and the strong emphasis on his Irishness, increases the sense that, given Simms's carelessness with plot and plausibility, there is something significant in the episode, over and beyond its convenience as plot.

If this is so with the Teddy McNamara episode, it is even more true with another character in the story, Hugh Grayson. He is one of two brothers, the older of whom, Wat, is one of Craven/Harrison's most loyal and resolute aides among the frontiersmen. Hugh, however, the more potentially able of the pair, is rebellious, jealous of Harrison's ascendency over Bess Matthews, and at one point almost does in the captain by foul murder, but his better instincts prevail. Hugh Grayson is one of the *Sturm und Drang* figures, popularized by Klinger, Goethe, and the German preromantics and coming into English literature by way of William Godwin, that Simms and other American writers liked to introduce into their fiction and drama from time to time. Such Hamlet-like characters, "sicklied o'er with the pale cast of thought," are given to dark passions and conflicting emotions, customarily expressed in soliloquy form. They serve the burgeoning needs of the romanticism of the day through providing a means to portray the man of ambition, sensibility, and introspection, doomed to live among mundane, ordinary folk who know not the divine discontent, and fated to loneliness and frustration because of his inability to discover an outlet for his talents. Depending upon his nature and the particular circumstance involved, he can opt for good or for evil.

We first encounter young Hugh Grayson with his brother, who taxes him for his jealousy of so admirable a figure as Captain Harrison. Hugh replies: "I cannot like that man for many reasons, and not the least of these is, that I cannot so readily as yourself acknowledge his superiority, while, perhaps, not less than yourself, I cannot help but feel it. My pride is to feel my independence—it is for you to desire control, were it only for the connexion and the sympathy which it brings to you. You are one of the million who make tyrants. Go—worship him yourself, but do not call upon me to do likewise."[8] Nothing, of course, about the fact that the captain has captured the affections of the girl that Hugh loves, Bess Matthews, is mentioned. A little later in *The Yemassee* Hugh's mother also recognizes his discontent and takes him to task for his unreasonable dislike for the captain merely because he seems to be a gentleman. Hugh agrees.

> Aye, that is the word, mother—he is a gentleman—who knows, a lord in disguise—and is therefore superior to the poor peasant who is forced to dig his roots for life in the unproductive sands. Wherefore should his hands be unblistered, and mine asore? Wherefore should he come, and with a smile and silly speech win his way into people's hearts, when I, with a toiling affection of years, and a love that almost grows into a worship of its object, may not gather a single regard from any? Has nature given me life for this?[9]

The truth is that Grayson has no basis whatever to suspect that Harrison is a nobleman in disguise; nor has the captain refused to get his hands blistered in the dirty work of preparing for frontier defense. At this point in the proceedings Hugh Grayson seems to be all set for villainy, motivated principally by jealousy of Craven/Harrison's way with Bess Matthews. But there is more to Hugh Grayson than this: "Mother, I am a slave—a dog—an accursed thing, and in the worst of bondage—I am nothing," he declares. And (the speech is long, but worth quoting):

> I would be, and I am not. They keep me down—they refuse to hear—they do not heed me, and with a thought of command and a will of power in me, they yet pass me by, and I must give way to a bright wand and a gilded chain. Even here in these

woods, with a poor neighborhood, and surrounded by those who
are unhonoured and unknown in society, they—the slaves that
they are!—they seek for artificial forms, and bind themselves
with constraints that can only have a sanction in the degradation of the many. They yield up the noble and true attributes of
a generous nature, and make themselves subservient to a name
and a mark—thus it is that fathers enslave their children; and
but for this, our lord proprietors, whom God in His mercy take
to himself, have dared to say, even in this wild land not yet their
own, to the people who have battled its dangers—ye shall worship after our fashion, or your voices are unheard. Who is the
tyrant in this?—not the ruler—not the ruler—but those base
spirits who let him rule,—those weak and unworthy, who,
taking care to show their weaknesses, have invited the oppression which otherwise could have no head.[10]

The widow Grayson is alarmed at such talk, and understandably so. Why cannot her boy be content? she asks.
Hugh responds that content is for the sluggard and the idle:
"Discontent is the life of enterprise, of achievement, of
glory—ay, even of affection." When his mother asks why he
must think all these strange thoughts, he tells her that it is
because "I have thought for myself, mother—in the woods,
by the waters—and have not had my mind compressed into
the old time mould with which the pedant shapes the skulls
of the imitative apes that courtesy considers human."[11] And
so on. His mother urges him not to cherish such hate for the
captain and contempt for his brother, to try to live at peace
with himself, and above all not to go around being so unhappy all the time. Hugh is not very optimistic about the
prospects for being able to do so, but he promises to do his
best, and the scene ends.

Ultimately he repents, and thereafter uses his energies
and talents for good causes, for as Simms tells us: "Hugh
Grayson, with all his faults, and they were many, was in reality a *noble fellow*. Full of a high ambition—a craving for the
unknown and the vast, which spread itself vaguely and perhaps unattainably before his imagination—his disappoint-
ments very naturally vexed him somewhat beyond prudence,
and now and then beyond the restraint of right reason"[12]
(italics added). Fortunately Craven/Harrison, despite almost
being murdered by Grayson during one of those moments of
vexation beyond prudence, recognizes Hugh's latent leadership abilities, puts him in charge of a troop of defenders, and,

when the Yemassees are driven off and after Hugh has shown his true mettle, invests him with full military command of the county of Granville as his deputy and spokesman. It is in so doing that he finally reveals his identity as the lord palatine, whereupon Bess Matthews falls into his arms and everybody present shouts for joy. Even Grayson is reconciled: "'I take your commission, my lord,' replied Grayson, with a degree of firm manliness, superseding his gloomy expression and clearing it away—'I take it, sir, and will proceed at once to the execution of its duties. Your present suggestions, sir, will be of value.'" [13]

Joseph V. Ridgely describes the characterization of Hugh Grayson as displaying a southern "fieriness" that Simms saw both as a virtue and potential menace. [14] But Grayson is not an aristocratic young southern hothead such as Ralph Colleton in Simms's previous novel, *Guy Rivers*. It is far more likely that Grayson's function, so far as Simms's imagination goes, is to embody an issue that, especially for the youthful Simms of the early 1830s, was of much emotional importance. For when he wrote *The Yemassee*, Simms had not yet married Chevillette Roach and become a gentleman-planter by marriage. He was still nursing the wounds of his losing battle against the nullifiers as editor of the Charleston *Gazette*; he bitterly resented the class system of Charleston and what he considered his rejection by that city's elite. Throughout his life he felt himself unappreciated by a politically obsessed squirearchy, even though, as we shall see, he ended up adopting many of its tenets. There can be little doubt that Hugh Grayson is expressing views about democracy and the common man that the young Simms also held and that made him describe himself to a northern friend a few years later as "a Democrat of the Jackson School" and insist that "I believe in the people, and prefer trusting their impulses, than the craft, the cupidity & the selfishness of trades & Whiggery." [15] Hugh Grayson is, in a real sense, a portrait of the youthful Simms, lonely and without status in class-conscious Charleston with its mercantile-planter aristocracy, denied a college education, apprenticed to an apothecary, given to wandering by himself in the woods and thinking his own thoughts.

For as noted, there is little reason for Grayson to have attributed to Gabriel Harrison the lordliness that he identifies him as exhibiting; in his behavior among the settlers the lord palatine-in-mufti has not behaved as if deference and obeisance were due him by right. It is as if, for a brief moment, Simms the storyteller has become so caught up in what Hugh Grayson represents that he transfers his narrative persona from Craven/Harrison to the unhappy young frontiersman in order to express his resentment of highborn authority and inherited privilege, which as Grayson declares is even in the early days of the Carolina colony already imposing hierarchy and subordination upon free men in the forests of the New World. The passion with which Grayson denounces such subservience seems excessive for the *Sturm und Drang* set piece; indeed, so genuine does it come across that it causes the reader, for the moment, to view Grayson and his attitude toward imposed authority quite sympathetically.

But if this is so—and it appears quite obvious—then there is a basic social tension present in Simms's thinking, and that tension manifests itself in the relationships exhibited in *The Yemassee*. Whatever the believability of his Jacksonian social views, Hugh Grayson is not the hero of the novel, and except for his brief set piece it is Charles Craven, alias Gabriel Harrison, upon whom the author centers his attention. We have already seen how the sectional politics of the 1830s intrudes into the novel in terms of the need to defend slavery. The incipient North-South schism also makes itself felt in other ways, as in the characterization of the dissenting minister who is Bess Matthews' father. Pastor Matthews, dour, self-righteous, convinced of his own rectitude, and unwilling to tolerate differences of opinion and belief, has little historical legitimacy for being on the Carolina frontier in the year 1715; what he really is, beyond question, is a New England Calvinist, who but for the time and place would be an abolitionist. Simms rings the changes on his smug, holier-than-thou attitude, his naïveté that enables him to believe that the hostile Yemassees are his friends. It is almost as if a slave revolt rather than an Indian uprising were in the offing! When Simms declares of Matthews that "he was a bigot himself, and, with the power, would doubtless have tyrannised after a similar fashion," the parson's antebellum political role is unmistakable: "The world within him was what he could take in with his eye, or control within the sound of his voice. He could not be brought to understand that climates and conditions should be various, and that the popular good, in a strict reference to the mind of man, demanded that people should everywhere differ in manner and opinion."[16]

Matthews is depicted as a Puritan, and Craven/Harrison is set in direct opposition to him as a Cavalier. When the humorless parson chides the captain for his seeming levity, Harrison replies that he will undertake to reform his ways

> when you shall satisfy me that to laugh and sing, and seek and afford amusement, are inconsistent with my duties either to the Creator or the creature. . . . It is you, sir, and your sect, that are the true criminals. Denying, as you do, to the young, all those natural forms of enjoyment and amusement which the Deity, speaking through their own nature, designed for their wholesome nurture, you cast a shadow over all things around you. In this way, sir, you force them upon the necessity for seeking of less obvious and more artificial enjoyments, which are not often innocent, and which are frequently ruinous and destructive. As for the irreverence to religion, and sacred things, with which you charge me, you will suffer me respectfully to deny.[17]

But it is not merely the English civil war of the previous century that Simms is importing into the Carolina frontier in 1715; the laughing Cavalier–dour Puritan dichotomy he is using was a staple of the rhetoric of the sectional division of Simms's own time. It was customary for southern pamphleteers to depict the North, and especially New England abolitionism, as made up of Roundheads and Levellers, and the South as the home of Cavalier chivalry. According to the rhetoric that came to dominate the schism, "the Yankee was a direct descendant of the Puritan Roundhead," as William R. Taylor writes, "and the Southern gentleman of the English Cavalier. . . . Under the stimulus of this divided heritage the North had developed a leveling, go-getting utilitarian society and the South had developed a society based on the values of the English country gentry."[18]

If we look closely at Simms's language, it becomes clear that his idea of democracy was not one that principally focused on the notion that all men are equal and that therefore human distinctions are without a basis in nature. What he has Hugh Grayson denounce is hereditary rank and caste, distinctions that are institutionalized into a caste system, and that prevent or hinder true merit from rising. Hugh Grayson, we have seen, was a "noble fellow"; what he objected to was a system that kept his innate nobility—his powers of imagination and leadership—from being properly recognized.

The enormous popularity of Andrew Jackson in the United States of the 1820s, 1830s, and 1840s was in part a corroboration of the notion of "nature's aristocrat," the remarkable man who, living in a country in which the hereditary institutions of the Old World no longer acted to stifle individual merit among all but the aristocracy, was able to rise by virtue of his own genius to heights previously reserved for kings and members of the nobility. Melville's great Invocation to the Muses in *Moby-Dick*, his apologia for daring to make a Nantucket whaling captain into a tragic hero, is a memorable statement of the theme. Like Simms an enthusiastic member of the Young America literary movement, Melville makes the specific analogy with Jackson: "Bear me out of it, thou great democratic God! who didst not refuse to the swart convict, Bunyan, the pale, poetic pearl; Thou who didst clothe with doubly hammered leaves of finest good, the stumped and paupered arm of old Cervantes; Thou who didst pick up Andrew Jackson from the pebbles; who didst hurl him upon a war-horse; who didst thunder him higher than a throne! Thou who in all Thy mighty, earthly marchings, ever cullest Thy selected champions from the kingly commons; bear me out in it, O God!"[19] In a Western society that had only recently been rocked by the French Revolution and the rise of Napoleon Bonaparte from obscurity into a position of power and might that had sent long-established kingships toppling, and whose armies, staffed with marshals who had found careers open to talent, had won victory after victory, the belief that the individual who possesses the requisite genius and follows his star is fated to achieve fame and glory was nowhere more popular than in a new nation founded on the stated belief that all men are created equal. The career of Jackson seemed to exemplify the principle.

If we think of this ideology in terms of the young, ambitious, obviously talented William Gilmore Simms, self-educated, without assured social credentials, growing up in a city in which caste and class were considered highly important, it is hardly surprising that the fame and success he coveted would be strongly infused with the notion of lofty position and that the shape it would assume would be that of the gentleman-planter, the possessor of a landed estate. Just as Andrew Jackson rose from obscure beginnings in the Waxhaws of Simms's native state to military glory, political supremacy, and the occupancy of the Hermitage near Nashville, Tennessee, so Simms aspired to literary fame, political influence, and a country seat of his own. His exemplar of achieved status, Charles Craven, in the Carolina colony of 1715, and the young frontiersman who so resents his own humble status, Hugh Grayson, can be seen as separate halves of what, a century later, Simms believed need not be separate and discrete individuals but one and the same person. Republican virtue, intense ambition, lofty status, and noble bearing could and should coexist in the same person. The New World was indeed the Land of Opportunity, the frontier was the place for democratic aspiration, the plantation would be the sign and seal of virtue and success, and the gentleman-planter would be the Cavalier who replicated the landed aristocrat of Old England, the symbol of successful achievement.

So thought Simms, and in *The Yemassee* he showed what would make it possible. In this novel of his early literary maturity there was much that grew out of his deepest emotional needs and fondest hopes. Yet, as we have noted, when we compare it with James Fenimore Cooper and his Leatherstocking Tales, what is largely missing in the South Carolina author's novel is the conflict between individual freedom in the wilderness and the needs and commitments of society. Simms's frontier folk may go out into the woods, may even do so, as Hugh Grayson tells his mother, to "walk—out of sight—in the air—I must have fresh air, for I choke strangely."[20] The wilderness may have things to teach the free man who, like Grayson, learns to think for himself "in the woods, by the waters," and thus avoids the rote learning of pedantry and custom. But there is nothing in *The Yemassee* of that self-identification with the forest, the deliberate choosing of the wilderness as a way of escaping from the complexity of civilized society, with its falseness and hypocrisy, such as sends Cooper's Natty Bumppo beyond the settlements.

Leatherstocking, as we have seen, as mediator between the forest and the town, can achieve for himself that access of freedom possible to a life in which, to quote his own

words, he is able to "eat when hungry, and drink when adry;
and ye keep stated hours and rules: nay, nay, you even over-
feed the dogs, lads, from pure kindness; and hounds should
be gaunty to run well. The meanest of God's creaters be made
for some use, and I'm formed for the wilderness; if ye love
me, let me go where my soul craves to be ag'in!"[21] Thus the
veteran frontiersman of *The Pioneers* reaffirms his purpose
to stay clear of society. But he pays a price for that freedom:
he remains celibate, alone. There can be no marriage, no
children, no inheritors, for these are the product of social
existence and require for their survival and their flourishing
the institutions of the social compact. And in paying that
price, Leatherstocking is but the first of a long line of figures
in American literature who discover the cost of living away
from society, in the wilderness, and therefore outside of history; I think of such diverse fictional characters as Huckleberry Finn, Isaac McCaslin, and the hunter Wilson in Hemingway's "The Short Happy Life of Francis Macomber."

With his characteristic understatement, D. H. Lawrence
has enunciated a truth concerning James Fenimore Cooper:
that novelist "loved the genteel continent of Europe, and
waited gasping for the newspapers to praise his WORK." His
"actual desire was to be *Monsieur Fenimore Cooper, le grand
écrivain américain*," but his "innermost wish was to be:
Natty Bumppo." Lawrence very properly emphasizes the extent to which the dream of Leatherstocking represented escape for his author—flight from all that society was and what
the concerns of being an author and a property-owning
gentleman demanded of him. The Natty-Chingachgook
myth, he keeps repeating, "is a wish-fulfillment, an evasion
of reality."[22]

Simms's dream, then, turns out to be diametrically opposed to that of Cooper. It is a dream not of solitude but of
society and the attainment of a position of comfort and dignity within it. Simms's frontiersmen live at the edge of the
forest, which they are busy converting into farmland. The
freedom that Hugh Grayson declares ought to be the proper
condition of the settlers, and that is being negated by their
willingness to accept European notions of subordination and
class, is not one of escape from society into a classless (and
childless) state of nature, but of the right to pursue one's
objectives and to make the most of one's abilities within

society. Nor is that ideal merely one of the small farmer, Thomas Jefferson's virtuous husbandman who tills his own acres and owes not any man. It involves the dream of status, of recognized accomplishment among one's fellow men: the right, one might say, to *be* a Thomas Jefferson or an Andrew Jackson.

Life in nature is not romanticized in *The Yemassee* or elsewhere in Simms's border novels. The forest is the place of outlawry and violence, with few ennobling qualities for those whites who put the territories behind them. The summit of civilized attainment for Simms is, to repeat, the great plantation, and like most of his fellow white southerners of the time, he did not see the use of the slave labor that made it possible as importantly marring its perfection. In the inability to recognize the hideousness of such a blemish and in thus helping to doom any promise of lasting fulfillment, he only shared in the common failure of his time and place. As we have seen, fortunately for James Fenimore Cooper no such crucial moral awareness was required of him.

When that well-born New York novelist set out to compose a historical romance involving Indian fighting and woodcraft, he could not envision his practical, lowborn frontiersman, skilled in coping with life in the primitive forestland and its Indian inhabitants, as also possessing the sensibility and cultural sophistication needed for the hero's role in a love story. For the plebeian Simms no such division of labor was necessary; a cultivated English aristocrat could also be a hard-fighting, intensely practical border captain, and vice versa. At the close, when the lord palatine weds the parson's daughter, not only will Bess Matthews henceforth be a great lady, but the marriage will symbolize what Simms envisions as the culmination of the New World social experience: the union of the innate refinement and virtue of the nontitled American with the assured status and implicit dignity of the titled aristocracy of the Old World.

If the transaction makes possible the nature-schooled dignity of an Andrew Jackson and the imposing grandeur of the plantation house, however, it deprives the southern imagination of the dream of natural freedom in the wilderness, the mythic escape from history and society into the pathless forest that a Leatherstocking may inhabit. For Simms's dream is of fulfillment *in* society and history—just as a century following the publication of *The Yemassee* a parvenu named Thomas Sutpen would make his way into the Mississippi forest to clear the land, build his great house, and seek to establish his dynasty. But in Faulkner's magnificent novel the price to be enacted for such fulfillment on the terms sought, which Simms and his contemporaries could overlook, is all too clear. At the close of *Absalom, Absalom!* the weeds and thickets of the once virgin forestland reassert their timeless dominion over the fire-gutted ruins of Sutpen's Hundred.

Notes

1. C. Hugh Holman, Introduction to William Gilmore Simms, *The Yemassee*, ed. Holman (Boston, 1961), viii–ix.

2. Clemens' demolition of Cooper, "Fenimore Cooper's Literary Offenses," has been frequently reprinted, in various editions. I have used Walter Blair (ed.), *Selected Shorter Writings of Mark Twain* (Boston, 1962), 226–38.

3. Holman, Introduction to Simms, *Yemassee*, ix.

4. *Ibid.*, xi. Holman's writings on Simms are usually the best criticism available on his fellow South Carolinian. See the essays in Holman, *The Roots of Southern Writing: Essays on the Literature of the American South* (Athens, 1972).

5. Simms, *Yemassee*, 20.

6. *Ibid.*, 355–56.

7. Joseph V. Ridgely, *William Gilmore Simms* (New York, 1962), 56.

8. Simms, *Yemassee*, 45.

9. *Ibid.*, 209.

10. *Ibid.*, 209–10.

11. *Ibid.*

12. *Ibid.*, 304.

13. *Ibid.*, 357.

14. Ridgely, *William Gilmore Simms*, 55.

15. Simms to James Lawson, December 29, [1839], in Mary C. Simms Oliphant, Alfred Taylor Odell, and T. C. Duncan Eaves (eds.), *The Letters of William Gilmore Simms* (5 vols.; Columbia, S.C., 1952), I, 167.

16. Simms, *Yemassee*, 51.

17. *Ibid.*, 56.

18. William R. Taylor, *Cavalier and Yankee: The Old South and American National Character* (New York, 1961), 15.

19. Herman Melville, *Moby Dick; or, The White Whale* (New York, 1961), 124.

20. Simms, *Yemassee*, 211.

21. James Fenimore Cooper, *The Pioneers; or, The Sources of the Susquehanna: A Descriptive Tale* (New York, 1964), 434.

22. D. H. Lawrence, *Studies in Classic American Literature* (New York, 1923), excerpted in Edmund Wilson (ed.), *The Shock of Recognition: The Development of Literature in the United States Recorded by the Men Who Made it: Volume II: The Twentieth Century* (2 vols.; New York, n.d.), 951, 954.

JAMES M. COX

Reflections on Hawthorne's Nature

It is for me a pleasant occupation to think and write about Nathaniel Hawthorne. I am no expert on the subject, but I have both thought and written about him over the years. I once embarked on a book about him. I had an idea—or seed, as Hawthorne might say—and I wrote about 160 typescript pages on his work. Having written a book on Mark Twain, I was sure that, what with my germinal idea, I could complete the project on Hawthorne in a much shorter time than the ten years I had taken on Mark Twain. I made real progress, but the book would not take the form I believed necessary for its subject. I believed, and still believe, that a critical book on Hawthorne should be expansive where Hawthorne was compressed and compressed where he was expansive. That is, a critical book of, say, ten chapters, ought to have six chapters devoted to the tales and sketches, two chapters on *The Scarlet Letter*, one chapter on the three novels, and a concluding chapter on those abortive manuscripts Hawthorne left behind him. Yet, with all the will in the world I found myself falling into the fatal form of the conventional book on Hawthorne: an introductory chapter taking me from the beginnings through *Fanshawe;* two chapters on the tales; a long chapter (which could have been made into two) on *The Scarlet Letter;* and then the inevitable chapter for each of the three novels (or romances, to use Hawthorne's terminology), followed by a final chapter on the unfinished manuscripts. I completed all those chapters right through *The Marble Faun* before abandoning the project because I could not tolerate the form my book was taking. And so the manuscript has been in a large envelope for fifteen years.

Actually, I have always been secretly happy with my decision, secure in the knowledge that such a significant amount of writing will not see publication. The knowledge has a Hawthornesque aspect about it. It would be even more Hawthornesque to burn the manuscript. How exquisite it would be, on a cold Virginia winter day, to break the chill of my study by burning old writing. To imagine so much is to get close to what I like to think is the spirit of Hawthorne's nature. In lieu of burning that manuscript, I want to try, in relatively compressed form, to give my impression of Hawthorne as a writer. If I do not touch Hawthorne, I may yet succeed in giving a sense of how Hawthorne has touched me.

The great fact of his life was surely his retirement upon completing college at Bowdoin. In an age demanding get-up-and-go, Hawthorne began with early retirement to a room in his mother's house. Returning home, he had a hard time leaving. Twelve years later he emerged with a book of tales and sketches—and a signature. He had written more, beginning with a novel, a form and a length he would not get back to for twenty-two years. We know, by virtue of Randall Stewart's biography (and more recently from biographies by Arlin Turner and James Mellow) that he was not a recluse all that time, but Stewart, for all his efforts to create a "normal" Hawthorne, could not convince even his generation that Hawthorne was not retiring.

To think about his retirement is to open our imagination to his identity and his identity to our imagination. There would be a shyness about such a person, and we know from the notebooks and the testimony of his contemporaries that he was shy—even painfully so, if such a shrewd observer as O. W. Holmes is to be credited. Then there was indolence. You have only to read Hawthorne's prose in his notebooks and sketches to see his enjoyment of doing sufficiently nothing until facts and the outward world are pressured with daydream. He liked the Concord River because, unlike wild, free mountain streams, it could not be dammed and put to work. Moving idly, the river could reflect the heavens and the overarching trees so serenely that the reflection seemed more real than the objects themselves. And Hawthorne himself reflected long and long in the solitude of his writing chamber.

Finally, he observed. He looked out windows at figures passing as much as he inevitably looked inward, and, I like to
think, must have been caught looking by the figures passing
in the street. To look out a window, whether upon a street
or upon solitary nature, is surely an activity deserving the
most intense consideration. Who among us has not done it?
I do not mean glancing out but truly looking out. To see such
activity as voyeurism is too simple, though surely part of the
story, for the act puts the observer in a privileged position,
reflecting an inescapable element of both longing and curiosity in the outward gaze as well as a bodily passivity that
turns action over to the eye. Beyond that, the observer's vision is fatally framed. External nature and mobile society are
framed for the observer; the observer is in turn framed for
nature's eye. Thus, we have nature as scene and the observer
as a portrait.

All of which brings us to the primary Hawthorne, who
was, in those twelve years of retirement, making himself not
merely a writer but an artist. To think of the process is to
know that writing came before experience for Hawthorne.
He was so different from Melville in this respect. Melville
had gone to sea and, having seen the world, had returned to
swim through libraries in the process of both recovering and
interpreting the experience that was in turn being transformed with roving meditation. Thoreau was probably most
like Hawthorne in the self-consciousness of studied composition, refining his writing and cultivating paradoxes. Self-
conscious as these two writers were about style and the primary force of writing, they yet sought to connect themselves
to the original force of a nature or a journey outside them.
Hawthorne eschewed that kind of originality, wishing instead to inherit his material. That was why he liked the
past—liked books of antiquarian lore and oral tales, or traditions, as he was sometimes wont to call them. Despite
the romantic revolution, which had placed the esemplastic
imagination in creative priority over the fancy—the faculty
of mind that reflected nature on lines of association and similitude—Hawthorne's imagination retained an archaic attachment to allegory and fancy. For Melville, the whale embodied the monstrous force that all languages were, as he
makes clear in his "Extracts," heroically seeking to name, to
capture, and to signify; for Thoreau, Walden was the clear
and pure source that all his discipline could but imperfectly

translate; for Hawthorne, the fixed Scarlet Letter stood before his fiction, generating the fixation from which the narrative would unfold.

Alone in his dismal chamber, Hawthorne fully recognized that his reading and writing were taking the place of the experience he had refused to enter. His art was indeed preceding experience. *The Scarlet Letter* is the culmination of that precedence. In the inherited manuscript that Hawthorne claimed to have found in the "second story" of the Custom House, we are made to see how the scarlet *A*, a letter, precedes its own narrative. Placing the faded remnant of the letter upon his breast, Hawthorne feels his heart and mind glow not with the flame but with the embers of creative fire. In that glow, possessing both warmth and pain, the imagination is fired to forge the narrative. The letter is at once the source and symbol, the motive and the means, of unfolding the "second story" of the book. But that is not all. There is the first story of the Custom House, the extended preface introductory to *The Scarlet Letter*, in which Hawthorne places himself as the veiled author *before* his fiction. The act of veiling not only darkens our vision of the author but darkens his vision of his story. As in the instance of Father Hooper in "The Minister's Black Veil," the vision is not only darkened but rendered uncertain, charging the visionary field on both sides of the veil with implication rather than explication. The surest implication is that, if the *A* on Hester's breast stands for adultery as well as Arthur, it also stands for Author—the author who, standing before his fiction, literally displaces what had happened between Hester Prynne and Arthur Dimmesdale in the forest with his fictive discovery and *conception* of the fiction. That conception brings, by implication, the concluding moral of the novel back upon the author, showing him in the act of revealing if not the worst trait about himself, at least that by which the worst may be inferred.

That would be the veiled or darkened revelation of the artist as author. Those who wished daylight and biographical evidence of the priority of Hawthorne's presence before his vision of the external world could do no better than go to the second story of the Old Manse and see Hawthorne's name written with a diamond upon the windowpane. I do not mean that this signature should be seen as a tourist sees it, but as a true reader of Hawthorne might see it. It took him so long to sign that name to his fiction; then, too, he had, as Faulkner was to do almost a hundred years later, changed the spelling of his name. I find myself wanting to think that he had restored some earlier spelling, but it is better to see him gaining a finer tone to the pronunciation of the name than the harsh New England tongue allowed— much as Emerson had sought in changing his wife's name from Lydia to Lydian—and at the same time fully identifying his name with nature. It is good, when you are in the Old Manse, to look right through that signature upon the old leaded glass toward the battlefield and realize what it is to look through a window upon both nature and history. That would be to realize what I have been trying to say about looking out of windows and to sense what I am suggesting about Hawthorne the author being in front of his vision. The author's writing on that window is no allegory; it is an emblem.

But of course we are only beginning to touch the elements present in Hawthorne's experience in his solitary chamber. There would be the matter of secrecy—or, better, intense privacy—in his act of art, which *was* his experience. We know that Melville, after Hawthorne's death, told Julian Hawthorne that he was sure that Hawthorne had some great secret. We can never discount anything that Melville said, but at the time he talked with Julian, he had already moved far out into the dead reckoning of age, leaving his books— even *Moby-Dick*—so far behind that he was able to answer an Englishman, who had written hoping for more great books, that his past life of authorship seemed remote and in effect unimportant. There he was not unlike Hawthorne, who had much the same attitude about his literary productions. In any event, there has always been the sense of some secret in Hawthorne's life. He himself encouraged it, what with his act of veiling himself and writing tales and sketches having to do with secret guilts and hoarded privacies. Small wonder that Philip Young has recently emerged with a book that, in effect, stretches itself out for a blessedly short length yet manages a narrative deferral of the great secret, which turns out to be a record of incest on the Manning side of the family. Such unveilings may do for certain temperaments, but not for mine, which does not mean that I think there are no secrets in Hawthorne's life. I have not the slightest doubt that there were many. There would have been more secrets in his present than in his past—secret thoughts about his sisters, his mother, his dead father. The history, in the form of annals and legends, that he ransacked in search of possibilities for his fictions was surely the visible veil that obscured the life of fantasy, ambition, and desire that he was living in the chamber under the eaves. Anyone who has sat in a study, struggling to write even the most pedestrian essays about major American writers, knows the range of fantasy and daydream accompanying the effort to subject thought to sequence.

All this should go without saying, but the critical and scholarly world involves us in helplessly repressing our own secrets in writing about such a figure as Hawthorne. Speculating about Hawthorne's "secrets" and "problems," we burrow like Chillingworth toward the secret heart of the other in an effort to gratify the very desire we are repressing. Thus, Frederick Crews—in what I still think is a remarkable book on Hawthorne—finds himself exposing Hawthorne and lamenting the paralyzing force Hawthorne's involvement in ancestral guilt came to have on his writing and his view of art. Surely what Hawthorne had recognized in the chamber under the eaves was the fantastic human propensity to repress one's own secret sins and desires in the act of judging and exposing those of others. The repression and the act of judgment were for Hawthorne inseparably related—were indeed a single terrifying energy. His ancestors had been just such judges. However Hawthorne may have brooded on them, he profoundly knew the dynamics of such behavior. That is why he understood the nature of reformers in his own time. He saw precisely how the desire not only to judge others but even to sympathize with them came from an interior drama in which all those forces—inhibition, sympathy, and judgment—were in volatile and related formation.

Thus, in "Roger Malvin's Burial" he could take the scene of Indian fighting and convert it so beautifully into the interior history of generational family struggle. By concentrating on the cumulative guilt of Reuben Bourne, Hawthorne not only deflects attention from the manner in which Roger Malvin's ostensible charity actually buries Reuben, but also from the savage implications of the whole "progress" of western migration. The charity of self-sacrifice and the moral sanctity of the westward movement of civilization lie like secret enemies in the terrain of the story. The more we are led to probe Reuben's guilt, to penetrate his nature, the more Reuben's relations—Roger, Dorcas, Cyrus, the Indians, and the Indian wars—are exempted from their collaborative force in his life. To start thinking about relations in that story is not to stop inside the story but to remember that a tale itself is a *relation*, a narrative. However much we might pursue the unconscious motives that move young Cyrus to lead the declining family's migration westward and Reuben to lead it instinctively toward the wilderness scene where Roger Malvin died, we should know that it is finally the author of the tale who is managing the fatal journey. The fatality that brings Cyrus to the spot where Roger Malvin was not physically buried and where Reuben Bourne was psychologically buried is what leads the artistic design of the story to betray itself as arbitrary manipulative will. Although we might wish to exempt the author from that narrative manipulation with probings into unconscious psychology, Hawthorne could never, I believe, quite wish to exempt himself from the implications of guilt and responsibility involved in having written the story. His refusal to exempt himself is one of his great distinctions as a writer. Instead of throwing all the weight of his judgment outward as his Puritan colonial world, for all its emphasis on universal sin, was prone to do, Hawthorne's finely balanced restraint retains by implication guilt for himself as author. His restraint is nothing less than his great reservation; it is at the center of his imagination and his style. In his tales, he veils, but does not hide, his own original sin, just as he envisions himself not as creator or originator but as inheritor of his material. He knows, moreover, that original sin is at once inherited and original—the primal originating urge of creation that fatally and fully re-presses its ancient and endlessly repeated *generation* of the race, if not the fall of humanity. That urge is, for an author, at once his power to *conceive* a fiction and his wizard's power to cast a spell, to hold in thrall the mind, if not of a vast audience, of an individual reader.

Here Holgrave's story of Alice Pyncheon (in *The House of the Seven Gables*) comes to mind. The story is about a Pyncheon father in the third generation of descent from the original Pyncheon who seized land from the Maules, who, as he looks intently at a Claude landscape, in effect authorizes the mental rape of his daughter by a wizard descendant of the

Maules. Holgrave, the "present" descendant of the Maules, tells the story to Alice, the present descendant of the Pyncheons. He has "evolved" from wizard to artist in the line of descent, just as she has evolved to the identity of the innocent and "bewitching" domestication of New England girlhood. Telling her the story, Holgrave feels the power of his narrative hypnotizing Alice and finds himself at the threshold of having her totally within his power. That was surely Hawthorne's last tale, acting as a seed, an inside narrative, in a novel recounting both the progress and the decline of New England generation. It is a late-blossoming offshoot of one of Hawthorne's earliest tales, "Alice Doane's Appeal," in which he framed a tale of fratricide and incest with an outside narrative in which the narrator leads two innocent maidens to Gallows Hill, where, after "making" them sit and listen to his "wondrous" tale of Leonard and Alice Doane and failing to "move" them, he conjures up the "historical" vision of the witch trials culminating in the executions on the very spot where they are sitting. His vision is sufficiently powerful to make them tremble and seize his arms—and, "sweeter victory still, I had reached the seldom trodden places of their hearts, and found the wellspring of their tears." Leaving Gallows Hill, the narrator wishes that a monument of "dark, funereal stone" commemorating the witch trials might be built there to match the monument on Bunker Hill.

It is difficult not to read both these stories biographically, especially in light of Phoebe's resemblance to Hawthorne's idealized vision of Sophia Hawthorne and the resemblance of the two young ladies of "Alice Doane's Appeal" to Hawthorne's sisters. Seen in such light, Hawthorne's fiction discloses both a wish and an inhibition to violate, and sexually violate, the taboo and the trust of his nearest, and presumably dearest, feminine relations. It is there in the image of the hand—surely it is the author's hand—that constitutes Georgianna's birthmark. Determined to remove it, Aylmer, husband and artist figure, probes and pursues the stain to her very heart. The wish is there again when the artist of the beautiful, Owen Warland, in rage and anguish upon seeing Annie Hovenden touch with a needle the delicate machinery of his art, seizes her wrist with such force that she screams. The wish is at the heart of Hawthorne's power to conceive fiction; the inhibition, or fear, makes him need the strong moral negations that so prominently characterize his narratives. Those negations are the imaginative counterthrust to the compelling fantasy at the core of much of his fiction. They are there not only in the stories of Alice Doane and Alice Pyncheon but also in "The Birthmark," "Rappaccini's Daughter," "Drowne's Wooden Image," *The Scarlet Letter*, *The Blithedale Romance*, and *The Marble Faun*. To think of Melville, Emerson, Thoreau, Whitman, and Mark Twain is to remember that what distinguishes Hawthorne from so many "major" nineteenth-century American writers is the strength of his heterosexual imagination. Even Poe and Henry James, who show strong determination to represent women in their fiction, never came close to achieving the passionate, feminine force of Hester Prynne. She is, of course, the apotheosis of Hawthorne's strength, but it is also evident in Beatrice Rappaccini, in Georgiana, in Zenobia, and in Miriam.

The dramatic conflict between his fantasy and his fear enabled Hawthorne to envision his narratives as having the power of original sin, putting him in touch with the psychic center of both family and religion. Colonial New England was precisely and personally where, for Hawthorne, family origin and religion met in secular history. For him, that history was inevitably secular and not sacred. His determination to be an artist was but a confirmation of the history that separated him from the vision of his ancestors even as it left him related to them. Indeed this secular history, eventuating in the displacement of colonial New England with democratic America, was itself the relation—the narrative—defining both the separation and the relation. If the "progress" of that historical narrative enabled Hawthorne's nation and generation to see the sins of the Puritan fathers in the witchcraft trials, Hawthorne as individual artist in the solitude of his chamber could feel just how their sin was fully alive in his compelling fantasies of wizardry and desire. His capacity to feel both the seduction and the sin of art in a single instant is at the heart of his imaginative power.

So much for the sin and secret knowledge of the artist in his dismal chamber. Beyond that, there is the shame that is related to the sin and power of art. The shame would not merely be for having retreated or retired or withdrawn into the chamber, but for the ambition and aim of the retirement: the aim of publication. Not for nothing is the sin of creation in *The Scarlet Letter* figured forth in the shame of Hester's publication before the community. The reticence of the author, whether behind his veil or within his study, is a true measure of what Hawthorne must have felt about publication. I do not mean at all that my Hawthorne lacked ambition; he had a great deal of it—enough to aim to publish, to win in solitude the fame, he wrote in his notebooks, that had been won. There was surely irony in that notebook observation—not a wry but a calm irony that sounds almost to the point of plangency in his writing. Still, there was the ambition, and in it the pride, and in the pride the shame. The emotions of pride and shame went hand in hand for Hawthorne, and they met in the act of publication. He surely wanted to publish; yet, just as surely he felt exposed and vulnerable. Here again, I am amazed at scholars and colleagues who never seem to feel the shame of publication. I do not mean fear, which is another thing. I mean shame, and a shame that precedes the humiliation you might get from seeing a savage review and knowing that your enemies were happily devouring it. The shame I refer to has to do with the knowledge that what you have written in the deep privacy of your study is going to be published. You want it to be published—that is your mastering desire—and yet you feel the loss of it ahead of time, a strange diminution that no public praise can ever quite balance. Beyond that, there is your sense of the imperfection of everything you write, enabling you to see, especially after publication, the defects of your execution. This sense of imperfection is not a stain upon the soul—that, for Hawthorne would be sin—but a birthmark on the face of your text that you can see best in solitude and calm reflection. It would be hidden in the flush of passion or in the blush of public shame. Here Hester Prynne comes again to mind. She sums up so much as she displaces the veiled author who has himself displaced the narrative of her original sin with his Custom House narrative of himself. She is there, strong in both pride and shame, in full publication before the community. No wonder we sympathize with her as victim. We do not believe—and Hawthorne's great achievement was his utter confidence that no future audience would believe—that her sin was sinful in the first place, certainly not as sinful as the community's judgment that published her. Casting himself as editor, Hawthorne can censure her act from time to time. His editorial stance in his fictively inherited manuscript is his way of achieving his finely balanced style that moves between sympathy and judgment, a balance possessing its own muted passion, which, if it does not inflame our sympathy, keeps its glow alive for the published heroine.

To see that balance is to be reminded of the balance of Hawthorne's nature. If he veiled himself, he nonetheless published the veiled self, not only in his tales and romances but in his great prefaces to *Mosses from an Old Manse* and *The Scarlet Letter*, which realized the full possibilities of the sketches he had written. That balance in Hawthorne ran toward doubt rather than faith, toward a generative skepticism that gave his judgment a power equal to his sympathy. It is well to remember that, in the abrupt opening of "Young Goodman Brown," Faith, already troubled with bad dreams, doubts and fears her husband's intended forest journey, a point often overlooked in the many interpretations of that story. Hawthorne's power of judgment is nowhere more potent than in his judgment of sympathy in *The Scarlet Letter*. For it is when Hester feels, or thinks she feels, a vision of sympathy in the eye of a young woman on the street that, as the editorial text observes, she sins anew. Her own projective vision, like that of Goodman Brown, generatively creates a world but a world passionately conceived in uncertainty.

The sin, shame, sympathy, and judgment at play in Hawthorne's act of publication still do not account for that mastering desire to publish that overcame the profound reticence and privacy of his conceptual impulses. There was, as I have indicated, a wish for fame, and fame, for a reclusive writer all but hoarding his privacy, required publication. Publication was his way out of the dismal and squalid chamber—dismal because it must have become increasingly like a prison of the self rather than a freedom from the public eye. It was, after all, his publication that extricated him from the guilty solitude of haunting fantasies, hoarded privacies, privileged observation, and the shame of pinched financial dependence. Whatever pride Hawthorne could have felt about the worth of his unsigned publication could hardly make up for the shame he felt in the chamber of the self. And whatever freedom he had in the secrecy of his imagination could not make up for the guilt of indulged fantasies of hostility and sexual violation. The guilt, like all guilt, would have been itself an indulgence as dissatisfyingly unreal as the protective shield of unsigned publication. Evasion of the individual signature left individualism in a state of increasingly hostile and mordant isolation. Surely some such psychic experience must have fueled Hawthorne's sketches and tales during his years of solitude. The extraordinary battle between reticence and ambition seems to me to be a measure of the aggression Hawthorne must have felt about signed publication, as if it were both a violation of fantasy's freedom and a freeing of fantasy's violations. Yet, without a signature his publication had no claim of personal recognition and responsibility in the marketplace, the hard reality of a capitalist democracy. The reality was hard enough to turn a strong and reticent modesty into the weak self-pity of the struggling author born to blush unseen and unappreciated. Such a feckless and delicate author is evident in many of the sketches. These were the forces that I find myself imagining in Hawthorne's act of signed authorship, making it strong enough to face the world even as his spelling of it at once modified and qualified his relation to the generations of Hathornes that had eventuated in his public presence.

His publication brought him out of his self-imposed prison, just as *The Scarlet Letter* was later to free him from the prison of Salem. It brought him not merely to public life and identity but to political office that offered a financial security that his publications could not earn. It also brought him to marriage and a sexual reality of which the old fantasies could have but dreamed. If the political office afforded the financial security for Hawthorne to embark on marriage, the marriage in turn offered the sexual security for him to imagine adultery. Surely here it is well to remember that the chamber under the eaves had *originally* afforded him the security to imagine those strong early publications, no matter how squalid and dismal it may have come to seem to him. The same process seems evident in his marriage. The presence of Sophia freed his imagination to realize a richer representation of women in his fiction than he had ever been able to accomplish in his isolation, and culminated in the figure of Hester Prynne stepping forth from the prison door into the marketplace. Later, Sophia's presence all but enters the fiction in the figures of Phoebe, Priscilla, and Hilda—figures of innocence poised approvingly yet oppressively not only against his dark ladies, Zenobia and Miriam, but against his male artists. Thus, Priscilla is the white veiled lady initiating Coverdale into his peeping dream of Zenobia, her dark "sister"; and Hilda is the dovelike artist as copyist who morally stifles the original artist and originally sinful Miriam. In the face of those figures, Holgrave, Coverdale, and Kenyon give up their art, expose themselves as voyeurs, and are guided home.

But that was later. Marriage was surely at first a blessed reality, made possible by the publication and the political life and in turn making the past lonely struggle seem unreal. The political life of Hawthorne has always gotten the shortest shrift in the successive versions of Hawthorne that have come down to us through American literary history. Hawthorne himself sought to keep that part of his life separate from his artistic identity, as if it were an unfortunate necessity of the time in which he lived—a reality from which he recoiled into the spiritualized world of fancy and romance. This spiritualized artist became the Hawthorne of the genteel tradition that succeeded the world of literary transcendentalism and political antislavery in which Hawthorne lived and had his being. After the Civil War those volatile movements, by no means identical before the war, merged into the moral and intellectual respectability characterizing the New England literary establishment that dominated the literary scene. It was the age that forgot about Melville and could view Whitman only with averted eyes, just as Concord became the village whose library committee removed *The Adventures of Huckleberry Finn* from the library shelves. In our age, F. O. Matthiessen, at the threshold of World War II, set forth what we might call a pentagonal constellation of writers in which he introduced the New Yorkers, Melville and Whitman, into the company of Emerson, Hawthorne, and Thoreau. They constituted his American Renaissance to match the Elizabethan Renaissance that accompanied the defeat of the Spanish Armada. And after World War II these figures became, with the addition of Poe (scandalously omitted by Matthiessen), Twain, and Dickinson, our "major" nineteenth-century writers to match our secure position as a world power. Matthiessen at least faced Hawthorne's political identity, appreciating the Jacksonian democracy of it, yet clearly uncomfortable about Hawthorne's refusal *ever* to enlist himself with the antislavery forces of his time.

Without going into the intricacy of pre–Civil War politics, I do want to emphasize the public and political side of Hawthorne in relation to his artistic nature. I do so because

Hawthorne himself was determined to emphasize it in his extended preface to his finest work. As a resident of New England and as a descendant of Puritans, Hawthorne had both pride in his region and shame in its, and his, history. He admired the directness, courage, and sturdy reality of the Puritans, as who does not? But he recognized just how their oppressively righteous sense of mission became repressive. The attention focused on his unquestionable interest in and relation to the Puritan past in all that has been written about the major writer Hawthorne continues to obscure his political identity as a Jacksonian Democrat. In our own age we have substituted a darker Hawthorne, a tragic Hawthorne, for the more ethereal genteel Hawthorne; yet, I think that our Hawthorne is no less spiritualized. He is the Hawthorne touched with Calvinism, the conservative Hawthorne who distrusts radicals and revolutionaries; he is cast always as part of the New England that so dominates American literary scholarship. That scholarship has made the Puritans dominate the study of American literature as much as the New England of Hawthorne's own age was bent on finding the sources of American freedom in the Mayflower Compact and the Puritan resistance to tyrants. Hawthorne of course knew of and admired that resistance, but he remained freer with and freer from the Puritans than, it seems to me, Perry Miller and Sacvan Bercovitch have remained. The vision of New England as the cradle of liberty or the source of American guilt in the American imagination unfortunately subordinates the Enlightenment and the eighteenth century to the essentially dismal gloom of the Puritans and Puritan writing. Hawthorne, born on July 4, 1804, was close to that century, to its balance of mind, to its skepticism, to its detachment, and to its own deep passion for freedom—freedom, we must remind ourselves, from tyranny and not from slavery. He was without question as sensitive to eighteenth-century style as he ever was to Puritanism and allegory. He had the skepticism of that century so firmly rooted in his style and imagination that he could genuinely contemplate the Puritan past with a freedom that is enviable. He had, let me say, the freedom truly to imagine it, and whatever ambivalence he had in relation to it (and he had much) he was never in bondage to it. He saw, I think, in transcendentalism, as well as in the antislavery movement, a potential threat of the tyranny of the imagination in literature and of righteous morality in politics that might be as great as the tyranny of religious superstition that Jefferson had so profoundly sworn to oppose.

To think steadily about this side of Hawthorne is to see how bent he was upon democratizing literature. Any sensitive reading of "The Artist of the Beautiful" will disclose how attributes of the artist behind the story are diffused in and distributed among all the characters in the story: the cold, materialistic scrutiny of the watchmaker, Peter Hovenden; the strength and self-confidence of the blacksmith, Robert Danforth; the maiden beauty of Annie Hovenden, who, in conjunction with Danforth, can create real life; their child, the real life that at once makes the created butterfly glow with preternatural beauty and, grasping it, crushes it into "a heap of glittering fragments"; and the persistent yet precarious struggle of the artist of the beautiful, Owen Warland, to realize in material form the ideal butterfly of his imagination. Indeed, the child's grasp of the butterfly at the end of the story is the fulfillment of Owen Warland's own dream, expressed in his design upon the ebony gift box containing the butterfly, a design that depicts a child reaching for a butterfly. Every character in that story reflects the intricate motives of the artist who made and released it for publication.

This democratic imagination is even clearer in *The Scarlet Letter*, in which Hawthorne again distributes the motives of the artist and democratizes the guilt among the characters and the community. In presenting himself before the story, Hawthorne veils, but does not hide, his own political life and identity as a political appointee in the Custom House. Stephen Nissenbaum has, in an incisive introduction to his edition of the novel, rightly emphasized that Hawthorne's preface conceals the partisan political conduct of his behavior as surveyor of customs. Exposing the manner in which Hawthorne's modest presentation of himself as an artist of the beautiful condemned to the torpor of the Custom House obscures the active Jacksonian Democrat who removed Whigs and enforced party discipline, Nissenbaum sees Dimmesdale and Hester as contradictory portraits of the artist. Dimmesdale is the exposure of the figure that the preface hides, the spiritualized version of the artist who has hidden, or striven to hide, his ambition; Hester is the portrait of Hawthorne's ideal artist who never seeks to put her art to work for a career or *office*—she "never uses—or misuses—her art to gain wealth or fame." In Nissenbaum's view, Hester finds, or Hawthorne finds for her, at the end of the novel a wealthy and aristocratic but invisible male patron who supports her in her declining years. That patron would be the wish fulfillment of the patron Hawthorne had hoped and sought to find in the federal government, which had proved to be so fickle.

In my view, all the characters in the novel are at once the motives and the offspring of Hawthorne's conception in the "second story" of the Custom House. Dimmesdale is indeed the ambition for career and fame, forming so large a part of Hawthorne's struggle throughout his career, yet hidden behind the public, spiritualized, nineteenth-century artist and public man Hawthorne was happy to present himself as being. Hester is both the object and subject of his imagination—the muse and sister of his whole literary ambition, if you will—who authorizes and releases the ambition into the shame and honor of publication. These two figures, or motives, meet in *adultery*, a sharing of the passionate ambition that is in *both* of them and a violation of their separate integrity. The offspring of the adultery is Pearl, the passionate innocence—both abrasive and unyielding—at the heart of Hawthorne's conception. She is the character of flame and the "child of nature" emerging from Hawthorne's glow of passion in conceiving the novel; she is the adamantinely innocent messenger of anguish accompanying the shame of publication and, in the course of the narrative, demanding that the spiritual father publicly acknowledge the hidden flesh behind the word. As the innocent, not sinful, child of their adulterous union, she is the hardened nature of innocence, as well as the hardened innocence of nature, at first separating and finally uniting the honor and shame of publication with the sin and guilt of public confession. Finally, there is Chillingworth, not only the cold observer that Hawthorne as artist always knew himself to be, but also the figure of vengeance lurking in Hawthorne's imagination as the self-judging critic at the threshold of his fantasies. In this novel he is the vengeful critic as passionate detective (Hawthorne had indeed read his Poe, who died on October 7, 1849, when Hawthorne was in the throes of composing *The*

Scarlet Letter), probing the motives of the minister for the sexual impulse at the heart of spiritual presence.

Thus, the whole of *The Scarlet Letter*, Custom House preface and ensuing narrative, discloses original, authorial creation merging with original sin; thus, the Jacksonian politician in the Custom House transforms himself into author of what in this particular light is a true political novel. Not only does the fanciful and romantic author reveal himself in his political identity at the outset; he discloses how his motives as a fired political official are, by virtue of passage through the veiled fire of his authorial conception, reborn as figural forces reconstituting what was the society of the Puritan world and what would be the erotic dream of romance. Thus, if his narrative sexualizes the forms of Puritan society with the energy of romantic fantasy, the fantasy is utterly socialized by the forms of the imagined society. Similarly, the incestuous tension present in the purity of romantic love is displaced by the adultery that resides in the novelistic imagination. It is hardly accidental that the Scarlet Letter is found in the second story of the Custom House and not in the romancer's chamber. Indeed, the narrative of the Scarlet Letter is nothing less than the second story of the Custom House; the actions of the characters instantaneously assume public, political, and official character. The Scarlet Letter itself must, in the course of the narrative, *do* its office.

The public life and identity of the society almost seems to define the figures in the novel more than the figures can define it. That is why the society seems not merely real but preternaturally solid in *The Scarlet Letter*—surely as solid as that represented in any "realistic" American novel. It is a society possessed of moral and political authority. Yet, the private thought and actions of Hawthorne's figures, forced into public light and identity by the very determination of the society, possess the motive force to shake the community to its foundations and make it equally share the passion, shame, and guilt of individual private life. That equilibrium and equality of force is the achievement of Hawthorne's democratic and political imagination.

Hawthorne's political nature and involvement in public life relate him to Milton, a fact hard to be lost on this Custom House author who was himself so profoundly related to the Puritans and who chose as the setting for many of his works New England at the very time when Milton's political party was killing a king. The Custom House preface corresponds to Milton's repeated invocations in *Paradise Lost,* which disclose the poet's justification of God's ways and veil his own involvement in satanic rebellion against a king. Milton's very ability to *see* Satan in the great, "original" beginning of the poem leaves him blind as he emerges from the epic journey into the hell he has both lived and imagined. Praying for inner illumination of holy light, the epic poet leaves the satanic self bound to a hatred of everything it sees of earth. Hawthorne's narrative, like Milton's epic, carries charges of self-judgment, particularly in the figures of Dimmesdale and Chillingworth. At the same time, both epic and novel refuse to let self-judgment displace judgment of others; they retain the aggressive pride and power to challenge the world that has judged them. The worthies of Salem who had opposed Hawthorne could have taken little more comfort in the action of Hawthorne's narrative than they could in his portrait of Custom House life.

But of course Hawthorne was not Milton. He was no Latin secretary to the council of state immersed in fierce public debate and revolution. He was merely a surveyor of customs in a provincial custom house—a minor official, subject to dismissal whenever his political party should be defeated in popular election. If he had been turned out of office, he had not been fined and forced to surrender his property, feel the threat of death, and suffer spiritual exile under a restored monarchy. Hawthorne kept his head sufficiently to be able to joke in his preface about having been decapitated, relating himself not to Milton but to his own countryman Irving. Remembering that Chaucer and Burns also worked in custom houses, he maintains throughout his account a modest humor, yet preserves enough formality to give it a touch of gravity. Instead of writing for fit audience though few, he hopes it may be pardonable to imagine a kind and apprehensive friend listening to him "prate of the circumstances that lie around us." Sufficiently casual and self-detached to judge himself even as he keenly judges the nature of the community occupying the Custom House, Hawthorne discloses his play of mind at work upon democratic political life in the customs of his country.

Reflecting on this modesty of tone in Hawthorne's extended account of himself brings us back to his democratic politics, for political life was somehow as essential for him as the life of literature. His dismissal from the Salem Custom House by no means ended his political life. When, two years later, his Bowdoin classmate, Franklin Pierce, became the Democratic presidential nominee, Hawthorne wrote the campaign biography and zealously planned its distribution; when Pierce was elected, Hawthorne, busily advising him in the matter of political appointments, amusingly referred to himself as Pierce's prime minister. Concluding a letter to Richard Henry Stoddard on how to behave in seeking a political appointment, Hawthorne wrote, "A subtile boldness, with a veil of modesty over it, is what is needed." That sentence, as fine a description of *The Scarlet Letter* as has been written, reflects the passionate if adulterous union between politics and literature in Hawthorne's imagination. It affords the opportunity for seeing the essential democracy of his literature.

Seeing the fatal tyranny of vision—of all vision and all ideals—Hawthorne balanced it with all his skepticism. Instead of trusting the self, he doubted it. He was wonderfully experimental in his notebooks, toying with his ideas. Those ideas for stories are speculations in the full sense of the word—speculations about imaginative possibilities and speculations for possibilities in the marketplace. Trials of a mind held always on a tentative line of force, they are experiments for invention. Hawthorne's passion for and profound knowledge of the glow of composition excited the dialectical vision in his mind of the artist as inventor in search of devices and linkages and gear reductions that would make his machines go. Far from weakly spiritualizing art (though he often entertained that impulse), he boldly materialized it, showing always a capacity to expose the artist's mechanisms. His exposure was at once a judgment on the "sin" of art and a reminder that an artist was, after all, an artisan. That was why Hawthorne so much liked the workshops of painters and sculptors, where he could see art as material object. Similarly, he saw nature as scene, and his descriptions of it in his notebooks are efforts both to describe it and to test its possibilities. He liked it less as primal energy than as a model of composition. Seeing the whole world as a model for the artist, he strove in his style for a composure that would reflect it.

He saw human nature in a similar light. His record of his

stay at North Adams in 1838 abounds in observations of
the run of ordinary American life. He sees potential stories
in the faces and forms of the figures in the North Adams
inn where he stayed. He liked bars and obviously enjoyed
drinking. No wonder he claimed his custom-house kin with
Chaucer, for there is a Chaucerian quality in Hawthorne's
observation of society. He clearly enjoyed the figures he met
in North Adams—the hawkers, drunkards, maimed people,
and waitresses, and the sharpers who mixed religion with
selling. He drew them out, unfailingly recognizing and appreciating their humor. Their humor almost always redeems
them in his eyes; it is both the struggle and the performance
by means of which individuals establish agreeable society in
the face of life's loneliness and defeats. Its counterpart in solitude is idleness, the passivity that the mind seeks as a defense against the anguish of isolation. Hawthorne likes to
wander in nature, to be secreted in its recesses, where he can
look up at the sky and see clouds floating above the trees;
similarly, he delights in watching the shadows of the clouds
moving resistlessly over hills and valleys.

Sensing these qualities in Hawthorne is essential in defining the composure of his style, the poise of his skepticism. The skepticism enabled him to see the tyranny in
the antislavery movement and to see how it might produce a
tyranny of freedom—which in many ways it has. How thoroughly he would recognize our present helplessness to remove the weapons that have been invented to secure our
freedom. He had seen the helplessness of his own society before the slavery that had accompanied American independence. To gain our present ideal of freedom from that slavery,
seven hundred thousand young men perished in a war. We do
not regret their deaths any more than Hawthorne ever regret-
ted the American Revolution. He accepted readily the progress of history's narrative, yet steadily recognized the irony
of that idealized romance. Knowing that American independence had slavery at its core, and knowing, too, that the great
Jefferson himself could not get rid of it, he sought whatever
freedom he could find in his own present time, choosing
not to join the antislavery movement, unlike Emerson and
Thoreau, who were finally constrained to do so. Seeing so
much, of course he could see the tyranny rooted in the romantic and transcendentalist imagination. That was why he
raised his doubt of art to an imaginative power, exposing, as

part of his creative enterprise, his artist figures and himself to the rigor of withering judgment and at the same time relating both them and him to the common arts of lime-burning, blacksmithing, watchmaking—areas of endeavor where the same forces and obsessions were at work. A student of Hawthorne, John Nettleton, once pointed out in a fine paper how "Drowne's Wooden Image," in its relation of an "artist" who creates living art to sell, exposes the relationship between the artist and the southern planter. Hawthorne, endowed with the power to create such living art and burdened with the necessity to take it to the marketplace, could hardly have failed to entertain the similitude. He would have sought the freedom of entertaining it rather than the necessity of confronting it.

Hawthorne sought as best he could the freedom from tyranny and slavery and art. He knew that he was an artist as well as any writer could know it; yet, he feared the identity of being an artist. In a profound way he did not want to be anything—wanted an idleness for the eternal reflections that would keep him free. Boating on the Concord River he could hear the secret whisper of nature: "Be free! Be free!" But even there he could hear something sinister in the seduction of the whisper, and so he returned to the circle of family and society. The home and the hearth were sacred; his study gave him the freedom to imagine all the tyranny of the generations of men and women who, from Satan down, had sought freedom. No wonder that he persistently relied upon the device of multiple choice in activating the interpretative machinery within his fictions. Reflecting the doubt at the root of all interpretation, the device preserved freedom of choice for his readers even as it implicated them in the personal responsibility of any interpretation.

How right that he died in the Civil War, just as Grant was emerging from the Bloody Angle of Spotsylvania, determined to move relentlessly toward a Union free from slavery. It was a new Union that Hawthorne did not live to see. He died so silently in Plymouth—not Plymouth, Massachusetts, but Plymouth, New Hampshire—that Franklin Pierce, his old loyal Bowdoin friend, did not hear or realize whatever quiet struggle Hawthorne might have had in leaving the world.

TERENCE MARTIN

Telling the World Over Again: The Radical Dimension of American Fiction

Emerson tells us that "the man who has seen the rising moon break out of the clouds at midnight has been present like an archangel at the creation of light and of the world." Thoreau observes that an American is "advantageously nearer to the primitive and the ultimate condition of man" than is an Englishman. Thomas Paine proclaims, "We have it in our power to begin the world over again." And John Quincy Adams defines the signing of the Declaration of Independence as an event unprecedented in "the annals of the human race": "The earth was made to bring forth in one day! A nation was born at once!"[1] Despite their rhetorical extravagance, none of these statements is merely decorative. In each case the writer appropriates a point of genesis that serves the purpose of his argument: with a prophetic sense of national glory, Adams celebrates the anniversary of American independence; with an imminent sense of radical change, Paine projects a euphoric vision of the future; with a persistent sense of the original purity of existence, Thoreau satirizes British pomp; and with an assured sense of how nature mimes the absolute, Emerson brings a domesticated Neoplatonism to his view of history. The effect, characteristic of though by no means limited to American writing, is not only to magnify the importance of the subject at hand but to affirm a world bright with possibility.

In narrative, the impulse to re-present the world issues into designs both synecdochic and metaphorical that attempt to *tell* the world over again. *The Aeneid* and *Paradise*

Lost, for example, fasten boldly on events that generate a sense of authority and wholeness. The histories of Herodotus and Eusebius take shape from similar tactics, the first by invoking the Persians as the source of tradition and hearsay (the raw *stuff* of history), the second by asserting that anyone wishing to understand the Church must "go right back to Christ himself" and "start with the beginning." Novels as different as *The Virginian* (1902) and *One Hundred Years of Solitude* (1967) suggest how making a fictional world seem *early* can enhance the significance of setting and release the flow of narrative. Owen Wister anticipates the dramatic movement of his story by juxtaposing the squalor of a raw western town with the pristine atmosphere of "creation's first morning"—out of which "Noah and Adam might come straight from Genesis." Gabriel Garcia Marquez constructs his deconstructive fable on the foundation of a "world . . . so recent that many things lack names." No one has yet died in the village of Macondo. What the reader knows as established discoveries are made in fierce privacy: emerging from intense and wasting meditation, José Arcadio Buendia proclaims to his family, "The earth is round, like an orange"— after which his wife smashes his astrolabe to the floor. In each of these cases a beginning or congeries of beginning moments fulfills what Edward W. Said calls a "primordial need" to be certain of one's story—the prerequisite for structure and coherence.[2]

Out of a feeling that radical beginnings were accessible for narrative, that they could be possessed imaginatively, came the American habit of telling the world over again. Not (obviously) that everyone wrote in the same way: the many novels that focus on individual lives, issues, events, and communities follow well-established conventions of their own. A profound respect for history leads Hawthorne to identify *firsts,* shaping points of departure that yield the tale: the showman in "Main-street" not only identifies the first settler of Salem but structures the panorama around the life of the first "town-born" child. Firsts are a kind of American hobby, beginnings in familiar guise. In his *Chronological History of New-England . . . from the Creation* (1736), Thomas Prince records many, among them the death of Isaac Johnson on Thursday, September 30, 1630, at "about 2 in the Morning." Johnson was buried "at the upper end of his *Lot*" in the square between Cornhill and Tremont Street, Prince writes—

"which gave Occasion for the *first Burying Place* of this Town to be laid out round about his Grave." More than a century later Hawthorne made use of this same detail to establish the matrix of *The Scarlet Letter*, referring (near the outset of Chapter 1) to "the first prison-house, somewhere in the vicinity of Corn-hill," and the "first burial ground, on Isaac Johnson's lot, and round about his grave, which subsequently became the nucleus of all the congregated sepulchres in the old church-yard of King's Chapel."[3]

Along with Prince's *Chronological History*, Washington Irving's *History of New-York, from the Beginning of the World to the End of the Dutch Dynasty* (1809) stands as an excellent example of how readily the habit of appropriating a beginning took form. Adapting the model of James Ussher's *Annales* from the seventeenth century, Prince starts with Adam (in the "year one, first month, sixth day"), traces a "Line of Time" to the Puritans, and makes sense of the whole procedure by arguing that history has been moving toward New England as its ultimate glory. In the bumbling idiom of Diedrich Knickerbocker, Irving links creation, Noah, and Christopher Columbus to the city of New York by a "latent" and parodic "chain of causation."[4] Each of these works is ambitious. More important, each assumes a direct and causal relation between acknowledged beginning points and the founding of American colonies—Prince with straightforward simplicity, Irving with studied naïveté. Considered together, they suggest the assurance (if not the mode) with which Americans could connect a point of genesis to their own history.

In the work of James Fenimore Cooper, Willa Cather, and William Faulkner, one finds narrative heightened in implication by the accoutrements of genesis or by the grandeur of elemental forces. In *The Pioneers* (1823), Natty Bumppo remembers looking out at creation from his ridge in the Catskills—and thus establishes himself as presocial, coeval with a primal reality. In *The Professor's House* (1925), Tom Outland experiences a oneness with nature on the Blue Mesa, as if he is somehow "breathing the sun"—and thus brings a legacy of peace to the disordered world of Godfrey St. Peter.[5] Isaac McCaslin in *Go Down, Moses* (1940) carries the idea of ownership back to Eden—and thus claims kin with an *original* sin. Attempting to tell the world over again does not, of course, guarantee novels of high quality. But it does suggest the manner in which American writers have courted the absolute in their work. And it demonstrates how relentlessly they have explored the national experience to give it full significance.

Because it pits the overwhelming power of a national origin against personal endeavors that Cooper associates with genesis, *Wyandotté* (1843) offers a troubled instance of what can happen when one beginning moment overtakes another. With a beguiling enthusiasm the narrative describes the joys of "diving into a virgin forest, and commencing the labors of civilization." The pleasure of subsequent activities is hardly to be compared with these original feelings—which are akin to those of "creating . . . pregnant with anticipations and hopes." By means of metaphor and incident Cooper enhances the account of Captain Willoughby's move into the wilderness. The captain and his party travel into a world in which settlements, including Cooperstown, "did not [yet] exist, even in name."[6] They drain a beaver pond (practical action that makes the labor of clearing unnecessary) and have sudden access to four hundred acres of postdiluvian farmland. Drawing on resources both biblical and local, Cooper thus sketches an unnamed world, associated with creation and proximate to the Flood, in which Captain Willoughby will undertake his orderly labors.

But Cooper in *Wyandotté* cannot gainsay the force of the Revolution, a "civil war" dividing families even as it promotes greed and social upheaval. With a sure sense of an unfolding national drama that has no room for doubt and demurral, he brings a copy of the Declaration of Independence into the novel, into the very hands of Captain Willoughby, who pronounces it "creditable" and "eloquently reasoned," though he has no wish to celebrate the birth of the new nation. From his caustic perspective in the 1840s Cooper broods over the document that brings life to the nation and ruin to the captain; the commemoration of national independence on July 4 has become an "all absorbing and all-swallowing jubilee" that overshadows every other holiday.[7] Anomalous and austere, *Wyandotté* closes out a personal world of possibility because of a national beginning Cooper cannot credit.

Out of an effort to incorporate the shaping power of beginnings into narrative come a number of Cooper novels, not only tales of settlement, such as *The Pioneers* (1823) and *Sa-*

tanstoe (1842), but those that reach to primal and mythic points as the condition of their existence—among them *The Crater* (1848) and *The Deerslayer* (1841).[8]

More than any other work in the Cooper canon, *The Crater* presents a radical beginning in pure and insistent form. The Pacific reef on which Mark Woolston is stranded inspires a feeling of proximity to creation: rock, surf, and atmosphere all appear to have come "fresh and renovated from the hands of the Creator." Cooper explains how Mark (of necessity) brings a nurturing world into existence, *making* a rudimentary kind of soil and exposing it to the air and water so that it might nourish seeds that are happily part of the ship's cargo. Soon, a reef that had lain "for thousands of years, in its nakedness," is "blest with fruitfulness." The beginning is elemental in nature: once Mark produces earth, the other three elements—air, water in the form of rain, and fire as rays from the sun—combine to bring life into being. As Cooper notes approvingly, Mark has participated in a "new creation."[9]

What takes *The Crater* beyond an account of the tactics of survival on a naked reef is that all of the nurturing and Crusoe-like chapters function as a prelude to the spectacular account of creation in Chapters 11 and 12. Put another way: creation, personal and domestic, issues into creation, primal and extravagant, and becomes the imaginative center of the novel. Cooper works with care and purpose in this part of the narrative. For the idea of an underwater volcanic eruption he apparently drew on Charles Lyell's account of Graham's Island in the Mediterranean Sea, which emerged from under the surface in 1831 only to disappear in the same year.[10] And he describes the devastation of Mark Woolston's violent fever in a way that surpasses Defoe's meticulous account of Crusoe's illness. Purgative and rugged, the fever leaves Mark empty, in "communion with his Creator," ready for the unique experience of witnessing creation. In a scene generated by an audacious display of metaphor, Cooper first blends the tremors of earthquakes with the sound of volcanic eruption, then describes a seething upheaval from within, a boiling over of primal, preelemental, matter. "Internal fires" burst forth in streams of flame, and molten earth emerges from the ocean. While Mark looks on, a new world is "created" in "the twinkling of an eye," after which he becomes a combination of Columbus and Adam, grateful discoverer and joyous namer.[11]

There is no doubt that a homiletic tone afflicts the final section of *The Crater.* As Cooper muses on the increasing dissension in the colony, he warns us that "everything human" moves toward excess, that "those who would substitute the voice of the created for that of the Creator" should recall "their insignificance and tremble." To look closely at Cooper's effort to capture the world in narrative, however, is to see that what robs the colony of its original purity is not demagoguery or mobocracy but the ownership of property. Even before the "serpent of old" (in the form of ministers, a lawyer, and a newspaper editor) comes to "this Eden of modern times," the forces of the novel are at cross-purposes. The colonists fear attack because they might lose their property; Mark (witness at creation, now governor for life) does not want to abandon the reef, largely because "there was too much property at risk." Cooper's unswerving faith in private property as a principle of social order is reaffirmed in the character of his protagonist: Mark Woolston believes "that civilization could not exist without property, or property without a direct personal interest in both its accumulation and its preservation." Moreover, Bridget will shortly inherit "an amount of property that, properly invested, would contribute largely to the wealth and power of the colony, as well as to those of its governor."[12]

What we have finally in *The Crater* is Eve as heiress, Adam committed to the accumulation of property, and Eden growing in wealth—all undone by the messy politics of equality. In other words, we have a Cooper catechism of hopes and fears, tattered by time, superimposed on a non-historical situation—something bound to break the narrative in two. Cooper's colony, let us note, is never a utopia: the mélange of roles and issues in the novel brings on a confusion very different from the geometrical coolness of utopian communities. Moreover, such communities traditionally banish private property as a matter of principle. Although the vitality of the creation chapters marks achievement of a high order, *The Crater* suffers from internal contradictions and a consequent lack of continuity. Much less sophisticated than Marquez in *One Hundred Years of Solitude,* Cooper has no means to deconstruct his fable according to expectations previously set up and no understanding that an emphasis on property has set the conditions for failure. Thus, he virtually abandons his new world, sinking it back into the Pacific with no witnesses present, not Mark Woolston and certainly not the reader.

In *The Deerslayer*, the final novel of the Leatherstocking series, Cooper invokes the harmony and isolation of "a world by itself," intact in its natural brilliance, and bids us discover an America fresh from the hands of the Creator. "Not a tree," Natty Bumppo says, has been "disturbed even by redskin[s] . . . but everything left in the ordering of the Lord." Although Cooper places his story in the 1740s, the ambience of the novel yields a controlling sense of timelessness: protected spatially and temporally, as H. Daniel Peck demonstrates, the world of *The Deerslayer* "suggests a time *before* history."[13] Into such a setting Cooper puts the youngest Natty Bumppo of all, not only resurrected from his death in *The Prairie* (1827) but granted his octogenarian wish for "twenty and the wilderness." Faulkner tells us in *Go Down, Moses*, that Isaac McCaslin was "born old," that he became "steadily younger and younger until"—nearing eighty—"he had acquired something of a young boy's high and selfless innocence."[14] If the differences between Isaac and Natty Bumppo are obvious, the similarities are nonetheless striking. Natty, one might say, was "introduced old" in *The Pioneers* (1823) and made erratically younger until—in *The Deerslayer*—he acquires an innocence that matches the purity of the setting.

Only Natty Bumppo properly values the splendor of this original world. Whereas Thomas Hutter and Hurry Harry witness a sunrise with lumpish indifference, Natty—as if newly born—is overcome with awe at the sight of the woods and of Lake Glimmerglass. "He loved the woods," Cooper writes, "for their freshness, their sublime solitudes . . . and the impress that they everywhere bore of the divine hand of their creator." Cooper enhances the primeval quality of his fictional world by remarking that Glimmerglass is "the first lake Deerslayer had ever seen."[15] Indeed, having taken pains to make the setting of *The Deerslayer* a direct embodiment of creation and thus a radical beginning world, he provides a number of episodes that constitute personal beginnings for Natty Bumppo. Natty's initial response to Glimmerglass cuts both ways, embellishing the pristine image of the lake even as it establishes a *first* in his life. The ritualized contest in which Natty kills his first Indian (and receives the name Hawkeye from his dying foe) evokes an important soliloquy from the youthful victor: "Well, this is my first battle with a human mortal, though it's not likely to be the last. I have fou't most of the creatur's of the forest . . . but this is the beginning with the redskins." And, as Cooper reports, the scene in which the vengeful Hurons admire the courage of the captured Natty is "the commencement of the great and terrible reputation" that Leatherstocking came to have among Indian tribes.[16]

Whether the action of *The Deerslayer* compromises Natty Bumppo as a part of the setting has been a moot point among the best of critics. Joel Porte, along with Peck, sees the novel ending on a note of stasis that includes and even features Natty Bumppo. John P. McWilliams assesses the general carnage in the narrative and concludes that "by entering Eden, man corrupts it." Neither position seems entirely accurate. Beyond doubt, Cooper's setting remains timeless. When Natty, Chingachgook, and young Uncas visit Lake Glimmerglass fifteen years after the bloody denouement of the story, "all was unchanged." Nature has reasserted its primal mastery: "the seasons rioted" in Hutter's unroofed castle; "a few more gales and tempests, would sweep all into the lake, and blot the building from the face of that magnificent solitude."[17] What man has done passes; what the Creator has done remains. Such is the lesson of Cooper's indestructible setting.

But *firsts*, generated in this context by the model of an individual life, imply a later development, a movement *through* time. And that movement is already under way in *The Deerslayer*. Natty Bumppo's killing of three more Hurons, for example, validates his feeling that the victory over le Loup Cervier was "the beginning with the redskins." In the final pages of the novel Cooper contrasts the tranquillity of a changeless wilderness with a mood at once nostalgic and expectant. Natty Bumppo returns to Lake Glimmerglass "on the eve of another, and still more important war." Offering a reprise on his subtitle, Cooper tells us that this had been the region of the "First War-Path" for Natty and Chingachgook, that it contained memories of tenderness and triumph, and that along with Uncas the two friends depart for a specific destination, the Mohawk, where they will "rush into new adventures, as stirring and as remarkable as those which had attended their opening career on this lovely lake."[18] In this novel, Cooper greets an already well-known Natty Bumppo at the beginning of a turbulent and preachy career. The logic of such a beginning suggests a movement through time rather than stasis.

For a socially embattled Cooper, *The Deerslayer* enacts the desire to recapture the promise not simply of childhood but of childhood dreams. Conceived long before as a character associated with creation, Natty Bumppo is the appropriate vehicle for a symbolic journey home. It is a satisfying alliance, that between a youthful Natty and an original wilderness. But radical beginnings in American fiction are primarily narrative strategies accessible as points of reference and departure. In one way or another, they are for leaving. Emerson may speak for the possibility of eternal youth; Thoreau may bid us to wake each day as if it were the first day of our lives. As a writer of narrative, however, Cooper uses beginnings differently. In *The Crater* he celebrates the wonders of a new world fated for destruction. In *The Deerslayer* he projects a timeless setting he had already subjected to time in *The Pioneers*. But he does not cast Natty Bumpo into a posture of changelessness. Quite the contrary: his radical beginning becomes the matrix of adventures that characterize Natty's youthful experience. And nothing accentuates narrative movement more surely than a set of anticipatory firsts guaranteed by a life already lived.

Significant to the fiction of Willa Cather is the sense of an original confrontation with the continent. In *My Ántonia* (1918), Jim Burden's immediate recognition of all that is absent on the Nebraska prairie gives him a sense of being "erased," "blotted out," taken "over the edge" of the world, "outside man's jurisdiction." As he rides out to his grandparents' home at night, he sees nothing familiar, "no fences, no creeks or trees, no hills or fields. If there was a road, I could not make it out in the faint starlight. There was nothing but land: not a country at all, but the material out of which countries are made." The task of Cather's narrative is to bring the prairie within the "jurisdiction" of her narrator's imagination, to fashion a country out of material almost threatening in its lack of form. An even more extreme formlessness emanates from the mesa plain in *Death Comes for the Archbishop* (1927). Despite its appearance of great antiquity, the plain nonetheless looks incomplete, as if, "with all the materials for world-making assembled, the Creator had desisted, gone away and left everything on the point of being brought together, on the eve of being arranged into mountain, plain, plateau." In this case, with the locale "still waiting to be made into a landscape," it is the task of Cather the artist to complete the act of creation.[19]

From the prairie and the Southwest come the stimuli that lead Cather to imagine the world from the beginning. And if the elemental harmony of the Southwest can yield spiritual health, the bleakness of the Nebraska prairie can threaten despair. The incipient fear in Jim Burden's initial account of the prairie is heightened by Mr. Shimerda's suicide even as it is tempered by the nostalgia of a narrative voice committed to memories that cohere in the bountiful figure of Ántonia. Without such a mediating vision, however, Cather's early fiction abounds in fatalities brought about by the unrelieved blankness of the locale. The Bohemian protagonist of her first story, "Peter" (1892), shoots himself in the manner of Mr. Shimerda. A Russian woman in "The Clemency of the Court" (1893) drowns herself "in a pond so small that no one ever quite saw how she managed to do it." More elaborate than these stories, "On the Divide" (1896) features a succession of brutal metaphors that dramatize in absolute terms the plight of the seven-foot Canute Canuteson. Choosing liquor rather than suicide, Canute travels "through all the hells of Dante," with the "skull and the serpent . . . always before him, the symbols of eternal futileness and eternal hate." He has seen the prairie "smitten by all the plagues of Egypt," ravaged by drought, by rain, by hail, and by fire, "and in the grasshopper years he had seen it eaten as bare and clean as bones that the vultures have left." Throughout this story Cather insists (to the point of rhetorical indulgence) on "the eternal treachery of the plains," which every spring turn green "with the promises of Eden."[20]

Not until *O Pioneers!* (1913) did Cather fashion a character with a deep commitment to the land and its promise. To the same Divide she brings Alexandra Bergson, whose faith and determination virtually force the land into yielding the riches she believes it to possess. Risking a tentative first to establish Alexandra's special relation to the land, Cather writes that "for the first time, perhaps, since that land emerged from the waters of geologic ages, a human face was set toward it with love and yearning." What had been forbidding to others seems beautiful to Alexandra, "rich and strong and glorious." Crucial to her faith is a sense of a glorious future latent but stirring under the high ground of the Divide. The accomplished early chapters of *O Pioneers!* in which Alexandra virtually weds the land, pose the question of survival and success sharply; the novel turns to a story of destructive human passion only after Alexandra has won a living from something that is bleak and new. If "the history of every country," as Cather writes, "begins in the heart of a man or a woman," Alexandra Bergson is a maker of history, just as Jim Burden's Ántonia Shimerda is "a rich mine of life, like the founders of early races."[21]

Willa Cather's fiction of the American Southwest celebrates elemental beginnings as a source of nourishment and balance. After expressing a fascination with the region in "The Enchanted Bluff" (1909), Cather established the terms of her vision in *The Song of the Lark* (1915). Thea Kronborg finds a sense of wholeness in the sun-drenched village of the Cliff Dwellers. She knows that these ancient people "had felt the beginnings" of human endeavor and rejoices that her life is united with the "seed" of effort and desire. A decade later, as we have noted, Cather "overcrowded" Godfrey St. Peter's residence in *The Professor's House,* and then—with Tom Outland's story—opened the window and "let in the fresh air" from the Blue Mesa. The stone village that Tom discovers sits high on the mesa with "the calmness of eternity." Every day he feels fresh, vital, in touch with "solar energy in some direct way."[22] In both of these novels, contact with an original world figures as an interlude, quick with significance but inevitably subordinate to larger issues.

In *Death Comes for the Archbishop* (1927), however, Cather engaged the imaginative possibilities of the Southwest in a way that sustained an entire narrative, enveloping character, event, and history in a unity of place and spirit. Presented by means of subtle shifts in perspective as both old and early, Cather's setting remains consistently proximate to creation. Not only is the locale "still waiting to be made into a landscape": gazing at mountains bright with sunlight through vistas of rain, Bishop Latour thinks that "the first Creation morning might have looked like this, when the dry land was first drawn up out of the deep, and all was confusion." Later, beneath the floor of a cave, he hears the flowing of a vast underground river, "a flood moving in utter blackness under ribs of antediluvian rock." As he listens to the majestic force, might made audible, he knows that he is hearing "one of the oldest voices of the earth."[23] Primal, elemental, anterior to human endeavor, such images and impressions pervade the atmosphere of Cather's narrative, providing an astonishing reprise of Genesis for this bishop of gentle French birth.

Cather's story also establishes contact with the origins of Christianity at every opportunity. On his first missionary journey through central New Mexico, Latour loses all sense of direction amid the miles of "conical red hills." The image of a "blunted pyramid," Cather writes, "repeated so many hundred times upon his retina," evokes the sense of wandering in a "geometrical nightmare." Only when he sees the cruciform tree is he able to feel at ease with his surroundings. In keeping with the general strategy of her narrative (as she preferred to call *Death Comes for the Archbishop*), Cather associates novelty with tradition, conical red hills with Egyptian monuments, and then resolves Latour's confusion with the primary symbol of his religion, the form of the cross. The bishop must learn to see his territory directly, to experience a quality of landscape, atmosphere, and history alien to the heritage of the classical world. But the cross, transcending cultures, exists in living vegetation, a natural part of the landscape to which Latour has journeyed. Befitting the ambience of the narrative, the bishop and Father Vaillant plan confidently for the future. Problems of distance yield to possibilities of space. Throughout the book the stimulus for narrative movement derives from a need to fill a spiritual void, to carry Christ into the emptiness of the desert. "Not since the days of early Christianity," Father Vaillant once says, has the Church had such opportunity to lift the human spirit.[24] Repeated allusions to the work of the early Church enforce the idea that missionary labors in the New World are themselves authentic beginnings.

David Stouck has commented on the "ever-present continuum" in *Death Comes for the Archbishop*, the collapsing of past and present into an embracing foreground.[25] Making such an effect possible is a style cultivated for the occasion.

As Cather said, she had long wanted to do something in the manner of legend, something "without accent . . . absolutely the reverse of dramatic treatment. . . . The essence of such writing," she continued, "is not to hold the note, not to use an incident for all there is in it—but to touch and pass on." Assisted by the detail and straightforward tone of William Joseph Howlett's *Life of the Right Reverend Joseph P. Machebeuf* (1908), Cather fashioned her account of missionary life in the Southwest with a disciplined lack of highlighting or "accent."[26] Commenting on Cather's style generally, Wallace Stevens wrote "that it is easy to miss her quality" because "she takes so much pains to conceal her sophistication."[27] Such an estimate applies to the quiet audacity of *Death Comes for the Archbishop* in a particularly accurate way.

Although the narrative takes careful account of external time as it draws to a conclusion, it continues to flatten out internal perspective and subsume background and foreground into an immediate present. Cather controls her fully shaped materials by moving their accumulated substance *into* the consciousness of Bishop Latour. As an aging man, the bishop observes that there is "no longer any perspective in his memories." What Cather calls "calendared time" has ceased to be a factor in his life. Released from the sequential nature of reality, "he sat in the middle of his own consciousness; none of his former states of mind were lost or outgrown. They were all within reach of his hand, and all comprehensible."[28] Such an account of the bishop's wandering mind safeguards even as it asserts the presence of everything that has gone before and thus serves the narrative with a retroactive significance. For the imaginative authority of *Death Comes for the Archbishop* derives from its relation to vital sources of beginning. Cather's achievement is that now, at the end, nothing has been lost, nothing has been outgrown; all is proximate—and fully comprehensible.

Almost a century after Cooper created his most pristine setting in *The Deerslayer*, William Faulkner made conversation the astonishing and heuristic instrument of discovery in *Absalom, Absalom!* (1936) and *Go Down, Moses* (1942). The conversations and questions and tortured analyses of Shreve McCannon and Quentin Compson re-create the American South in *Absalom, Absalom!* just as the compulsive labors of Thomas Sutpen enact in primitive caricature the story of the colonist in the New World—and virtually enslave Quentin's imagination. The swirling dialectic of *Go Down, Moses* reaches back to Adam, to Columbus, and to the American Civil War as Isaac McCaslin explores the implications of ownership and the exploitation of the wilderness in the Mississippi setting Faulkner knew so well. With immense range *Go Down, Moses* engages the turbulent issues of American history, alludes to the discovery of an already tainted promise in the New World, and appropriates the biblical story of dispossession from Eden to its thematic purpose. Perhaps no other novel articulates the fundamental themes of American history so precisely.

It is by means of an aggressive negating language (the same kind of language with which Jim Burden described the blankness of the Nebraska prairie) that Faulkner evokes what he calls the "anachronism" of Old Ben, the bear, and fashions the wilderness that will be Isaac McCaslin's "mistress and his wife."[29] But the wilderness—threatened long before by "the axes of the choppers," as Natty Bumppo remembers in *The Prairie*—is the doomed victim of accelerated progress in *Go Down, Moses:* Isaac has seen it retreat "year by year before the onslaught of ax and saw and log-lines and then dynamite and tractor plows."[30] Having outlived Old Ben and Sam Fathers, he incorporates their spirit into his feeling that he and the wilderness are coeval. Despite his similarities with the figure who came into existence at age seventy in *The Pioneers,* Isaac has no Glimmerglass to provide a life after death. But Faulkner does grant him a corollary vision of himself and the wilderness "running out together, not toward oblivion, nothingness, but into a dimension free of both time and space," in which all the hunters he has known can move "again among the shades of tall unaxed trees and sightless brakes where the wild strong immortal game ran forever before the tireless belling immortal hounds, falling and rising phoenix-like to the soundless guns."[31] It is a harmless hunting ground that Isaac envisions, sport made eternal by the extravagant negation of all that is finite.

Again in *Go Down, Moses* property becomes a central issue, this time morally because it involves the ownership of human beings, this time dramatically because it involves a character who will not accept his patrimony. From the opening page of the novel we learn that Isaac "owned no property and never desired to." Scorned by Lucas Beauchamp for not having insisted upon the McCaslin inheritance, insulted finally by a cranky Roth Edmonds for being old and monotonous, Isaac takes the case against ownership to its ethical extreme: he rejects the idea that he has repudiated his inheritance, because, as he says (in beginning an argument that equates ownership with original sin), "It was never mine to repudiate."[32] If the ownership of property brings on the destruction of Mark Woolston's colony in *The Crater,* in the world according to Isaac McCaslin it has already brought about the fall of man, first in the Old World, then in the New.

Only once in *Go Down, Moses* does Isaac succumb to the pressures that would have him accept his family inheritance. And then only temporarily. During their brief marriage, his wife, intent on possessing what she calls "The farm. Our farm. Your farm," coerces a promise that the conversations with McCaslin Edmonds could never extract. Faulkner's scene implicates sexuality and the eternal Eve with the desire for property; what social pressures cannot bring to pass, she will. Ike hears "the bell ring for supper," locks the door and undresses at his wife's command, sees her nakedness as "the composite of all woman-flesh" since the creation of man, feels the pressure of her fingers tugging at his wrist ("as though arm and hand were a piece of wire cable with one looped end") while he says, "No . . . I wont. I cant. Never," until he surrenders to passion with "Yes" and the thought that *"We were all born lost."* Following the amazing theological drama of this encounter—profound in implication, comic in manner—Ike becomes, as Faulkner says, "unwidowered but without a wife"—and ultimately "uncle to half a county and father to no one."[33]

Whereas some critics have regarded Isaac McCaslin as a lonely hero who seeks a private purity in the midst of a corrupt world, others have seen him as one who flees to an impossible innocence to avoid the responsibilities of being human.[34] In either case Isaac remains the character who extends the issues of the novel to a radical dimension. By means of Isaac's stance, Faulkner projects in high relief what he calls the agony of "a whole land in miniature"; by means of Isaac's hop-skip-and-jump logic, Faulkner implicates the world in a family problem.[35] Admittedly, "Delta Autumn" shows us that Isaac is thoroughly encumbered by the social attitudes of his time and place and that his conception of innocence comes under the unremitting pressure of a history in which we are all involved. But the example of Ikkemotubbe, who murders his nephew and sells his son (Sam Fathers) to Carothers McCaslin, validates Isaac's perception about power and property in an ever-falling world. Toward the end of "The Bear," an eighteen-year-old Isaac sees an enormous snake, "the old one, the ancient and accursed about the earth." Echoing words once used in tribute to nature by Sam Fathers, Isaac salutes the snake with the words "Chief . . . Grandfather," and thereby associates Ikkemotubbe and Carothers McCaslin with the eternal source of evil. The ludicrous spectacle of Boon Hogganbeck laying claim to a tree full of squirrels follows immediately. In the final words of the story, Boon shouts at Isaac: "Dont touch them! Dont touch a one of them! They're mine!"[36] Thus, Faulkner concludes with a synoptic meditation on evil and a comic view of the serious matter of owning nature—something that seems instinctive and innocent, yet insistent and troubling, in this childlike brute of a man.

In the chapter on property in his *Two Treatises on Government*, John Locke argues that money and ownership have brought the world to its present sorry condition—far different from what it was originally. For, "in the beginning," he concludes, "all the World was *America*, and more so than that is now."[37] The essential American narrative, the story that attempts to tell the world over again, is a version of Locke's statement: in a variety of ways, it reaches to the "beginning" and delivers us to the "now." And in doing so, it cultivates a radical dimension that defines the self in its relation to innocence and experience, to the continent and to the world.

Notes

1. Ralph Waldo Emerson, "History," in Emerson, *Essays and Lectures* (New York, 1983), 245; Henry David Thoreau, "A Yankee in Canada," in *The Writings of Henry David Thoreau* (Boston, 1906), V, 83; Thomas Paine, *Common Sense and Other Political Writings*, ed. Nelson F. Adkins (New York, 1953), 51; John Quincy Adams, *An Oration . . . on the Sixty-First Anniversary of the Declaration of Independence* (Newburyport, Mass., 1837), 12.

2. Eusebius, *The History of the Church from Christ to Constantine*, trans. G. A. Williamson (New York, 1983), 33; Owen Wister, *The Virginian* (New York, 1957), 11; Gabriel Garcia Marquez, *One Hundred Years of Solitude*, trans. Gregory Rabassa (New York, 1970), 1, 5; Edward W. Said, *Beginnings: Intention and Method* (New York, 1975), 49.

3. Thomas Prince, *A Chronological History of New England . . . from the Creation* (2 vols.; Boston, 1736), Vol. II, Part ii, Section 2, p. 2; Nathaniel Hawthorne, *The Scarlet Letter* (Columbus, Ohio, 1964), 47. As Michael J. Colacurcio demonstrates, a tale as ultimate in theme as "Young Goodman Brown" (1835) nonetheless takes its meaning from the issues of local history. See Colacurcio, *The Province of Piety: Moral History in Hawthorne's Early Tales* (Cambridge, Mass., 1984). And in such postapocalyptic tales as "The New Adam and Eve" (1843) and "Earth's Holocaust" (1844), Hawthorne's emphasis is on the human heart rather than on a radical starting point.

4. Prince, *Chronological History*, Vol. I, Introduction, Section 2, p. 4; Washington Irving, *A History of New-York, from the Beginning of the World to the End of the Dutch Dynasty*, in *The Works of Washington Irving* (4 vols.; New York, 1904), IV, 38.

5. Willa Cather, *The Professor's House* (New York, 1925), 201.

6. James Fenimore Cooper, *Wyandotté; or, The Hutted Knoll*, ed. Thomas and Marianne Philbrick (Albany, 1982), 29, 26.

7. *Ibid.*, 100, 83. Cooper draws a much more extended portrait (primarily satiric) of a Fourth of July celebration in Chapter 21 of *Home As Found* (1838).

8. Wayne Franklin includes *The Crater* in his excellent analysis of Cooper's tales of settlement. See Franklin, *The New World of James Fenimore Cooper* (Chicago, 1982), 183–212.

9. James Fenimore Cooper, *The Crater; or Vulcan's Peak*, ed. Thomas Philbrick (Cambridge, Mass., 1962), 49, 101–102.

10. Harold H. Scudder, "Cooper's *The Crater*," *American Literature*, XIX (1947), 109–26.

11. Cooper, *Crater*, 139, 160–61, 166.

12. *Ibid.*, 444, 459, 390, 272, 300, 286.

13. James Fenimore Cooper, *The Deerslayer; or, The First War-Path* (1859–61; rpr. New York, 1870), 157, 34; H. Daniel Peck, *A World by Itself: The Pastoral Moment in Cooper's Fiction* (New Haven, 1977), 159.

14. James Fenimore Cooper, *The Prairie* (1859–61; rpr. New York, 1870), 37; William Faulkner, *Go Down, Moses* (New York, 1955), 106.

15. Cooper, *Deerslayer*, 299, 110. Interestingly, Natty Bumppo is pleased that Lake Glimmerglass has not yet been named by Christians.

16. *Ibid.*, 131, 313.

17. Joel Porte, *The Romance in America: Studies in Cooper, Poe, Hawthorne, Melville, and James* (Middletown, Conn., 1969), 39; Peck, *World by Itself*, 159–60; John P. McWilliams, *Political Justice in a Republic: James Fenimore Cooper's America* (Berkeley, 1972), 289; Cooper, *Deerslayer*, 595–96.

18. Cooper, *Deerslayer*, 596–97.

19. Willa Cather, *My Ántonia* (Boston, 1918), 7–8; Cather, *Death Comes for the Archbishop* (New York, 1950), 95.

20. Virginia Faulkner (ed.), *Willa Cather's Collected Short Fiction, 1892–1912* (Rev. ed.; Lincoln, 1970), 516, 494–97.

21. Willa Cather, *O Pioneers!* (Boston, 1913), 65; Cather, *My Ántonia*, 353.

22. Willa Cather, *The Song of the Lark* (Boston, 1915), 306; Cather, *The Professor's House*, 201, 240.

23. Cather, *Death Comes for the Archbishop*, 95, 99, 129–30. In "Cather's Felicitous Space," *Prairie Schooner*, LV (1981), 185–98, Judith Fryer examines Cather's fusion of inner and outer landscape in *Death Comes for the Archbishop*.

24. Cather, *Death Comes for the Archbishop*, 18, 210.

25. David Stouck, *Willa Cather's Imagination* (Lincoln, 1975), 134.

26. Willa Cather, "On *Death Comes for the Archbishop*," in *Willa Cather on Writing* (New York, 1949), 9. Edward A. and Lillian D. Bloom provide a full discussion of the manner in which Cather used Howlett's biography in *Willa Cather's Gift of Sympathy* (Carbondale, Ill., 1962), 212–27.

27. Holly Stevens (ed.), *Letters of Wallace Stevens* (New York, 1966), 381.

28. Cather, *Death Comes for the Archbishop*, 290.

29. Faulkner, *Go Down, Moses*, 193, 326.

30. Cooper, *Prairie*, 264; Faulkner, *Go Down, Moses*, 354.

31. Faulkner, *Go Down, Moses*, 354.

32. *Ibid.*, 3, 256.

33. *Ibid.*, 312–14, 281, 3.

34. Richard P. Adams provides an excellent analysis of Isaac McCaslin

and the alternative views of his decision in *Faulkner: Myth and Motion* (Princeton, 1968), 137–52. As Adams shows, even Faulkner was ambivalent about Isaac.

35. Faulkner, *Go Down, Moses*, 293.

36. *Ibid.*, 329–31.

37. John Locke, *Two Treatises of Government*, ed. Peter Laslett (Cambridge, England, 1960), 319.

DANIEL AARON

The Unholy City: A Sketch

There is an amusing passage in Theodore Dreiser's autobiography symptomatic of a shift in American literary sensibility. Young Dreiser has escaped from the shabbiness and poverty of his Indiana boyhood and happily savored metropolitan variety as a newspaperman in St. Louis, Chicago, Cleveland, and Pittsburgh. Twenty-three years old and "blazing with sex," he cannot wait to see the great and glittering New York City, center of "ease and luxury." Who knows? He might "bag an heiress or capture fortune in some other way." Brother Paul, the songwriter, has urged him to pay a summer visit and promised to show him Broadway and to introduce him to some prominent journalists. Dreiser begins to save his money for the trip east.

But then Dreiser, not yet the American Gorki or the Hindenburg of the American Novel, happens to read George Du Maurier's *Trilby,* the book that seemed "to connect itself with my own life . . . and the tragedy of not having the means to travel." His thoughts turn to his Missouri sweetheart, with whom he has been exchanging "sentimental" letters. He feels an "uncontrollable impulse" to see her. So he leaves Pittsburgh one hot July day and arrives at the small country town where she has been living with her parents. The idyllic setting and the gracious if somewhat seedy family embody for him "the spirit of rural America, its idealism, its dreams, the passion of a Brown, the courage and patience and sadness of a Lincoln . . . the dreams and courage of a Lee

or a Jackson . . . a fixedness in sentimental and purely imaginative American tradition in which [he significantly adds] I,
alas! could not share."

And why not? Because he had been exposed to what he
calls "the other life" in pulsing cities: "I had seen Pittsburgh. . . . I had seen Lithuanians and Hungarians in their
'courts' and hovels. I had seen the girls of that city walking
the streets at night." After such excitements, pastoral Missouri was pale and insipid, his sweetheart "no more than a
frail flower of romance," her parents appealing in their goodness—but "asleep."[1]

Dreiser's declaration expresses a sentiment rarely heard,
though sometimes covertly entertained, in American literary annals before he lumbered into the cultural scene—an
unabashed opting for "the other life." It may be crafty and
cruel and brutal and may affront the ideals dear to a middle-
class "Christian" America, but for better or worse it is real.
The sprawling, unholy city delights and dazzles him; its
most wretched spots are "as good as meat and drink" for
him. "Impish . . . larkish," never "tame, disconsolate, or
hang-dog," the city coerces his imagination.[2]

Writers and intellectuals from the beginning of recorded
history have looked upon cities as both menacing and magnetic, as sinks of depravity and founts of enlightenment. But
in Western literature, and especially in American literature,
the city has been denigrated and invidiously contrasted with
uncontaminated rural life more often than celebrated. Innocent and gullible, the "young man from the provinces" comes
to the city, succumbs to its enticements, is overwhelmed and
disenchanted, and goes back to where he started. The wicked
and alluring city is the Devil's turf. Characters have "experiences" there, learn from them, and pay for them. God reigns
in the cloistered countryside.

For obvious and not so obvious reasons, American writers until at least the beginning of the twentieth century exhibited a marked anti-urban bias. This is not to say that they
were indifferent to the city, only that they were slower than
European writers to respond to its depths and complexities;
slower to yield to its attractions, to capitalize on its mysteries, to mythologize it; slower to explore it and use it as a
background for their fictions; and slower to feel at home in
it. How and why this happened and the part played by writ-

ers of immigrant stock in bringing the city into focus and fa-
miliarizing the unfamiliar is the burden of this sketch.

My story begins in 1819 (incidentally the same year in which
Balzac opens *Le Père Goriot*) with an essay in the *North
American Review* on Charles Brockden Brown, that prolix
and powerful psychological novelist and the first American
writer to feature the city in his gothic plots. The author of
the essay, Richard Henry Dana the elder, argued in it that
American cities were "unsuitable" for romantic treatment:

> Our cities are large but new, and they constantly suggest to us
> the gainful habits and secure homes of a recent and flourishing
> population; the labouring and happy are seen everywhere and
> not a corner or recess is secret. The deserted street at midnight
> produces no awful sense of solitude or danger, and the throng
> that passes us by day would scarcely suggest the thought that
> anyone was alone in the crowd, buried in contemplation, and
> perhaps brooding over mischief in darkness. We hear of crimes,
> but they usually appear so vulgar and selfish, so mean or cruel,
> that the imagination sleeps under abhorrence or disgust; we re-
> gard them as public evils, and think it enough to leave them to
> the benevolent reformer and the laws of the land.

Not even the lurid imagination of Brockden Brown could
strike fear and terror from sober Philadelphia or bustling
New York. No writer, in fact, who tried to depict violent
and sensational incidents in such "stubbornly familiar and
unpoetical" surroundings could sustain the illusion; "his
events and characters" would be "exceptions to everything
most Americans had ever known."[3]
    Only a few decades after Dana's reflections, American
cities had taken on some of the unwholesomeness associated by him and his contemporaries with Old World blight.
The lonely figure in Poe's famous story "The Man of the
Crowd" (1840) haunted the streets of London, possibly because no American city possessed for him the required size
and density or the right atmosphere of mystery. Yet, even
then the man alone in the crowd had ceased to be an anom-
aly in the United States. If not poetical, the larger cities were
at least susceptible to literary attention and had acquired
enough "mystery" and texture to attract the romancer and
the novelist of manners. Dana's own son, the celebrated author of *Two Years Before the Mast* (1840), would periodically

masquerade in his discarded sailor's garb and cruise the slummy sections of Halifax, Boston, and New York, interrogating and admonishing prostitutes. In 1845 Poe's friend, the reformer and journalist George Lippard, published a violent pornographic fantasy on the depravities of the Philadelphia gentry, and seven years later Herman Melville painted glaring scenes of New York lowlife in his novel *Pierre.*

Although not really "seen," the antebellum city was beginning to supply American romancers with symbols for their fables and sermons. Emerson wrote to Carlyle that the delights to the eye and mind New York offered to its citizens almost compensated "for the sale of their souls." As for himself, he felt "some loss of faith on entering cities." They seemed to him "great conspiracies" of "masquers who have taken mutual oaths of silence not to betray each other's secret and to keep the other's madness in countenance."[4] I read in this remark an inadvertent but confirmative gloss of Hawthorne's "My Kinsman, Major Molineux." The rich and ambiguous setting of this tale, with its more than passing reference to the lawless and the illicit, might have suggested to those writers (including Hawthorne) who constantly complained about the paucity of inspiring subject matter in pedestrian America, that other towns beside colonial Boston were exploitable.

It took a Walt Whitman to stretch the poetic dimensions of the American city by cataloging the teeming variety of Mannahatta, in his eyes a great poem of life. Hawthorne and Melville, on the other hand, saw the city differently—rather as death in life. To the former, it was a "paved solitude."[5] To the latter, it was a surreal stone desert where the isolato Bartleby and the ill-fortuned Pierre Glendenning were literally and metaphorically imprisoned. Both writers depreciated the city not so much on moral grounds, though allusions to Tartarus and Vanity Fair abound in their writings, but rather as a correlative of an impending mechanical and heartless society in which lonely men were isolated or barred from the community.

Such presentiments were disquieting in a society still ostensibly attached to the dream of a Protestant Jerusalem and to the openness and equality guaranteed in Jefferson's agrarian republic. The city had its booster chorus of politicians, merchants, land speculators, newspaper editors, and professional men whose personal fortunes and self-esteem fluctuated with its fortunes, but about 1860 the vague apprehensions about city life that tinged a good deal of American writing before that time hardened into aversion and fear. Cities had grown even more lonely, impersonal, cold, faceless, artificial, irreligious, disreputable, agitated, exhausting; conditions contradictory to republican ideals more conspicuous; the gap wider between rich and poor, worker and employer, native- and foreign-born. The great cities, Whitman charged, reeked "with respectable as much as non-respectable robbery and scoundrelism." Most shocking to the alter-ego hero of William Dean Howells' *A Hazard of New Fortunes* was the absence of any "intelligent and comprehensive purpose" in New York's "huge disorder." The Chicago of Robert Herrick, a distant relative of Hawthorne and as sensitive as Howells to the big city's moral obliquity, stood for greed and the "terrible power of an uncontrolled selfishness."[6] The American city, in short, had become the stage upon which the most foreboding manifestations of national life were being enacted.

And it was not merely the chaos or the pervasiveness of big-city knavery that sickened many of the writers who wrote about urban America in the Gilded Age and after. Much of their city phobia sprang from outraged aesthetic sensibilities. The city emerged in their collective panorama as a trap of "brick and granite," a warren of filthy alleys swarming with criminals and drunks, with "smut-faced factory girls" and "the hot-lipped hiccoughing harlot."[7] The city stank. It assaulted the ear with noise, and it was fouled with dirt—not clean country dirt but city dirt, excremental dirt, smut. It was a sink or jungle or brothel, a great sore curable or incurable, depending upon the philosophy of the observer. In the urban novels of the period, it is the ugliness of the city that the authors keep harping on, especially the Chicago novelists of the 1890s and early 1900s.

Rebuilt immediately after the fire of 1871 had consumed it, Chicago had blossomed rankly into an enormous organism whose feeding, digesting, and excretory processes were visible for all to see. Kipling stigmatized Chicago in 1889 as a city of savages and likened it to Calcutta, all "turmoil and squash," a "maze of wire ropes overhead and dirty stone flagging underfoot." That was the way the Chicago novelists,

too, saw it, but they were challenged by the city as well.
Henry Blake Fuller wrote to Howells in 1895 that since he
was condemned to live on the Chicago "muckheap," he felt
obliged to "edit it" by "ordering, formulating, and characterizing its various delectabilities" and thereby "raise this
dirt pile to some dignity and credit."[8]

Fuller and his fellow midwesterner Hamlin Garland did
manage in their fashion to annex the city "to the principality
of literature," but neither palliated what Fuller called its "hideousness and impracticability." From his aerial perspective,
the "mighty but unprepossessing landscape" beheld "through
swathing mists of coal-smoke" had a kind of nasty grandeur
if, he added, the viewer ignored "the lofty articulated iron
funnels," the "numberless tanks" that squatted "on the high
angles of alley walls," and "the little pools of tar and gravel
that ooze and shimmer in the summer sun." Garland con-
ceded even less than Fuller. His Chicago surveyed from a
high rooftop was a "stretch of roofs, heaped and humped into
mountainous masses, blurred and blent and made appalling
by smoke and plumes of steam. A scene as desolate as a
burnt-out volcano—a jumble of hot bricks, jagged eave-
spouts, gas-vomiting chimneys, spiked railings, glass sky-
lights, and lofty spires, a hideous and horrible stretch of
stone and mortar, cracked and seamed into streets. It had no
limits and it palpitated under the hot September sun, bound-
less and savage. At the bottom of the crevasses men and
women speckled the pavement like minute larvae." The sur-
charged violence of Garland's alliterative malediction (Chicago illumined as an industrial hell) betrays a more passionate rejection of the city—that insult to holy nature—than
Fuller's. His rage energizes his prose and momentarily raises
the tension of a lackluster novel.[9]

Whether exalted or sickened by what they saw, the novelists who wrote about Chicago at this time were "doing" the
city rather than getting at it from the inside. Frank Norris
worked himself into a lather over Chicago's magnificent vitality, not a whit disturbed by its grime and murk, its scream-
ing mills and roaring traffic. He hailed the crudity, sanity,
and health of "the Heart of the Nation" and rejoiced in its
brutal ambition, "formidable, and Titanic." Robert Herrick
dug deeper than the rhetorical Norris, and though he was
willing to grant Chicago an "eccentric impressiveness," his
antipathy glowed through his descriptions. Herrick hated

Chicago, according to critic and novelist Floyd Dell, because he thought it warped and degraded "the finest instincts of her people." Tawdry, slack, dirty, vulgar, Chicago epitomized for Herrick the disorder he loathed and feared. India or certain Spanish-American countries, he wrote of Cottage Grove Avenue in one of his novels, "might show something fouler as far as mere filth, but nothing so incomparably mean and long. . . . From the cross streets savage gusts of the fierce west wind dashed down the avenue and swirled the accumulated refuse into the car, choking the passengers and covering every object with a cloud of filth."[10]

What Dell said of Herrick's Chicago ("a pervasive influence—a condition and not a place") applied to the Chicagos of Norris and the others. Yet, if Herrick was blinkered by his preconceptions and moral squint, he differed from most of the genteel literati in his speculations about the centrality of cities in the novel of the future. There they were, "undeniably ugly," to be sure, "with their slovenly approaches, their needless crowding," hardly more than "huge industrial camps" composed of "massive buildings, rather than agreeable homes of human beings." All the same, American writers would have to come to terms with these "camps" and not avert their eyes from the mechanical men and women, "somewhat hard and metallic in their nature," who inhabited them. Whether perceived as "squalidly ugly or infernally beautiful," the modern city offered the most propitious material for literary fictions, Herrick believed. He allowed for the dreadful possibility that writers could grow used to urban ugliness and even fall in love with the abnormal. That risk must be taken. Certainly the neat, sterile suburb was no alternative. It might turn out to be the "social salvation" of America, but it was surely its "aesthetic purgatory."[11]

Herrick, Floyd Dell pointed out, never yielded to the enchantment of "a suddenly beautiful and impressive aspect of a familiar spot, the miraculous strangeness of the known."[12] Perhaps his adopted city did not touch off these little epiphanies. It inspired its own brand of big-shouldered, meat-and-potatoes poetry, but compared with New York, less poetic intensity.

By the time Herrick set down his thoughts on the city and the novel (the year was 1913), Stephen Crane had already conveyed in his expressionistic prose New York's seductive and sinister power, caught the flamboyant color of its slums

where "the street lights glittered red like embroidered flow-
ers" and cable cars "shining with red and brass" moved
"dangerful and gloomy" through mud-spattered streets. And
Henry James had responded in a vein beyond the capacities of
the Chicago school to New York's "particular type of dauntless power," its web of bridges and bristling skyline, and
the ominous hang of the "special skyscraper" over Trinity
Church, "the vast money-making structure quite horribly,
quite romantically" redeemed by the looming fog that conferred upon it "an insolent cliff-like sublimity." But no matter how differently they registered urban vibrations, did either Crane or James really know New York in any deeper
sense than Fuller or Herrick knew Chicago? And weren't
they as ingenious in finding ways to distance themselves
from the scenes and people in their respective canvases? The
New York that James returned to repelled, overwhelmed, and
baffled the "restless analyst." Its monstrous growth had occurred so rapidly and recently and with such momentum
that it seemed to him "beyond any possibility of poetic, of
dramatic capture." Ellis Island and the East Side ghetto were
visible signs to him of the "profane overhauling" New York
had undergone since his youth, and the realization that he
and his dispossessed countrymen must perforce share their
American consciousness "with the inconceivable alien"
haunted and saddened him.[13]

Herrick thought he knew why writers like James felt out
of place in the melting-pot cities of America, why, disliking
the present and fearing the future, they looked backward to
simpler times and places, and why he himself could not
think of one novel "deeply identified" with an American
city. Old-stock American writers, he decided, simply lacked
the education to confront and absorb the new. Inheritors of
traditional letters and learning, they were "American in the
old sense of the word" and represented an America that no
longer existed except on the top fringes. The non–Anglo-
Saxon and preponderant America (German, Slav, Scandina-
vian, and Italian) lay below the upper surfaces, acknowledged to a degree by journalists and short-story writers but
ignored by the novelist except as a collection of oddities or
targets of ridicule. Herrick doubted if there would ever arise
any writer of "the old tradition" with "genius enough to give
these foreign brethren their due position in the picture." He

was not thinking particularly of the city's foreign-born and their recent descendants when he wrote these words, but it followed logically enough that those of them confined to cities were the least likely to get their due so long as novelists only poked around the urban edges and wrote about cities as if they were "huge hotels" where their characters ate and slept, or refuse heaps peopled by the offscourings of Europe.[14]

Who, then, would reveal the city from the inside? Herrick did not say, but Hamlin Garland two decades earlier had had a premonition. It would require a new breed of writer, born and bred in the urban briar patch, at home in it, and privy to its secrets. "The novel of the slums," he declared, "must be written by one who has played there as a child, and taken part in all its amusements; not out of curiosity, but out of pleasure seeking. It cannot be done from above nor from the outside."[15] Strictly applied, Garland's prescription would have ruled out Theodore Dreiser (whom he later tepidly championed), because Dreiser first encountered the city as an adolescent. But it took a writer of immigrant background, uninhibited by genteel culture or class fastidiousness, to accept the city as it was, blowsy and dangerous but marvelously beguiling or, as Dreiser would say, "Aladdinish."

To most of his literary predecessors, the city had remained unfamiliar and threatening, a jungle crawling with alien fauna. Muckrakers and naturalistic novelists had escorted their readers on quick trips through bad neighborhoods where the poor languished and the "dangerous classes" spawned. Radical writers had scared them with prophecies of class war, and evangelical uplifters had concocted plots demonstrating how the spirit of Christ worked wonders on Skid Row. Dreiser's cities were crude and violent and dirty, but he did not recoil from them or regard them as "problems" or temples of sin to be exorcised. Sister Carrie has a rough time in Chicago, but she is in harmony with it all the same, and she adjusts to it, as she does later to New York, without suffering the moral agony that afflicts the characters of Howells and Herrick and Fuller. And the same can be said of the so-called "hyphenate" writers, Dreiser's Jewish, Italian, and Irish sons and beneficiaries. They did not necessarily like or enjoy its promiscuous contacts in his or Whitman's rapturous vein, but they found nothing foreign about it.

Before the arrival of these immigrant "pioneers," the alleys and side streets and ghettos appeared as incomprehensible and designless to the old-stock writers as the forest mazes did to Cooper's civilized whites. They stepped warily along the city trails, seeking familiar landmarks. Consider an experience Frederick Jackson Turner reported to his sister in 1887 after the historian of the American frontier accidentally strayed into a Boston ghetto swarming with unspeakable Jews. Turner was appalled by the sounds, smells, and sights of this enclosed quarter, packed, he wrote, as tight as buckshot in a glass with immigrants of all ages. Some of the Jewish "maidens" were pretty, "as you sometimes see a lily in the green muddy slime," but he could not feel at ease until, after much elbowing, he spotted the Old North Church "rising out of this mass of oriental noise and squalor like a haven of rest."[16] Perhaps the note of pessimism in his famous announcement of the closing of the frontier derives in part from his memories of immigrants penned up in cities and doomed to remain alien and un-American because denied the cleansing frontier experience.

Henry James's response to a similar scene was more thoughtful and sympathetic. He did not especially relish his swift passage through the "longitudinal" and "meanly intersected" streets of New York's "foreign quarter," but though he gasped no less than Turner did at the "swarm" of Jewry "heaped as thick as the splinters on the table of a glass-blower," he evinced no Turnerian panic. The trained observer acquainted with the darker and fouler ghettos of Europe recognized the East Side as a new and more vital Jerusalem. Without speculating at length on the import of this "hotchpotch of racial ingredients," he noted that the foreigners looked "at home" in the ethnic cauldron, that the plethora of "baited" shops reflected the aspirations of their shabby customers and "a new style of poverty."[17]

The American Scene is objective and emotional at the same time; fact and imagination interanimate. F. Scott Fitzgerald's New York is camouflaged by a mist of sentiment, "bewitched . . . suspended by the stars . . . glittering and white." E. E. Cummings' New York, rising "incomparably tall" into "firm hard snowy sunlight" is largely spectacle. James the poet has a less gullible eye. His New York (like the Chicago of the Chicago novelists) is both a palpitating organism and a machine—a "bad bold beauty," a "spaciously organized cage for the nimbler class of animals in some great zoological garden," a "colossal hair-comb turned up."[18] The New York of James the reporter is studded with exactly remembered details—doorsteps, fire escapes, curbstones, gutters, roadways. Still, for all his clairvoyant imagination and accuracy of recollection, he can only give a rough translation of the city's hieroglyphs and do no more than hint at its lower layers, which he neither knew nor cared to know.

It took acculturated neo–Natty Bumppos, the outsiders-turned-insiders, to make sense of the urban Babel. These sons and daughters of the exotic swarm that so jarred the sensibilities of Turner and James had absorbed the city through their pores. It was their natural and national habitat (as Hamlin Garland opined it must be if the city in fiction were ever to be realized), one in which they no longer lived as aliens, however alienated they might feel within it. The New York of Michael Gold, Henry Roth, and Alfred Kazin, the Chicago of James T. Farrell, Nelson Algren, and Richard Wright, and the Kansas City of Edward Dahlberg were unedenish, but they were depicted by writers "at home" with pavements and drainpipes, neighborhood schools, grocery stores, and candy shops, tenement cellars, and manure-littered streets, writers for whom the city was never "strange" or "picturesque." Henry Miller might have spoken for them all when he recalled how he walked the streets of his boyhood Brooklyn "with a thousand legs and eyes, with furry antennae picking up the slightest clue and memory of the past."[19] In their books, adjectives like *jagged* and *spiked* that speckled the sentences of earlier cityscapes had a neutral value. *Seamy, squalid, savage, filthy, hideous,* or *appalling,* when used at all, betrayed no squeamish revulsion. Their city could be transfixed in the image of a "wheeling and diving" gull with garbage in its beak.[20] Thanks to them and to others of similar background, the city for a time was demystified and comprehended after over a century of partial or myopic readings.

Theodore Dreiser was the first major American novelist to incorporate the raggedy, sexy city into the hitherto-monitored precincts of American literature and to do so innocently and without shudders or apologies. No one before him, Whitman excepted, so happily orchestrated discordant city clamor, odors, and shapes—rancid alleys, oily rivers, splendid hotels, pretty women—or was made so "ecstatic" by delicious congestion and the "sublimity" of crowds, by

"cars, people, lights, shops!" Who else but Dreiser could remark on the New York whose horrors (read his account of
the city morgue and Bellevue Hospital) tortured him almost
beyond endurance and yet whose glaring disparities allured
and elated him: "After the peace and ease of Pittsburgh—
God! But it was immense, just the same—terrific."[21]

Stuart P. Sherman, the humanist critic, denied Dreiser's
vision and veracity. He traced what he sarcastically called the
"new note in American literature" that Dreiser supposedly
typified to "that 'ethnic' element of our mixed population"
and placed him "outside American society."[22] Sherman's in-
terdict in effect subsumed a large percentage of city ethnics,
the "foreign bodies" that had swelled the amorphous crowds
in the works of nineteenth-century viewers-with-alarm. But
by the time Sherman shot his bolt (1915), the urban night-
mares that had haunted writers as diverse as Henry George,
Charles M. Sheldon, Ignatius Donnelly, Upton Sinclair, and
Jack London had pretty well subsided. No longer dark, per-
ilous, and uncharted, the unholy city shimmered in the fan-
cies of a young literary generation, drawn to it, as Dreiser had
been, by the prospect of wealth and fame and, even more, by
the promise of endless unsupervised diversion.

Notes

1. Theodore Dreiser, *A Book About Myself* (New York, 1922), 420–26.
2. *Ibid.*, 65–66.
3. Richard Henry Dana, Sr., in *North American Review and Miscellaneous Journal*, IX (June, 1819), 64–65.
4. *The Correspondence of Thomas Carlyle and Ralph Waldo Emerson, 1834–1872* (Boston, 1883), I, 269.
5. Nathaniel Hawthorne, "The Grey Champion," in Hawthorne, *Tales and Sketches* (New York, 1982), 240.
6. Walt Whitman, "Democratic Vistas," Whitman, *Complete Poetry and Collected Prose* (New York, 1982), 937; William Dean Howells, *A Hazard of New Fortunes* (New York, 1952), 200; Robert Herrick, "The Background of the American Novel," *Yale Review*, n.s., III (1914), 224.
7. Quoted in Robert H. Walker, "The Poet and the Rise of the City," *Mississippi Valley Historical Review*, XLIX (1962), 91.
8. Rudyard Kipling, *From Sea to Sea and Other Sketches of Travel* (2 vols.; London, 1900), II, 152; H. B. Fuller to W. D. Howells, June 3, 1895, in William Dean Howells Papers, Houghton Library, Harvard University, Cambridge, Mass.
9. Henry Blake Fuller, *The Cliff-Dwellers: A Novel* (New York, 1893), 2–4; Hamlin Garland, *The Rose of Dutcher's Coolly* (Chicago, 1895), 210.
10. Frank Norris, *The Pit: A Story of Chicago* (New York, 1903), 62–63; Floyd Dell, "Chicago in Fiction," *Bookman*, XXXVIII (November, 1913), 275; Robert Herrick, *The Web of Life* (New York, 1900), 199.
11. Dell, "Chicago in Fiction," 275; Herrick, "The Background of the American Novel," 222–25.
12. Dell, "Chicago in Fiction," 275.
13. Stephen Crane, "An Experiment in Misery," in Crane, *Prose and Poetry* (New York, 1984), 538–39; Henry James, *The American Scene* (New York, 1907), 72, 80–81, 83.
14. Herrick, "The Background of the American Novel," 229–31.
15. Hamlin Garland, *Crumbling Idols*, ed. Jane Johnson (Cambridge, Mass., 1960), 61.
16. F. J. Turner to Ellen Turner, June 30, 1887, in Frederick Jackson Turner Papers, Huntington Library, San Marino, Calif.

17. James, *The American Scene*, 98, 118, 132.

18. F. Scott Fitzgerald, *The Crack-Up*, ed. Edmund Wilson (New York, 1945), 30, 33; E. E. Cummings, *The Enormous Room* (New York, 1922), 286; James, *The American Scene*, 106, 130, 136.

19. Henry Miller, *Black Spring* (Paris, 1936), 20.

20. *Ibid.*, 17.

21. Theodore Dreiser, *Dawn* (New York, 1931), 159, 366, 298, 392.

22. Stuart P. Sherman, "The Barbaric Naturalism of Theodore Dreiser," in Sherman, *On Contemporary Literature* (New York, 1917), 87, 95.

LOUISE COWAN

Innocent Doves: Ransom's Feminine Myth of the South

The poems of John Crowe Ransom have been held in high regard during his lifetime and well beyond, widely heralded despite their apparent lack of kinship with other modernist verse. Nearly all of them were written before 1927, though Ransom revised individual pieces from time to time throughout his career. His alterations, apparently, were made more in an attempt to augment meaning than to improve style—an indication that, as he contended in several critical essays, ideas and rational argument, too, have their importance in poetry.[1] Indeed, his slender body of distinguished verse may be regarded, I think we may contend, as a kind of microcosm in which can be located the principles of an authoritative literary and cultural criticism.

One aspect of this small treasure house of poems has been inordinately admired by perceptive readers: its fastidious dryness, of the sort predicted by T. E. Hulme in "Romanticism and Classicism," his famous essay written early in the century and posthumously published by Herbert Read.[2] If we accept Hulme's criteria, we can say that Ransom is without doubt a classicist, viewing human nature as limited, adhering to the "sane classical dogma of original sin," recognizing the necessity of form and organization, and finding his imagery in hard, dry things. At least it is fair to say that his most frequently anthologized poems may be satisfactorily accounted for in these terms. "Bells for John Whiteside's Daughter," "Dead Boy," "Here Lies a Lady," "The Equilibrists," "Antique Harvesters"—these are all classical poems in Hulme's sense. Ritualistic, courtly, spare, ironic, elegiac, they express piety and tenderness, without so much as a grain of sentimentality. Like Ransom's other poems, they conform to what might be considered his aesthetic credo, stated overtly in a slight little lyric, "Agitato ma non troppo," first published in the April, 1923, *Fugitive* and later placed at the beginning of *Chills and Fever*.[3]

> I have a grief
> (It was not stolen like a thief)
> Albeit I have no bittern by the lake
> To cry it up and down the brake.

The poet contrasts his demeanor with that of Dante and Shelley, who, at least according to his own liking, demonstrate their emotions rather a bit too noisily. He goes on to cite questions raised by his readers concerning what they consider to be an unnatural restraint. Where are the standard clichés, they ask, if he has any feeling at all? He concludes by making clear the discrepancy between man and nature:

> I will be brief,
> Assuredly I have a grief
> And I am shaken, but not as a leaf.

True to this antiromantic bent, Ransom has instructed poets, critics, and those who he believes should be the best and most influential readers—the teachers of literature—on the theme of not being agitated "too much." Poetry, as he conceives of it, implies a formed, respectful attitude toward life and is born, not out of a first, immediate thrill but out of "second love." Hence, in a time unfriendly to self-denial, Ransom's poems and essays, through sheer intellect and charm, have revived the cultivated asceticism of the gentleman. His own objects as poet, as he once described them to Allen Tate, indicate an attitude at once reverential and stoic. His aims were, as he wrote, to "find the Experience that is in the common actuals," to allow this experience to bear—by association—"the dearest possible values to which we have attached ourselves," and then to confront their "disintegration or nullification" as "calmly and religiously as possible." Thus, Ransom's context of meaning, his students and followers have seen, provides a rich ambiguity, implying a passionate devotion to life yet seasoning the implication with detachment and wit. His style is inclusive and ironic, with "scrupulous shadings of attitude," as Robert Penn Warren has pointed out, maintaining in its acceptance of contradictions a dualism that, though never resolved into a synthesis, is under the control of form.[4]

Yet, as we read and reread the poetry, it takes on a disturbing and almost frightening strangeness. Have we ever really seen it for what it is? Or has the wry elegance and reticence of the man himself inhibited our understanding of his verse? One of his poems, "Vision by Sweetwater," may serve as an illustration of my point.

> Go and ask Robin to bring the girls over
> To Sweetwater, said my Aunt; and that was why
> It was like a dream of ladies sweeping by
> The willows, clouds, deep meadowgrass, and the river.
>
> Robin's sisters and my Aunt's lily daughter
> Laughed and talked, and tinkled light as wrens
> If there were a little colony all hens
> To go walking by the steep turn of Sweetwater.
>
> Let them alone, dear Aunt, just for one minute
> Till I go fishing in the dark of my mind:
> Where have I seen before, against the wind,
> These bright virgins, robed and bare of bonnet,
>
> Flowing with music of their strange quick tongue
> And adventuring with delicate paces by the stream,—
> Myself a child, old suddenly at the scream
> From one of the white throats which it hid among?[5]

Something ominous intrudes in these lines, far more horrifying than the rueful instruction in "much mortality" that we have become accustomed to uncovering in Ransom—something darker and more appalling than the classic tragic spirit discerned by such perceptive readers as Thornton Parsons and Miller Williams in this chilling poem.[6] For it is not so much Greek tragedy that is called to mind in this brief vignette of shock and dread as it is the pretragic world of mythology itself. Asked to have Robin "bring the girls over to Sweetwater," the speaker suddenly has an experience of *déjà vu:* in the "dream of ladies sweeping by," he goes fishing in the "dark" of his mind. He remembers something from the past, from another world entirely, from what Jung calls the collective unconscious, and fuses his memory of horror with the loveliness and domesticity of the present scene.

The poem is a record, like Yeats's "Second Coming," of a

vision out of which poetry itself emerges: it is an account of the poetic process. The flash that illumines it, however, is not, like Yeats's "rough beast," an enigmatic and apocalyptic image breaking in from the future, to be explored and interpreted as symbol of the present situation. Rather, Ransom's abrupt peripety comes from a nightmarish vision dredged up from "the dark backward and abysm of time." The terror of this apparition, superimposed as an image on an imagined idyllic future, is recognized from its effects, not its specific appearance. Whatever is to happen to one of the soft, gentle "wrens," wading by the "steep turn" of Sweetwater, chattering in their "quick, strange tongues," the fearful possibility is perceived as an inevitable part of the feminine presence. What is the content of this disturbing vision? Not simply death, but violation—and, in particular, the violation of women. The "bright virgins" who are to be "brought over" to Sweetwater, conducted and protected as agents of all the graces and delicacies of life, are to be channels for a nameless horror. An invisible evil preys upon their gentleness and softness and calls forth out of the white throat the scream that has been "hiding" there, always potentially present.

The terror expressed here has it roots in the recognition of a psychic fact embedded in the substratum of consciousness. The feminine grace and charm of the southern scene itself seemingly rouses an archetypal power that can burst forth and despoil the sacred. Several recent commentators on southern culture have sought to identify such a summoning event more specifically. Kathryn Lee Seidel, describing the attitude toward young women in the traditional South, finds in that culture an ambivalence that she attributes to a "constant and pervasive fear" that southern women were "about to be raped by black men." Hence, "fictional rape," she continues, "represents a mythic cultural pattern and is indicative of the position of women in the southern society." She describes the precariousness of their station: "The southern belle is the designated object or work of art of her culture; the emblem of her as a statue on a pedestal represents the projection of her society's attitudes toward women and sexuality, toward blacks and guilt, toward itself and its weakness and loss." A decade earlier Anne Firor Scott had similarly delineated the uncomfortable iconic status of the southern lady: "Southern women, already an ideal by the time of the

Civil War, became the central goddesses of the southern mythos by becoming a symbol for the South itself." And William R. Taylor, speaking of the South's tendency to mythologize and so elevate its situation in general, explained that southerners "grasped for symbols of stability and order to stem their feelings of drift and uncertainty and to quiet their uneasiness about the inequities within Southern society."[7]

It seems unlikely, however, that myth, as opposed to a mystique or a phobia, could take its origin in self-exculpation or idolatry. And the southern character, whatever one may consider its moral confusion to have been, evidences the consistency of myth. In the sense that I am speaking of it, myth is the unifying interior pattern of a people, bestowed upon them by a spiritual force outside themselves, providing an unmistakable design for their corporate life, their mythologies, sagas, codes, customs, and arts.[8] Imprinted upon them before their conscious knowledge of themselves, a "word" spoken in the darkness of their prereflective lives, myth provides a sense of shared identity and enables them to form order out of chaos. In living out their myth, people do not know what it is that they live by, though their ideals, frail as they are, are based on this intuited order. The mythopoeic poet like Ransom discovers his community's forms; the later literary artist like Faulkner assumes and tests them.

The southern myth did indeed place woman at its center, but not out of fear or guilt. In an undeservedly neglected essay, "The Southern Quality," published in 1947, Marshall McLuhan describes the Ciceronian tradition as the basis for southern thought: "Wherever this classical and forensic education spread, it carried with it the full gentlemanly code of honor, dignity, and courtesy, since that was inseparable from the reconstituted program as it was propagated by Castiglione, Sidney, and Spenser. It was no mere archaeological revival. It had the full vitality of medieval chivalry and courtly love in every part of it." McLuhan goes on to explain the transmission of this tradition to the American South and to speak of its propensity for producing the man of passion, with his idealization of feminine beauty: "There is basic in any tradition of intellectual and social passion a cult of feminine beauty and elegance. A feeling for the formal, civilizing power of the passionate apprehension of a stylized feminine elegance, so obvious in Southern life and letters, stems from Plato, blossoms in the troubadours, Dante, and the Renaissance Platonists, and is inseparable from the courtly concept of life."[9]

Southern society missed the founding influence of Puritanism and, because it devoted a large part of its energy in the nineteenth century to the defensiveness and introspection induced by a tragic situation, kept to its original character up to the First World War. In both its social and poetic images of itself, the South was more clearly aligned with the traditions of the Old World than the New. As Lewis Simpson has pointed out, "the culture which began to develop with the founding of Jamestown . . . has sought its literary destiny . . . in an association with the European literary consciousness." Simpson cites Allen Tate's remark that the southerner was "the last European."[10] The South was an agrarian, hierarchical order, feudal rather than modern in its organization, and its central values were never efficiency and productivity, as were those of the North and East. Rather, hospitality and chivalry became the governing southern social ideals. In the exercise of these virtues, women held a paramount position. Their beauty and grace came to represent the highest possible development of civilization.

"Vision by Sweetwater" takes place in an atmosphere suffused by the southern mythic sense of the sacredness of woman. It goes on to apprehend, however, a force in brute necessity that threatens her privileged position. Thus, a single impelling psychic event seems to have ignited Ransom's poetic imagination, in this as in many other of his poems: the assault upon the myth—the violation of culture by raw power. And it is in the very nature of things for this violation to occur. Courtesy and *gentillesse* would have it otherwise, but the rationalist must accept and act upon the callous indifference of nature. Ransom commented on this dualistic aspect of his outlook in a letter to Allen Tate, who had designated the conflicting principles behind Ransom's poetry as "Rationalism" and "Noblesse Oblige": "I am obliged to see that in rationalism and Noblesse Oblige you have picked out two cues that penetrate very deep into my stuff—and I rather like, too, the more synthetic concept of the Old South under which you put them."[11] And later he commented again on the same topic, making clear that his poetry was not essentially southern.

About Rationalism & *noblesse oblige:* You do me the honor to let me be a mouthpiece for a very noble historic culture. But this is the accidental and perhaps the questionable feature of your interpretation, and certainly the less important feature. What is important in your witness was that my stuff presents the dualistic philosophy of an assertive element *versus* an element of withdrawal and Respect. Your terms *Rationalism* and *noblesse oblige* are nearly as ultimate and pure as could be stated in discourse. If you are right, I am happy—I've put unconsciously into my creative work the philosophy which independently I have argued out discursively.[12]

Later, in "Poetry: A Note in Ontology," Ransom named the two terms *idea* and *image,* viewing those who unduly espouse ideas, Platonists and scientists, as working by abstraction. The attempt of abstraction, Ransom maintained, is "to get its 'value' out of the image. . . . People who are engrossed with their pet 'values' become habitual killers. . . . It is thus that we lose the power of imagination." In a balance of the two we find culture, religion, and art: "The aesthetic moment appears as a curious moment of suspension; between the Platonism in us, which is militant, always sciencing and devouring, and a starved inhibited aspiration towards innocence which, if it could only be free, would like to respect and know the object as it might of its own accord reveal itself."[13]

Ransom's concern, which he considered to be philosophic and ahistorical, was the destruction of the civilized attitude of respect and love by the predatory approach of conquest and control. But for all his protests of timelessness, his outlook was nevertheless part of what Lewis Simpson has called "the culture of alienation," the revolt against modernity, and it early found in the southern way of life its central poetic *topos:* the possible ravishment of culture by brute power.[14] An early poem, "In Process of a Noble Alliance" (*Fugitive,* December, 1922), depicts this violation as a marriage.

> Reduce this lady unto marble quickly,
> Ray her beauty on a glassy plate,
> Rhyme her youth as fast as the granite,
> Take her where she trembles, and do not wait,
> For now in funeral white they lead her
> And crown her queen of the House of No Love:
> A dirge, then, for her beauty, Musicians!
> Ye harping the springe that catches the dove.[15]

This is a lovely and arresting poem that remains enigmatic without some understanding of Ransom's dominant metaphor: the victimization of woman, who in her softness and vulnerability is like a bird—a dove or a wren. In this poem her violation is symbolized by marriage, in a union that, like a trap, represents a condemnation to death.

Erich Neumann has written of the marriage of death in his commentary on Ovid's version of the Amor and Psyche myth:

> The procession forming for the dreadful wedding, the torches burning low . . . [the music] changed to the melancholy Lydian mode. . . . The ancient, primordial motif of the bride dedicated to death, of "death and the maiden," is sounded. . . . Seen from the standpoint of the matriarchial world, every marriage is a rape of Kore, the virginal bloom, by Hades, the ravishing, earthly aspect of the hostile male. . . . The marriage of death is a central archetype of the feminine mysteries. . . . For the male—and this is inherent in the essential opposition between the masculine and feminine—marriage, as the matriarchate recognized, is primarily an abduction, an acquisition—a rape.[16]

Contained within the figure of the virgin is the "primordial motif" of the bride dedicated to death. Ransom enacts his version of this "death and the maiden" theme in "Piazza Piece," in which the lady "young in beauty" is waiting for her lover's kiss. She is accosted instead by the gray "gentleman in a dustcoat," a figure of time, winter, old age, death, Hades—who must soon have his "lovely lady." That the approach is erotic is confirmed by the young woman's startled and affronted cry: "Back from my trellis, sir, before I scream!" As Louis Rubin has pointed out, accurately intuiting the archetypal undertone, we might be justified in speaking of the old gentleman as time, the grim raper.[17] Something of this same dark implication is hidden in "The Tall Girl," "Hilda," "Moments of Minnie," "Emily Hardcastle, Spinster," "Blue Girls," "Janet Waking," and "Of Margaret."

Most of Ransom's poems, as a matter of fact, like Henry James's novels, center on women and sexuality. In his *Selected Poems* (1969), thirty-two of the offerings are about women or love and marriage, eleven are about "the manliness of men," and sixteen are about the human situation in general. Without some grasp of what Ransom is doing with his major metaphor, one is likely to miss the import of an attitude that may seem to be a mere courtly mask. The predatory attitude characteristic of the brutal lover, Ransom indicates, may also be characteristic of cultures—may, in fact, represent a fundamental metaphysical attitude. Examining his metaphor further, then, we discern the implication that just as the sexual union—even in love and marriage—is a kind of rape unless carried out with the restraint and humility that are the mark of the gentleman, so, too, in creating works of art, gaining knowledge, and building civilizations, the pursuer must make his approach with love and respect.

In several of his poems Ransom depicts the piety of the lover, the poet, or the gentleman. "Spectral Lovers," for instance, shows two lovers "out of that black ground suddenly come to birth," who walk the earth in April. "Lovers they knew they were, but why unclasped, unkissed?" Painfully conscious of the implicit violence in lovemaking, the man's heart is "pinched" by "considerations" when the lady is prepared to yield, and he rejects the act of consummation but not the love. He tells himself:

> Blessed is he that taketh this richest of cities;
> But it is so stainless the sack were a thousand pities.
> This is that marble fortress not to be conquered,
> Lest its white peace in the black flame turn to tinder
> And an unutterable cinder.

The danger in this unmitigated nobility is that of angelism, and these lovers, who walk the earth "clad in the shape of angels," barely touch each others' fingers, these two spectral lovers, "whose songs shall never be heard." In a similar situation in "April Treason" (an early piece reinstated, with some revision, in the 1969 *Selected Poems*) the lover, an artist who has been painting an idealized portrait of a woman, forgets his role and becomes for one April day a mere man. "He and Venus had their will." Disgusted, he destroys the painting and is left with fingers "cold as ice" for the lady, who is immeasurably reduced.

"The Equilibrists," one of Ransom's most accomplished poems, portrays the perfect balance of the two principles, here represented as love and honor, by means of a bizarre metaphysical conceit—twin stars that revolve about each other. Neither love nor honor is relinquished, and neither is diminished. The poem enacts the drama of the lover's making this choice, for, though consumed by desire for the lady, he is reluctant to seize her.

> Full of her long white arms and milky skin
> He had a thousand times remembered sin.
> Alone in the press of people traveled he,
> Minding her jacinth, and myrrh, and ivory.

His restraint, however, is fully as strong as his lust; consequently what results in the poem is a precarious and unspeakably lovely equilibrium—like a dance. The responsibility of protecting the inviolably pure feminine principle and the concomitant urge to possess bring the lovers to a brilliant, ever-moving "still point" where the polarities are held in suspension.

> And rigid as two painful stars, and twirled
> About the clustered night their prison world,
> They burned with fierce love always to come near,
> But Honor beat them back and kept them clear.

The observer, a third party who has advocated the sensible procedure of choosing one or the other of the alternatives, eventually perceives that the lovers are not in fact in a "torture of equilibrium," but are "orbited nice," with flames "not more radiant than their ice." He has become one who understands, the necessary receiver of the noble message, and thus himself takes on the task of preparing the tomb in which the two will lie in the "quiet earth" and of composing lines "to memorize their doom."

> Equilibrists lie here; stranger, tread light;
> Close, but untouching in each other's sight;
> Mouldered the lips and ashy the tall skull,
> Let them lie perilous and beautiful.

The hypothetical intruding stranger to whom the initiate speaks is warned to "tread light" because of the splendidly achieved and vulnerable equilibrium. With heavy footstep, the outsider, unaware, may jostle together the elements that should remain forever asunder, though joined in a close untouching equipoise. The ending speaks of this achievement as history; by the time of the poem the lovers have become fabulous. The vital surging of spirit against spirit is no longer present but past, though constitutive of present culture. Their feat must be remembered and rendered imperishable in its bravery and fidelity. Ransom is of course speaking here, as in much of his other poetry, of the act of giving form and permanence to value by composing poems. But he is also imply-

ing the difficult feat of balancing the mythic and the primordial in a culture—myth (what one upholds as the ideal)
represented by the feminine, with its need for cherishing
and respect; and the primordial (necessity) represented by
masculine lust, which could debase and destroy the desired
object in a predatory satisfaction of appetite.

Ransom's poetic gift was the ability, as Tate said of Emily
Dickinson, to "grasp the terms of the myth directly and by a
feat that amounts almost to anthropomorphism, to give
them a luminous tension, a kind of drama, among themselves."[18] Certainly this seems to describe Ransom's peculiar
relation to the South and his ability to embody its fundamental values in concrete and specific figures. But further, as I
have been suggesting, Ransom's direct apprehension of the
myth involves at the same time a vision of the primordial—
and this is the source of the wry and ironic distortion present in his poems.

If we consider as mythic those sacred principles and beliefs
on which a particular and unique culture builds its social
harmonies, its prescriptive codes of conduct, and its shared
nuances of feeling, then we may go on to consider as primordial the dark ground of *physis* out of which emerge the unyielding terms of human existence for all people in all ages—
the archetypes. It is something of this sort that Ransom
points out in his essay "Forms and Citizens," in which he
speaks of the overwhelming power of the raw experience of
sexuality and death, advocating the humanizing force of
codes to govern courtship and funerals: "The natural man . . .
is a predatory creature to whom every object is an object of
prey . . . while the social man, who submits to the restraint
of convention, comes to respect the object and to see it unfold at last its individuality, which if we must define it, is its
capacity to furnish us with an infinite variety of innocent
experience: that is, it is a source from which so many charm-
ing experiences have already flowed, and a promise, a possibility of future experiences beyond all prediction."[19]

Ransom illustrates his point further, describing the possible conduct of a man toward the woman he desires: "He
may approach directly, and then his behavior is to seize her
as quickly as possible. No inhibitions are supposed to have
kept the cave-man . . . when life was 'in the raw' from taking
this severely logical course. If our hero, however, does not

propose for himself the character of the savage, or of animal, but the quaint one of 'gentleman,' then he has the fixed code of his *gens* to remember, and then he is estopped from seizing her, he must approach her with ceremony, and pay her a fastidious courtship."[20] A woman addressed in such a manner, he tells us, becomes "a richer object," her value enhanced in proportion to the delay in attaining her. Out of some such piety arises the figure of the gentleman, who depends for his action upon commonly held codes of restraint. But when the codes break down, when a society begins to disintegrate, as Jung tells us, a strange and weird image may emerge in the mind of the poet as spokesman for the community: "It is a primordial experience which surpasses man's understanding. . . . It arises from timeless depths: it is foreign and cold, many-sided, demonic, and grotesque."[21] In it, he continues, the artist penetrates "to that matrix of life in which all men are embedded, which imparts a common rhythm to all human existence."

Ransom's poetic vision, though not situated in the primordial, is subject to this disruption. It is this emergence of the archetypal, the inevitable reality of things, that is the experience giving rise to his poems. He is aware of the myth of his people—in fact, stands within it and is loyal to it—and yet he is cognizant of its displacement. This peculiar perspective gives his poems their grotesque and sometimes weird distortion. They are not merely rueful and ironic. Many of them are fantastic and strange, having to do with seemingly archaic legends and fables. They speak of spectral presences, phantoms, monsters, fairy tales, allegorical debates, and bestiaries. Some of Ransom's readers have commented on the jarring features of his style: Thornton Parsons, for instance, who provides some excellent readings of individual poems, rails at Ransom's "absurd diction," his "attitudinizing," his "inflated bookish epithets," his "pompous mannerisms," his "mixture of floridity and flatness," and ends by considering as successful only eleven poems of the entire canon.[22] But Ransom's verbal incongruities, his apparent infelicities of meter, as well as his staginess of dialogue and his exaggerated caricatures, far from being lapses, stem from an art that is adapted, with astonishing consistency, to his purposes. All the elements of structure and texture in his poems express an insight that is itself grotesque, rendering his poetic canon as bizarre and fantastic as any in the English language.

Wolfgang Kayser's *The Grotesque in Literature and Art* offers a useful definition of the grotesque: "It is the estranged world . . . our own world suddenly transformed into the ominous," the intrusion of the uncanny into a familiar scene, an alienation that "ominously permits of no reconciliation."[23] In Ransom's poetry this peculiar alienation was evident from the very beginning of his writing—even in his first volume, *Poems About God,* though in an awkward and not always successful fashion. A new manner, still grotesque, but urbane and polished, began to make its appearance in some of the *Fugitive* poems as he sensed more clearly the image that expressed his poetic concern: the elegant and stylized feminine figure—the lady—and the stance appropriate to her. His awareness that all she represents is the result of a "gentleman's agreement," the product of culture rather than nature, surrounded her with sinister possibilities. Thus, as he saw, her safety is maintained sometimes with grave difficulties. She must at times take consolation from small favors, as in "Here Lies a Lady," where she is made into a pretty picture of languishing and fretting. The attentions of her husband, her aunt, and her three-year-old child, however, along with "medicoes marvelling sweetly on her ills," afford her no doubt at least a modicum of comfort in distress. "Was she not lucky?" the poet asks:

> In flowers and lace and mourning,
> In love and great honor we bade God rest her soul
> After six little spaces of chill and six of burning.

The lady is enabled to play her part to the end and to die "in character," no small bit of good fortune.

The southern myth expresses itself predominantly in Ransom's poems, then, as a cult of the feminine, elevating woman to a station of supreme importance, a position maintained in his society, however, as he saw, with intense and sometimes almost neurotic effort. In such a view, the possibility of harm to a woman is an outrage not to be contemplated. An early poem, "In Mr. Minnit's House," published only in *Two Gentlemen in Bonds,* deals mock-heroically with this offense. Mr. Minnit, a harsh old tyrant of a grandfather, views with "rage and melancholy" his grandson Mortimer in the act of pulling his sister's hair. The boy, he fears, is likely to turn out like his father, who has mistreated Mr. Minnit's daughter, Mortimer's mother. The prospect is unthinkable. "It was the first time Mortimer had / Seen the old eyes crying and sad." If Mr. Minnit is the aged and infirm defender of a noble cause, then Mortimer, abusing his sister, is the new man, with no piety toward the myth, or at least so Mr. Minnit in his lugubriousness fears him to be.

"Lady Lost," a fable about a "timid lady bird" that flew up the lane and "eyed her image dolefully as death," knocking "on our window pane / To be let in from the rain," suggests a dastardly deed that has quite transfigured its gentle victim. The speaker, piteous-hearted and indignant, plans to go out and ask:

> Who has lost a delicate brown-eyed lady
> In the West End section? Or has anybody
> Injured some fine woman, in some dark way
> Last night, or yesterday?

What Ransom has done in this poem about a ladybird, as he has also done in his "Vision by Sweetwater," is to recreate the myth that in his poem "Philomela" he avowed himself incapable, as an American, of grasping.

> Procne, Philomela, and Itylus,
> Your names are liquid, your improbable tale
> Is recited in the classic numbers of the nightingale.
> Ah, but our numbers are not felicitous,
> It goes not liquidly for us.

The "improbable tale" of the rape of Philomela has spread throughout Europe, he tells us, its beauty and anguish creating, wherever the song is heard, a realm of transcendent value. It has moved from Greece, through the Romans, to the Germans, the French, and the English—but not to the Americans.

> Not to these shores she came! this other Thrace,
> Environ barbarous to the royal Attic;
> How could her delicate dirge run democratic
> Delivered in a cloudless boundless public place
> To an inordinate race?

The poet, who is, as he says, "sick of my dissonance," goes out to Bagley Wood, in England, in search of the nightingale. But even abroad he is still an American and a barbarian; the bird sings, but his ears fail him. He cannot hear the beauty of her song: "Her classics registered a little flat! / I rose and venomously spat." Moving from this inelegant language to a lofty lyricism, he ruefully renounces the perfection of the classical.

> Philomela, Philomela, lover of song,
> I am in despair if we may make us worthy,
> A bantering breed, sophistical and swarthy;
> Unto more beautiful, persistently more young,
> Thy fabulous provinces belong.

Ransom is here declaring that the American enterprise is not a direct continuation of the European classical civilization, that, in fact, this "bantering breed" must find its own "improbable tale" to express the poignant archetype of the feminine and its violation, a tale that will have to be carried on our shores not by nightingales but by wrens, ladybirds, doves, bluebirds, and pigeons.

Further poems about the feminine situation (the "Innocent Doves" section of the 1969 *Selected Poems* [24]) sound the variations on Ransom's major theme. Among others, there is "Miriam Tazewell," who, as a kind of perverse Proserpine, goes sullen because of a storm that "deflowered" her lawn ("To Miriam Tazewell the whole world was villain, / The principle of the beast was low and masculine"). "Emily Hardcastle, Spinster," in the process of being buried, has remained true to the loftiness of her station. The men in town had thought one of them would have her "by default," but she will not choose a husband until the Grizzled Baron comes, to bear her away to his "gloomy halidom." "Youngest Daughter" details the number of lovers who seek out Desiree, the Dowager's youngest daughter, but who marry someone else. In revenge Desiree is locked up as tight as in a nunnery; "When the ill-bred lovers come / We'll say, She is not at home."

The grotesque quality of these verses stems, as I have indicated, from Ransom's perception of two forces vying with each other in the southern way of life and in all high cultures that have begun to decline: the myth itself, requiring chivalry toward women, with its attendant fragility as a "vision of order"; and what Jung has called the "volcanic outburst from the very bottom of things" when cultures are entering a stage of disorder. [25]

If Ransom's muse directs his attention primarily to young women and the grim irony of the marriage awaiting them, she nevertheless enables him as well to envision the heart of the myth embodied in an aging mistress. Three of his poems—"Old Mansion," "Conrad in Twilight," and "Antique Harvesters"—imply a declining myth, one that is kept alive only by its loyal servitors. Among these, the darkest image of the southern culture is depicted in "Old Mansion," where the little life that is left is secluded like an invalid, shut away from the world behind closed doors. A passerby, a modern, who has many times seen the old mansion, seeks entry so that he may understand, from within, "a house whose annals in no wise could be brief / Nor ignoble."

> It was a Southern manor. One need hardly imagine
> Towers, white monoliths, or even ivied walls;
> But sufficient state if its peacock *was* a pigeon;
> Where no courts kept, but grave rites and funerals.

But the old mistress is ill; the mythic center, while still alive, will not reveal itself to the fact finder; later, "the antiquary would finger the bits of shard." The visitor, however, has a glimpse of himself "on the languid air" and, one senses, is changed by the encounter, incomplete as it is. He goes "with courage shaken / To dip, alas, into some unseemlier world." This is Ransom's equivalent of Allen Tate's "Ode to the Confederate Dead," in which an uninitiated modern muses on the chivalry of the dead soldiers who gave their lives "hurried beyond decision" and cannot find the entry into that world of shared heroism.

Another poem, "Conrad in Twilight," is, like "Old Mansion," about unmitigated decay; but in it is a loyal servitor— a lover—who will not forsake the old order. An aging Conrad sits in his "mouldy" garden, forgetting his ailments, cautioned by someone more sensible to come inside to his comfortable dwelling. But Conrad, stubborn and unyielding in his grotesque gallantry, is faithful as though to a declining lady—and of course both the earth and gardens are ancient matriarchal symbols. Conrad will not "uncurve" his back, even though his lungs are filling with "miasma," and his feet are "dipping in leafage and muck." Conrad, like the "Autumn days in our section," is "the most used-up thing on earth," but still he stays late in his garden, with "an autumn on him, teasing."

It is in "Antique Harvesters" that Ransom demonstrates most overtly the bonds forged by tradition, showing the way in which ritual functions in a society both to express and to reinforce the mythical pattern of the motherland. The poem is like a masque, a pageant in which are enacted the ceremonies that kindle belief. The atmosphere is one of "declension": leaves are "tawny," the crop is "meager," and the old men assemble, "dry, grey, spare, / And mild as yellow air," to croak like ravens and rehearse the past "in sable." They compel the young to participate, all unwilling, in the harvest festivities: plucking the spindly corn, recalling the past, honoring the dead heroes, hunting the fox, and in ceremony serving the myth.

> And by an autumn tone
> As by a grey, as by a green, you will have known
> Your famous Lady's image.

As Rubin has pointed out, "Antique Harvesters," in its concentration on the South as a beloved land, rather than as a decaying mansion or garden, is virtually a prescription for the Agrarian movement.[26] Fidelity to the land and the tradition is the theme of the elders. Like battle-scarred veterans of old wars, they seek to rally the young by warning them against those who would mislead them. To disloyal suggestions of giving up the struggle, their reply should be "angry as wasp-music."

> Forsake the Proud Lady, of the heart of fire,
> The look of snow, to the praise of a dwindled choir,
> Song of degenerate specters that were men?
> . . . .
> True, it is said of our Lady, she ageth.
> But see, if you peep shrewdly, she hath not stooped;
> Take no thought of her servitors that have drooped,
> For we are nothing; and if one talk of death—
> Why, the ribs of the earth subsist frail as a breath
> If but God wearieth.

The old men sit, like the elders of the doomed Troy, chirping like grasshoppers, remembering the heroic past, admiring the beauty of Helen, unafraid of death. The Lady herself has not been humbled. And as the aged tell the young, in a sudden peripeteia, not our lives but the verities are the standard for action. For we are in the hands of God; life itself is uncertain under any circumstance. Our task is to spend it on things of genuine worth—the heroic admonition heard throughout the ages.

The southern myth that nurtured Ransom and provided a coherent, rich, and inclusive panorama of life upon which an inquiring mind could speculate was based, as we have indicated, on the supreme value of feminine qualities, which when violated evoke a primordial fear and dread. So, too, it was dependent upon masculine heroism, "The Manliness of Men," the title that Ransom restored to one of the divisions of his 1969 *Selected Poems*. "Captain Carpenter" is a classic quixotic figure, brave, unyielding, foolish. Such heroic images are necessary in a chivalric society, one that has risked its deepest metaphysical self on the defense of the feminine. But heroism carries with it its own possibility of failure, the sense of which renders a man directionless and lost, beset by Furies. "Man Without Sense of Direction" and "Prometheus in Straits" demonstrate the disintegration of the myth and hence of purpose, so that even the natural qualities on which one could ordinarily rely are invalidated by the resulting emptiness.

It is in his revisions of "Prelude to an Evening," however, that we are given insight into Ransom's completed vision, inchoate in his earliest poems, gradually working itself out in his more mature pieces and in his constant revisions. His habit of revising, even to the extent of rewriting many of his poems, is a clue to the real nature of his poetic genius. Allen Tate has remarked that one must view Ransom's "compulsive revisions as a quite consistent activity, as an extension of his reliance on *logic* as the ultimate standard of judgment." Ransom himself commented, near the end of his life, about the poetic process: "A rational structure such as the argument of a poem is an abstract that never exists in nature by itself, but is merely one of perhaps countless structures operating in the same time and space and perhaps not interfering much with each other. And the rational mind cannot express such multiple combinations. The best the poet can do is to introduce words and phrases related to the argument, but partly going off tangentially and rather spectacularly as if heading for some other structures."[27]

It is obvious that a poem exists, for Ransom, somewhere behind the language itself, in a mental and spiritual experience that could be expressed in a number of choreographies.

Surprisingly, for this poet-critic who taught his pupils an absolute attention to words, to that "miracle of harmony" that
occurs when meaning and sound come together, the language of the printed poem has no finality. It is the strange
figure presenting itself to the imagination that bears the authority, like a numinous presence that once seen can never
be forgotten and that one can even perhaps come to know
better as the years pass.

Ransom has rewritten, among his other revisions, eight
poems that he paired with their original versions, appending
explanatory comments in the 1969 edition of the *Selected
Poems*. He made new poems out of old, apparently believing
that he had come to know more clearly what it was he meant
to say. And in the rewriting of "Prelude to an Evening," he
went so far as to correct his interpretation of the myth that
had been dominant in his poems almost from the beginning.
He had been wrong, he said, to allow the masculine principle
to dominate the feminine, though he was still not sure, as
were "some of my friends," that "an expiation is always in
the interest of a fiction."[28]

"Prelude to an Evening" depicts the conflict of which we
have been speaking—that between the feminine myth of
order and the primordial vision of horror, the feminine men-
aced not only by the aggression and appetite of the male, but
by his capacity for "wicked imaginings." It is a prelude to an
evening of lovemaking: the man, after his wanderings in the
world and his encounters with evil, wants passion and desire
in a Romantic dramatization of the dangers he has faced. The
civilizing "form," the restraint, is domesticity—family life,
gentleness, love of children, which are the woman's terms. In
its original version, the poem begins with the man's protest.

> Do not enforce the tired wolf
> Dragging his infected wound homeward
> To sit tonight with the warm children
> Naming the pretty kings of France.
>
> The images of the invaded mind
> Being as monsters in the dreams
> Of your most brief enchanted headful,
> Suppose a miracle of confusion:

Suppose, the husband thinks, that you could take on my
mood, could imagine the evil forces that I have imagined, so
that there would be, after our night together, "a drift of fog

on your mornings" and you would feel "invisible evil, deprived and bold." All day long, "the clock will metronome / Your gallant fear."

> Freshening the water in the blue bowls
> For the buckberries with not all your love,
> You shall be listening for the low wind,
> The warning sibilance of pines.
>
> You like a waning moon, and I accusing
> Our too banded Eumenides,
> You shall make Noes but wanderingly,
> Smoothing the heads of the hungry children.

Thus, in its original version, "Prelude to an Evening" ends with the corruption of the woman also—the masculine fantasy of primordial evil, of the Furies, prevails. In the 1969 edition, Ransom has added five stanzas and revised the entire direction of the poem. Why? Because, as he says, he would not let the feminine principle become the victim of the masculine fantasy. She will remain uncorrupted; the man will have to submit to her. He will dream other evil dreams but will return to her constantly. Ransom has changed his message, has modified his mythopoeic fable. The "plot," the *mythos*, has changed.

In the four stanzas added at the end, Ransom contrives a "frame" for the preceding stanzas, showing that the action of the poem has thus far been in the protagonist's mind. As he explains: "The poem is the man's soliloquy as he approaches his house. He is addressing the mother of his children, who awaits him, as if rehearsing the speech he will make in her presence in order to persuade her to share his fearful preoccupations and give him her entire allegiance."[29]

> I would have us magnificent at my coming,
> Two souls tight-clasped, in a swamp of horrors,
> But you shall be handsome and brave at fearing.
> Now my step quickens—and meets a huge No!

The no he encounters is his own, "forbidding tricks at homecoming." His peripety is swift and complete.

> I have gone to the nations of disorder
> To be quit of the memory of good and evil;
> There even your image was disfigured,
> But the boulevards rocked; they said, Go back.

I am here; and to balk my ruffian I bite
The tongue rehearsing all that treason;
Then stride in my wounds to the sovereign flare
Of the room where you shine on the good children.

The myth sustaining Ransom's poem is no longer simply the courtly cult of the lady; he has now recognized it to be "those patterns within the great Familial Configuration which had been ordained in our creation and were therefore the ones likely to be standard and permanent."[30] But his ideal figure is no less feminine, if less endangered.

Returning to his poems after some thirty years, Ransom was no longer pleased with the poetic figure of the feminine threatened and injured by the masculine. What changed his view was a greater understanding of the components of the myth, with the result that the elevation of woman did not remain so artificial and hence so fragile a construction. In his commentary on the revision Ransom speaks of having been enlightened by Charles Coffin's unfinished work on *Paradise Lost*, a portion of which was published as an essay. It deals first, Ransom says, "with the magnanimous creation of man in the Creator's image and then with the man's adventurous behaviors as they affected his relations with the Creator."[31] What struck him, Ransom says, was the account of the "friendly association" between the two, despite man's frequent rebellions: "The Creator always is prepared to extend his grace . . . as if He had allowed for [the faults] in advance."

Hence, behind the obscure layers of primordial necessity that had always seemed to lie beneath observable reality, Ransom discovered the "Great Myth," as he terms it in this commentary. This is the Old Testament myth of Creation and the Fall—the story of Adam and Eve and their exile from the Garden and, as he came to see, of God's grace in seeking man's reunion with him in love. In man's gift of freedom he has the power to imagine something other than the blessedness of the Garden, to participate in fantasies of the dark formlessness of Chaos, in which he encounters demons and drama, to build cities and destroy them. In reality, however, he is only "half-free," as Ransom indicates in his commentary, since his marvelously intricate body functions without his conscious will. But Eve is only one-quarter "free." Something in the feminine makeup must constrain her to rear children, not simply to produce them—the body takes care of that process—but to renounce self-fulfillment, dreams of evil, "freedom," in order to love and nurture a family. With this inborn virtue, woman is less subject than man to "wicked imaginings." If Adam is to have his Eve, it will have to be on her terms; she is not free to desert her children, not free to give up love and tenderness in order to be *for* herself or *for* Adam.

After the Fall, then, Adam is beset by the Furies: he wanders in darkness, he dwells in a world of primordial menace. The only recourse for his "good self" (for his "unfree" self) is to yield to the woman's influence and to help nurture the children, to construct a sacred order based on the family, so that there grows up within the wickedness of civilization a myth of culture, centering around the feminine, an analogue of the Garden if not the Garden itself, a realm moved by goodness and gentleness if still stained by sin.

It is eros that pulls Adam's freedom toward the love of woman, his body and psyche needing her and desiring her; she is the attraction impelling his free half to yield to her condition. And in so doing, his errant freedom is reconciled with the half of him that still belongs to his Creator and yearns for his love.

In discovering the "Great Myth"—the indestructible human reality, stubborn and persistent despite the Fall—Ransom found as well a pattern of right order informing the southern culture that had shaped his imagination. Poetry, for him, was indeed a unique mode of knowing, based on a distinct ontology. "The miraculism which produces the humblest conceit is the same miraculism which supplies to religions their substantive content," he wrote in 1938.[32] "It is the poet and nobody else who gives to the God a nature, a form, faculties, and a history; to the God, most comprehensive of all terms, which, if there were no poetic impulse to actualize or 'find' Him, would remain the driest and deadest among Platonic ideas." Less than a decade's experience of "meaning his metaphors" in poetry gave Ransom sufficient material for a lifetime of intellectual exploration. In his old age, fresh motifs and formulations of old conceits came to him, requiring again the adventure by poetry. His comments on "Prelude to an Evening," which he was at such pains to reconceive near the end of his life, seem to say that he had discovered something permanently true about myths of order, that value need not surrender to the darkness of the abyss. Implied in his statements is the recognition that culture is not ultimately a futile enterprise sustained by desperate heroism, but an analogue of that larger pattern, the *imago dei*, written on our hearts and discovered only by the poetic impulse.

Notes

1. Ransom reproved Cleanth Brooks for objecting to the paraphrase of a poem. John Crowe Ransom, "Why Critics Don't Go Mad," in Ransom, *Poems and Essays* (New York, 1955), 142–51. And he faulted Richard Blackmur for treating poetic ideas as though they have no importance in the real world, "even though they may be ideas from which, at the very moment, out in the world of action, the issues of life and death are hung. . . . No faith, no passion of any kind," he tells us, "is originated in a poem; it is brought into the poem by the 'imitating' of life . . . it is the fact which is the heart of the fiction." Ransom, "More than Gesture," in Ransom, *Poems and Essays*, 104, 107.

2. T. E. Hulme, "Romanticism and Classicism" in Hulme, *Speculations: Essays on Humanism and the Philosophy of Art*, ed. Herbert Read (London, 1924), 117.

3. This is one of the poems Ransom rewrote in his third edition of *Selected Poems* (New York, 1969). I have compared versions of this and other poems in order not to miss the intention of Ransom's revisions but have elected to use the more familiar, earlier versions in the 1945 edition of *Selected Poems* for the poems quoted, except where otherwise indicated.

4. John Crowe Ransom, Preface to Ransom, *The World's Body* (New York, 1938), viii; Ransom to Allen Tate, March, 1927, as quoted in Louise Cowan, *The Fugitive Group: A Literary History* (Baton Rouge, 1959), 178; Robert Penn Warren, "Notes on the Poetry of John Crowe Ransom on His Eightieth Birthday," *Kenyon Review*, XXX (Autumn, 1968), 319–49.

5. "Vision by Sweetwater" was first published in *Two Gentlemen in Bonds* (New York, 1927) and again in all Ransom's subsequent volumes except the 1945 *Selected Poems*.

6. Thornton H. Parsons, *John Crowe Ransom* (New York, 1969); Miller Williams, *The Poetry of John Crowe Ransom* (New Brunswick, N.J., 1972).

7. Kathryn Lee Seidel, *The Southern Belle in the American Novel* (Gainesville, 1985), 139, xv; Anne Firor Scott, *The Southern Lady: From Pedestal to Politics, 1830–1930* (Chicago, 1970), 139; William R. Taylor, *Cavalier and Yankee: The Old South and National Character* (New York, 1961), 146.

8. For a fuller discussion of myth conceived as a cultural form, as distin-

guished from mythological fables and archetypes, see my "Myth in the Modern World," in Robert F. O'Connor (ed.), *Texas Myths* (College Station, Tex., 1986), 3–22.

9. Herbert Marshall McLuhan, "The Southern Quality," in Allen Tate (ed.), *A Southern Vanguard* (New York, 1947), 109, 121.

10. Lewis P. Simpson, "Home by Way of California: The Southerner as the Last European," in Philip Castille and William Osborne (eds.), *Southern Literature in Transition: Heritage and Promise* (Memphis, 1983), 55; Allen Tate to Donald Davidson, August 10, 1929, in John Tyree Fain and Thomas Daniel Young (eds.), *The Literary Correspondence of Donald Davidson and Allen Tate* (Athens, 1974), 230.

11. Ransom to Tate, February 20, 1927, quoted in Cowan, *The Fugitive Group*, 234.

12. Ransom to Tate, March, 1927, quoted in Cowan, *The Fugitive Group*, 235.

13. John Crowe Ransom, "Poetry: A Note in Ontology," in Ransom, *The World's Body*, 114, 116, 129.

14. Lewis P. Simpson, *The Dispossessed Garden: Pastoral and History in Southern Literature* (Athens, 1975), 65.

15. Reprinted in *Chills and Fever* (New York, 1924) and, as "In Process of the Nuptials of the Duke," in *Grace After Meat* (London, 1924). Ransom did not include it in his later volumes.

16. Erich Neumann, *Amor and Psyche, The Psychic Development of the Feminine: A Commentary on the Tale by Apuleius,* tr. Ralph Manheim (New York, 1956), 61–63.

17. Louis D. Rubin, Jr., *The Wary Fugitives* (Baton Rouge, 1978), 32.

18. Allen Tate, "Emily Dickinson," in Tate, *Essays of Four Decades* (Chicago, 1968), 289.

19. John Crowe Ransom, "Forms and Citizens," in Ransom, *The World's Body*, 34.

20. *Ibid.,* 33.

21. C. G. Jung, *Modern Man in Search of a Soul,* tr. W. S. Dell and Cary F. Baynes (New York, 1933), 156–57.

22. Parsons, *John Crowe Ransom,* 26–30, 164–65.

23. Wolfgang Kayser, *The Grotesque in Art and Literature,* tr. Ulrich Weisstein (Bloomington, 1963), 185.

24. This sectioning was first used in *Two Gentlemen in Bonds* but was dropped from succeeding volumes until it was restored in the 1969 *Selected Poems.*

25. C. G. Jung, *The Integration of the Personality,* tr. Stanley M. Dell (New York, 1939), 12.

26. Rubin, *The Wary Fugitives,* 42.

27. Allen Tate, "Reflections on the Death of John Crowe Ransom," in Tate, *Memoirs and Opinions, 1926–1974* (Chicago, 1975), 43; Thomas Daniel Young, *Gentleman in a Dustcoat* (Baton Rouge, 1976), 464.

28. Ransom, *Selected Poems* (1969 edition), 148.

29. *Ibid.,* 151.

30. *Ibid.,* 157.

31. *Ibid.,* 153.

32. Ransom, "Poetry: A Note in Ontology," in Ransom, *The World's Body,* 140.

CLEANTH BROOKS

The Past Alive in the Present

The poets and novelists who made the Southern Renaissance in the twentieth century have received much praise from various quarters. But in my opinion, their most handsome compliment has come from Vann Woodward, the acknowledged dean of southern historians. In his recently published *Thinking Back: The Perils of Writing History,* he has provided an absorbing account of his own career as a historian. Early in the book he tells us of what the emergence of this new and exciting literature out of the South meant to him as he began his study of southern history. He writes that "no Southern youth of any sensitivity could help being excited by the explosion of creativity taking place during the early 1930s—in fiction, in poetry, in drama."

Yet, more than a vague general excitement was present. On a later page Woodward states very specifically the aspects of that literary movement that impressed him so deeply: the past was not dead but very much alive in the present; the southern past was presented without special pleading, the deficiencies alongside the virtues; and a serious attempt was made to remove the veil that hid much of the real southern past. In short, the new poets and novelists of the South were telling the truth—something like the whole truth—about the southern experience, past and present. Then Woodward adds a further point: the perspective to which they had won might enable them to provide some valuable and necessary insights into the American experience as a whole.

To this last point I mean to return later, but I want now to develop further Woodward's praise of the new southern writers for their consciousness of the past's presence, alive and significant, in the present, a sense of lived history that gave continuity and resonance to their renditions, even of contemporary experience. Can one provide concrete illustrations from the Southern Renaissance? Yes, indeed—from Faulkner, for instance. But in the 1930s and 1940s the issue of the past in relation to the present was sadly confused by most reviewers and literary critics, both North and South. Many of them felt that Faulkner simply could not face the realities of the modern world. Needless to say, the issues that interested Faulkner were far more complicated than that. The past could prove a support or it could prove an intolerable burden. But it could not with impunity be evaded any more than the present could be dismissed, for the present had grown out of the past.

In *The Sound and the Fury* Quentin Compson is hagridden by the past, but in a special way. His ancestors have set a pattern for him that he cannot fulfill. They were men of honor whose behavior had established standards that he cannot live up to. In his desperation he comes to believe that his only escape is into death, but it is an escape from an intolerable present situation—not merely into the past, for it is his personal past that judges and condemns that present.

That this is the true account receives full confirmation from what we learn of Quentin in the novel *Absalom, Absalom!*. One can, of course, argue that *The Sound and the Fury* and *Absalom, Absalom!* are two distinct novels and that the Quentin in one is not necessarily the same man as the Quentin in the other. But the problems of Quentin A and Quentin B are in essence the same problem: how to understand, and even more to shoulder, the burden of his past. That problem is given its personal urgency because he has failed to protect his sister's honor. In *Absalom, Absalom!* the fascination that the character of Henry Sutpen holds for Quentin is Henry's achieved defense of his sister's honor even if it demands killing his best friend. As for the past being alive in the present, Faulkner has presented it in the most powerful symbolism possible: Quentin's discovery of the emaciated form of Henry Sutpen himself. Henry had fled the country as a kind of Cain or Orestes and so, decades before, had become simply a part of the legendary history of Yoknapatawpha County. But on his midnight visit to the ruinous Sutpen mansion, Quentin sees Henry Sutpen, who has secretly come home—come home to die, as he tells Quentin. Hyatt Waggoner aptly describes Henry as a flesh-and-blood ghost, now living in a house long thought to be haunted. Could there be a more powerful symbol of the tragic past of long ago alive in the present? This memory of the withered body of Henry Sutpen lying on the yellowed sheets haunts Quentin. Months later, Quentin, lying in his dormitory room at Harvard, cannot put this vision out of his mind.

Yet, the past as a living force can exert its vigor in the mind of a southern boy under very different circumstances and for very different effects. Of Chick Mallison, in the novel *Intruder in the Dust*, Faulkner as author observes that "every Southern boy fourteen years old" is capable of reliving the moment just before Pickett's charge at Gettysburg as if the issue had not been already decided some eighty years before. For a boy like Charles Mallison, the moment becomes circumstantially alive: "The guns are laid and ready in the woods and the furled flags are already loosened to break out and Pickett himself . . . [is] waiting for Longstreet to give the word and its all in balance." Here again the long-past event is still very much alive in the present consciousness.

To call this passage, as one New York–based reviewer did, "literary, flamboyant, historically ridiculous in terms of America today" misses the point entirely. Faulkner himself, I have no doubt, had had the experience; I confess that I have had it, and I know many others who had. Make of it what you like, it is a cultural fact that has to be faced if we want to deal honestly with cultural history and to understand the psyche of the South in the first third of the twentieth century.

The fiction and the poetry of Robert Penn Warren is suffused with the sense of the past still alive in the present, a past that his characters fail to accept at their peril. The past must be accepted and, if possible, redeemed. For example, one of his most brilliant earlier poems is entitled "Original Sin," but Warren uses the theological term in his title as a metaphor for a deeply ingrained quirk in all men, however rational. We cannot live entirely by maps and schedules. They are never quite perfect enough. The best-laid plans of mice and men gang aglay—break up on that hidden rock of experience. But what looks like a vicious perversity may in fact yield its blessedness. Life is more exciting and finally more wonderful because of the very fact of our hidden affections, blind urges, faiths that resist all rational attempts to extirpate them. Yet, the poem is not a celebration of the irrational. Of course, we have to try to be rational, but we must never deceive ourselves that it is entirely possible. Life is too mysterious for mere calculation to encompass. If what I have just set down looks like moralization, do not put the blame on Warren's poem. The poem is a dramatic rendition; in fact, its subtitle is "A Short Story"—not a philosophical treatise, but a narrative of one man's experience.

Perhaps Warren's full-dress presentation of this theme in verse is *Brother to Dragons*. The poem imagines what might have been the impact on Thomas Jefferson of the terrible news that two of his nephews, out on the frontier of western Kentucky, had murdered one of their slaves for committing a trivial offense and then chopped up his body on a meat block, in the presence of the other slaves, to intimidate them and to make sure that they would fear to report the crime. Though there is nothing among the Jefferson papers to indicate how he responded to such tidings, he must have known of the murder. The killers were the sons of his favorite sister, Lucy. Moreover, the news did get out to other people. To Jefferson, such news obviously struck at family loyalty and pride. But its impact on Jefferson had to be even more special. He had entertained high hopes for mankind, placed as he was in the New World and so given a new start. It was Jefferson who had invested so much of his moral and spiritual capital in man's natural reasonableness and goodness.

Since there is no extant information as to what Jefferson's reaction was, Warren has been left free to imagine it: the shock and horror, the revulsion against his great dream for mankind, and his final reappraisal of his beliefs. His sister Lucy pleads with her brother not to disavow his dream but to accept the past even with all its horror and shame and to try to build a better dream on the only firm foundation it can ever have: an acceptance of the past, the actual past. Lucy tells her brother:

> Your dream, dear brother, was noble.
> If there was vanity, fear, or deceit in its condition,
> What of that? For we are human and must work
> In the shade of the human condition.

Jefferson, accepting the past, even the wickedness disclosed in his own blood line, concurs when his friend and kinsman Meriwether Lewis (of the Lewis and Clark expedition) exclaims:

> nothing we had
> Nothing we were,
> Is lost. All is redeemed
> In knowledge.

Jefferson adds:

> But knowledge is the most powerful cost.
> It is the bitter bread.
> I have eaten the bitter bread.
> In joy, would end.

It would be a pleasure to quote passages from the work of John Crowe Ransom, Donald Davidson, and others who made the Southern Renaissance of the 1930s and 1940s, the writers to whom Woodward pays special tribute. Moreover, one could find plenty of further illustrations from the succeeding generations of southern writers, for the historical consciousness is still to be found among them, even among some of our youngest writers. But there is one more of the earlier generation whom we cannot fail to consider: Allen Tate. He has two special claims on our attention here. The first is that of the essayist who has written most explicitly and extensively on "the peculiar historical consciousness of the Southern writer." Woodward quotes this very phrase in his account of the "heartening effect" exerted on his own work by the writers of the Southern Renaissance. A second claim for special attention is Tate's fine novel, *The Fathers*, which treats in dramatic detail the traditional man and the antitraditional man. But the issue as presented in that novel is complicated—all the more so by the new ending with which Tate furnished his revised edition.

The problem—at least as it has presented itself to some readers—is this: assuming that Major Buchan is the essential traditionalist, the man who honors the past and would preserve its values, and assuming that his son-in-law, George Posey, is the man of the future on whom the traditionalist values rest lightly and who is ultimately interested only in making money, do not both turn out to be equally destructive of any stable society? One of them seems to be blindly locked into the past; the other, utterly contemptuous of it. It is easy to see why Tate wanted to make the two protagonists direct antitheses, each of the other. But do Major Buchan and George Posey exhaust the human alternatives?

Lacy Buchan, the major's youngest son, relates, many years afterward, an account of the destruction of his family: Major Buchan refused to see what was at stake, believed that Virginia could keep out of the impending War Between the States, disowned his son Semmes for joining the Confederate army, and only after his own house had been burned by a regiment of German-speaking Union troops came to see his folly and so hanged himself. If not a Lear, Major Buchan turns out to be a kind of Gloucester: deceived in this instance not by his bastard son, but by his son-in-law, and, like Gloucester, sacrificing his own son in the process.

Posey scorns all the forms of the traditional society as irrational and therefore ridiculous. When he wins the prize at the tournament and so is allowed to crown with a chaplet the young lady of his choice as Queen of Love and Beauty, he cannot make himself place it on Susan Buchan's head but unceremoniously drops it in her lap. When he is insulted by another man, he scorns to meet him in the duel that custom requires, and simply knocks him down with his fists. Later on, when the same man insults him even more viciously, he simply draws his pistol and shoots him down like a dog. No tears need be shed for the man Posey killed; by common consent he deserved his fate. But again, Posey scorns the traditional forms for handling such matters. He believes in direct action—even impulsive action.

It is easy to see why George Posey would have proved an attractive, even glamorous figure to any teenage youth brought up in what must have appeared to him a stodgy home in which nothing exciting ever happened. But how can Lacy, fifty years later, an elderly man, looking back on the disaster to his family, possibly utter the following laudation of Posey? "As I stood by his grave in Holyrood Cemetery fifty years later [that is, in 1911] I remembered how he restored his wife and small daughter and what he did for me. What he became in himself I shall never forget. Because of this I venerate his memory more than the memory of any other man."

Are these words freighted with an irony that I have simply missed? Remember that George Posey, in a sudden spasm of anger, had shot and killed Lacy's brother Semmes, that he had driven his wife, Lacy's sister, insane, and that in the last glimpse we are given of Posey's little child, she is babbling, "Papa make money, Papa make money." This is her comment on his nearly constant absence from home. Tate has provided a short preface to the revised edition. Its subtitle reads: "Caveat Lector." Is it meant to sanction a measure of irony— even sarcasm—in Lacy's final appraisal of Posey? In this preface Tate says that the revision "gives the reader two heroes: Major Buchan the classical hero whose *hubris* betrays him; George Posey, who may have seemed to some readers a villain, is now clearly a modern Romantic hero." Let the reader indeed beware, but of just what?

Thus far I have been concerned with the appropriateness of the ending that Tate has supplied for his novel. But there is a deeper and more general problem: just what constitutes a historical consciousness? More specifically, does Major Buchan, a man of the tradition, possess any historical consciousness himself? The answer here is not as obvious as it may at first appear. Major Buchan has difficulty in imagining any civilized society that is different from his own, that of a Virginia gentleman living on his own acres. He is obviously not a particularly reflective man, but if he were, surely he would affirm the basic continuity of the past and the present. As a matter of fact, a reflective person, including the typical literary artist, until rather recent times always has. The characters of Shakespeare's Roman plays are not vastly different from Shakespeare's contemporary Elizabethans. The mind-set of men of different races and ages was held to be essentially the same. Calibans, of course, were something else again, but Caliban as Shakespeare portrays him in *The Tempest* is not altogether human. But an Antony or a Caesar could be easily accommodated, *mutatis mutandis*, to the Elizabethan scene—British higher education found little difficulty in basing itself on the classics of Greece and Rome, not only in the seventeenth century, but almost down to the present day.

The historical consciousness as manifested by T. S. Eliot, Ezra Pound, and Tate himself is a much more sensitive and specialized cast of mind. These writers have felt that the changes that had begun to occur in twentieth-century culture had gone far deeper and would radically alter the whole human perspective. Specifically, they saw a challenge to the value system by which mankind had lived for millennia past.

Tate was later to find his general prescription for society in a return to orthodox Christianity, specifically as embodied in the Roman Catholic Church. In later life he became a Roman Catholic himself. But earlier and more generally he had stressed "the peculiar historical consciousness" that was the southern writer's rightful heritage and urged him to write without any evasion or defensiveness of southern history. The writer was to render the whole truth about his own region and about his country, the United States at large. Although this position began to be foreshadowed in his early essays, it came to its full and final expression in 1959 in "A Southern Mode of the Imagination."

Where does all of this leave Major Buchan? Did he have, as a southerner, a "peculiar historical consciousness"? My reading of the text of *The Fathers* makes it quite plain that he did not. Tate would have surely approved of the major's belief that men of the past were recognizably like ourselves and, I suspect, would have seen the worth of the major's love of manners and ritual. Yeats, in his great poem "A Prayer for My Daughter," has put the matter in a form that I believe Tate must have applauded:

> And may her bridegroom bring her to a house,
>   Where all's accustomed, ceremonious.
> How but in custom and in ceremony
>   Are innocence and beauty born?

George Posey, by the way, did not bring Major Buchan's daughter Susan to such a house. The last section of *The Fathers* depicts it as an abode of living death.

Yet, a true "historical consciousness" includes an awareness of change and of the need to cope with it. The major entirely lacks such an awareness. He lives in a kind of virtual present in which he cannot envisage real change as ever occurring. Moreover, the major is guileless and something of a sentimentalist. Early in the novel, George Posey charms the major out of his sense of outrage at what the major regards as Posey's breach of good manners. Posey puts his excuse so prettily and apparently so innocently and plausibly that the major relents at once. Late in the novel, after Posey has shot Semmes Buchan to death, he sends a letter of apology that wins the major's heart. As Major Buchan tells Lacy: "He shot your brother in anger, and he explained everything that had led up to it. I have been particularly impressed by his contrition." Major Buchan is obviously a special case. He is not typical of the southern landed gentry of his time: compare Lee, Stephens, Jefferson Davis, Mary Boykin Chesnut and many another. Buchan has as little sense of history as has his son-in-law, George Posey.

Semmes Buchan, though no intellectual, at least saw what was happening to the country and to Virginia. Lacy's grandfather Buchan seems to me to have had an acute consciousness of history and a sound judgment of men. He, or at least his ghost, explaining matters to Lacy, gives an analysis of Posey's character that surely must reflect Tate's own: Grandfather Buchan knows about Posey's capacity for destruction, and from what it springs. George Posey, he tells his grandson, "is entirely alone. My son, in my day we were never alone, as your brother-in-law is alone. He is alone like a tornado. His one purpose is to whirl." It is a thumbnail sketch of the rootless, alienated man of our own day.

This magnificent novel through 203 pages (of the revised edition) renders with powerful drama a major universal theme. It is not merely a "southern" novel or even an antebellum novel. The essential problem is quite alive today. If much of our population is as well intentioned as was Major Buchan, it also shares his utter lack of a consciousness of history; as for George Posey, I suspect that if we look sharply about us, we could make out a goodly number of George Poseys among us. Our Poseys are as glamorous to our young Lacys and can beguile our Major Buchans as well as George ever did.

My denial of the historical consciousness to that obviously traditional man Major Buchan is not actually made in so many words by the text of the novel, and readers who regard Buchan as representing all that Posey is not may be somewhat bewildered, for does the author not set up these characters as polar opposites? In any case, to deny the "restorative" powers to Posey, as I have done, and to see him as a purely destructive force does clearly run counter to the last paragraph of the revised edition. (Neither does it accord very well with the concluding paragraph of the original version of *The Fathers*.) Most of all, my interpretation flies in the face of the long note that Tate supplied for the revised edition.

A full discussion of these matters must be reserved for another essay. Here it would constitute a further distraction from my main point: the historical consciousness exhibited by the writers who made the Southern Literary Renaissance, a movement in which Tate was a key figure and to which his own writings contributed so much—his essays, his poems, and *The Fathers* itself, save for that puzzling last paragraph.

WALTER SULLIVAN

The Novelist as Historian:
Andrew Lytle's *Forrest*

Let me say at once that my title is troublesome because if a novelist is not a novelist until he has published a novel, then Andrew Lytle was not a novelist when he wrote his biography of Nathan Bedford Forrest. He had published three undistinguished poems while he was at Vanderbilt—two in *Driftwood Flames*, one in the *Fugitive*. Later, at Yale he wrote some plays that were never produced or printed. Then he went to New York, where, while supporting himself as an actor, he worked on his contribution to *I'll Take My Stand* and did research on the life of General Forrest. His first story did not appear until 1932, a year after the publication of *Forrest*, and his first novel came four years later. If the definition of a novelist that I gave above is strictly applied in Lytle's case, then he was not a novelist until after he had written biography, and the question that I should be investigating is not what a novelist brings to the writing of biography but how history prepares an author for writing novels. Of course, the flaws in this line of reasoning are sufficient to make it frivolous, so let me put the matter another way: if Lytle was a born novelist, as he no doubt was and is, why did he write the one biography he would ever write before he turned his hand to fiction? And what did writing biography teach him about the art of the novel?

He was not the only member of his group to engage in such a beginning. Robert Penn Warren's *John Brown: The Making of a Martyr* appeared in 1929, long before any of his fiction and before most of his poetry. Allen Tate wrote biographies of Stonewall Jackson and Jefferson Davis and worked on a life of Robert E. Lee, which he never finished, before he began *The Fathers* or completed his revisions of "Ode to the Confederate Dead." Since most writing is a search, a process of discovery, it appears that all of these men were seeking to establish themselves more firmly in the tradition out of which they had come and that they could now see slipping away. The Civil War had been the most significant event in southern history, and if they were fully to understand it, they needed to write about it. This much they had in common, but each chose subjects to suit his own temperament and frame of mind. Warren, who was to contribute the essay on race relations to *I'll Take My Stand*—an essay he had painfully to answer for, first to Donald Davidson, who thought it too liberal, and for the next thirty years in strained interviews and public recantations to the world at large, which saw it as racist—chose an abolitionist of doubtful sanity who was to engage Faulkner's attention over a decade later in "The Bear." As Faulkner's McCaslin Edmonds points out, John Brown was a man of action, untroubled by theory. It was in this role, perhaps, that he appealed to Warren, who was to make much dramatic use of the dialectic of fact and idea.

When Tate selected his subjects, he still believed, erroneously, that he had been born in Virginia. He may have been guided by geographical pride, but complicated person that he was, he was more likely intrigued by Jackson's stern puritanism—an attraction of opposites—and by the flaws of Davis' character that doomed the Confederacy almost at its inception. He could not, however, finish his manuscript on Lee, because, as he told John Peale Bishop, he could not reconcile the private man with the public dimensions of his life. All of these elements, Jackson the hero and Davis the villain and Lee the unreconciled personality, are prominent in Tate's poetry and in *The Fathers* and indeed in his own life.

Why Lytle chose to write on Forrest has answers both simple and complex. The most basic facts of Forrest's life are sufficient to fire any author's imagination. He was a tall, strong, and ruggedly handsome man who, with less than a year of formal schooling, made a million dollars by the time he was forty and turned out to be a military genius when he went to war. Mistreated and betrayed by his commanders and hunted relentlessly by his enemies, he fought battle after battle, usually against superior forces, and never lost until the end, when he had no army left with which to fight. He was wounded four times, had twenty-nine horses shot out from under him, and killed thirty men in hand-to-hand combat. After the war he helped the widows of his fallen soldiers as long as he had means to do so, he tried and failed to build a railroad, and he served as grand wizard of the Ku Klux Klan in an effort to restore white-dominated order to the South. Lytle's claim that Lee called him the greatest general in the Confederate army cannot be documented. But Sir Douglas Haig studied his campaigns carefully, as did Irwin Rommel later, and an account of his battles was published in 1930 by Captain Eric William Sheppard, O.B.E., M.C. Employing his cavalry frequently as mounted infantry, Forrest devised basic tactics for the kind of mobile warfare that was fought by tanks and motorized infantry in World War II.

Such a life begs to be written, and authors less skillful than Andrew Lytle began to write it almost as soon as the Confederate banners had been furled. John Morton and William Witherspoon, both of whom had served under Forrest, wrote their memoirs. General Thomas Jordan and J. P. Pryor sent their manuscript to Forrest for corrections and brought out their life of him in 1868. Captain J. Harvey Mathes and Dr. John Allen Wyeth composed their biographies near the turn of the century and gathered material from the surviving veterans of Forrest's command. Lytle drew heavily from Wyeth and also talked to some ex-Confederates, but by the late 1920s their ranks had thinned and memories had grown dim. This seems to have been of no great consequence to Lytle. His book has no footnotes and only a scanty bibliography. His biography was going to be as much a work of the imagination as of fact; he was pioneering the form that Shelby Foote was to bring to brilliant fruition in his three-volume history of the Civil War.

Lytle was drawn to Forrest not only for the extraordinary dimensions of his character, but for what he represented in Lytle's vision of the South. In "The Hind Tit," his contribution to *I'll Take My Stand*, Lytle, using the early demographic studies of the Old South made by Frank Owsley and his own recollections of rural life, celebrated the yeoman farmer and drew an invidious distinction between him and the cotton snob. Forrest came from the plain people and remained loyal to his roots. He was born in Tennessee, son of a blacksmith who migrated to Mississippi in search of land, which in Lytle's view is the only material possession of enduring value because, though the land is a hard taskmaster, it sets one free. Lytle's ideal farmer, as described in "The Hind Tit," is almost totally self-sufficient, building his house with his own timber, growing his own food, making his own clothes. This is what Bedford Forrest and his family did. By the time the father died, their cabin was finished but there were still land to clear and fences to build, most of which Forrest accomplished. His brothers plowed; his sisters cared for the cows and the chickens, ran the spinning wheel, and sewed the clothes; Bedford tanned skins and made shoes and leggings for the family by firelight. Although his mother was a strong and strong-willed woman who bore numbers of children to two husbands, Bedford was the youthful patriarch in a society that Lytle conceived to be essentially patriarchal. Forrest did, or assigned to others, the basic work that made the land produce; he was therefore responsible for the survival of his people. As he began successfully to trade livestock, the fortunes of the whole family were augmented by his skill. But this account simplifies what was and remains for Lytle a spiritual matter.

Life, properly lived, requires that those who live it have a sense of order rooted in the transcendent. A principle of Agrarianism is that farmers, dependent as they are on weather and the seasons, understand better than any other group that sun and rain are gifts from God. And God is king, the supreme patriarch who makes all laws and shapes all fortunes. Neither heaven nor earth, neither the community of saints nor that of men is organized according to democratic delineations. Everyone knows this, but almost everyone treats the knowledge in a different way. Many want to challenge the nature of things by a program of self-aggrandizement. In 1930 Lytle warned against this by admonishing small farmers, particularly in the South, to halt what he saw as their rush toward destruction. The cotton snobs had been brought low by the Civil War, to be sure, but they had prepared their downfall by trading their self-sufficiency for money. They had violated the land by making it a producer of wealth. At the time *I'll Take My Stand* was published, small farmers, no less perverse than any other group of human beings, were preparing their own ruin by their own pursuit of riches, thereby emulating the cotton snobs, who by now had gone broke and moved to the cities. A tragic aspect of this development was that even should the small farmers succeed in becoming large-scale planters, they would have sacrificed their old life of piety and contentment for an uncertain, mundane existence based on abstraction, on wealth that had no intrinsic value.

Worst of all, in regarding the land not as provider but as capital, the plain people of the South were abandoning the old patriarchal order and affirming the plutocratic system that ruled in the cities of the North. The old mysteries of soil and sky, which were manifestations of the unfathomable Maker of the universe, were forgotten in favor of the mysteries of the futures market, where every day thousands of pork bellies were bought and sold by people who would neither make nor take delivery of the product, many of whom had never seen a pig. A drought in Mississippi might alter the price of cotton in Chicago, but for the traders the cotton, like the pork bellies, remained an abstraction on which the price would rise and fall mainly according to the manipulations of businessmen. And if a market for cow chips had been established, they would as willingly have dealt in them. There was Wall Street, too, where not even lip service was paid to such primary realities as cotton and hogs. Here one could buy shares in companies that made soap and bread and women's underwear, all of which the farmer once made for himself. In such a world it is Jay Gould or George Volkert who causes your shares to fall, but these cannot fill the role of patriarch left vacant when the yeoman farmer betrays his ancient system of order that included God. With the loss of the concept of God, all systems of order become relative and start to shift continually. Of most importance, without God the patriarch to serve as paradigm, the sense of the family as a patriarchy is lost. Mutual respect among members of the family deteriorates. Each person begins to elevate his own personal interests above those of the group. Thus, order is destroyed with the failure of discipline. When the family ceases to exist as a patriarchy, the larger social and political patriarchies—community, state, country—that take the family as their foundation are lost as well. Thus begins the plunge into general chaos. So Andrew Lytle argued in 1930 when he was writing his life of Nathan Bedford Forrest.

To put this another way, Lytle was called to write about Forrest because Forrest fit a philosophy that Lytle wanted to propound, but to say this engages a paradox. Shelby Foote, whose accomplishment demands that we respect his judgment, says that a proper writing of history requires the combined talents of historian and novelist and that these are rarely found in a single human frame. Most novelists lack patience to research properly, but they know that facts alone do not constitute truth, that truth is an order that exists within the facts and must be discovered. Historians, Foote maintains, are indefatigable at gathering material, but almost none of them knows how to write. Furthermore, they are not interested in learning. What is worse, they are ideologues who start with a position, a thesis; then they include in their work only the facts that help to prove what they have decided is true in the first place. If what I have said above is accurate, this seems to place Lytle not among the novelists, but in the ranks of the historians.

Lytle's two-part thesis is that the South would have been better off if it had won the Civil War and that it would have won if the authorities in Richmond had paid more attention to the western theater of operations and furnished the Army of Tennessee with better generals. Except for Forrest, who is the doomed hero, few commanders connected with that army escape Lytle's scorn. He castigates Albert Sydney Johnston for not taking the offensive in the opening stages of the war, when, Lytle believes, he might have fallen upon a divided Union army and destroyed it. Certainly, Johnston displayed more timidity and indecision than one expects of a great soldier, but Lytle ignores the fact that Johnston had little with which to fight. Not only was his army smaller than that of his enemy; the troops he did have were poorly equipped, many being armed with shotguns and many more possessing no weapons at all. Most commentators on this phase of the war give Johnston high marks for his fakes and parries, which kept the Federals at bay.

Once battle was joined at Forts Henry and Donelson, Johnston was guilty of poor judgment, but in this campaign there was more than enough culpability to go around. The missed opportunities, the heroic suffering of the soldiers, and the self-serving posturing of the commanders strike a theme that was repeated often both in Lytle's biography and in the sad history of the war in the West. Forrest refused to surrender. He told his superiors that he had promised the parents of his soldiers that he would take care of them and he meant to keep his word. Thus he becomes what he will remain for Lytle throughout the biography: the patriarch who is also a general, the father figure who controls and protects those in his care.

Larger figures than Floyd and Pillow and Buckner were needed to serve as foils for Forrest's greatness and to show why, even with Forrest on their side, the Confederacy lost the war, and these were easy to find. Chief among them, according to Lytle, was Braxton Bragg, an incompetent and vain commander, jealous of his own prerogatives, a stern and often cruel disciplinarian who wasted the lives of his men by fighting when he should have retreated and retreating when victory was in his grasp. That Bragg was less than a military genius is clearly evident even to amateurs who study his battles. After Chickamauga, his subordinate generals declared their lack of faith in him and asked that he be replaced. But Jefferson Davis, more loyal to his old friendship with Bragg than to the country over which he presided, did not replace him, and Bragg did not resign. Later, when the removal of Bragg could be delayed no longer, Davis, still more concerned with personal relationships than with public duty, called Bragg to Richmond, where as the president's military adviser, he could continue to work his mischief against the soldiers in the field.

Bragg was not completely without virtue. He drilled and worked his troops long and hard when they were in training. The soldiers complained, but they were tough and well disciplined when they broke camp and went into the line. Bragg was well schooled in tactics, and his incompetence and timidity may have been the result not so much of stupidity or cowardice—as Forrest thought and Lytle thinks—as of poor health. He suffered migraine headaches that came without warning and doubtless rendered him less effective throughout his career than he might otherwise have been. But when all that can be said in his favor has been said, he remains a blunderer. He is, for Lytle, the avatar of all the mistakes that Confederate commanders had made and were to make in the prosecution of the war, and he was the enemy and betrayer of Nathan Bedford Forrest. He is the antagonist, and when he enters the pages of Lytle's *Forrest*, the structure and tone of the book change: it ceases to be historical study, marshaling evidence to support a premise, and becomes historical narrative with a hero and a villain as distinctly identified as those in any novel. The Confederate bureaucracy with which Forrest must deal, the Union armies that he will oppose, even the generals commanding opposite him are abstractions when compared with the solid presence of Bragg, whose purposes are to elevate himself and to harm Forrest. Ideology is put aside for the sake of drama.

The first hundred pages of Lytle's book, those which I have characterized as historical study, can be understood, once Bragg comes on the scene, as preparation for the main story. The early successes of Forrest reach a climax with his capture of Murfreesboro soon after Bragg takes charge of the army. Bragg publicly commends Forrest's boldness and promises him command of all the cavalry in middle Tennessee. But he breaks this promise, places most of the troops that Forrest has recruited and armed under Joe Wheeler, and sends Forrest west to start over again. Once more, after Chickamauga, Bragg gives Forrest's troops to Wheeler, and in a famous scene reported by Dr. J. B. Cowan, who witnessed it, Forrest damned Bragg for his meanness, called him a coward whose orders he would no longer obey, and threatened to kill him if they ever met again. But this was not the end of the struggle between them. Late in the war Forrest proposed a campaign that embodied the last faint hope for Confederate victory: he would go into Tennessee, break Sherman's supply lines and relieve the pressure on Joe Johnston's army north of Atlanta. But Bragg was now in Richmond as the president's military adviser, and the answer was no. More than a dozen years later, riding in Forrest's funeral procession, Davis blamed his misuse of Forrest's talents on his generals. "I was misled by them," he said. "I saw it all after it was too late."

The protagonist and the antagonist in Lytle's *Forrest* were private men who had been elevated to roles of prominence. They fell into conflict with each other, and the fate of a country and a people hinged on the outcome of their clash of wills. One may object that under the best of circumstances, with the optimum use of their commanders and all their resources, the Confederates still would have lost the war. But Lytle does not believe this, and his narrative of Forrest and Bragg encompasses, almost completely, the public and private dimensions of a place and time. In their own beings, they were who they were absolutely: the untutored frontiersman and the graduate of West Point. In their official capacities they embodied the best and the worst of the Confederacy: the heroism of its soldiers and citizens; the genius and perversity of its leaders; the violence and romanticism and sense of honor that pervaded its society; and the southern devotion to the "peculiar institution" that was a proximate cause of the war—Forrest had dealt in slaves.

With his novelist's instincts, Lytle appears to have seen Bragg and Forrest as characters worthy of Tolstoy, and they confirmed him in the belief that would inform not only all his fiction but his criticism and memoirs as well: the belief that every serious work of literature must have both a public and a private dimension, and that if either is missing, the effort will fail. Look, for example, at his first novel, *The Long Night*. The initial action of this story is a conflict between Cameron McIvor, a private citizen, and Tyson Lovell, whose dealings in stolen slaves are a threat to the moral order of the community. When McIvor is murdered by Lovell's hirelings, Pleasant McIvor, Cameron's son, undertakes a program of vengeance by which he intends to kill every person who was even remotely involved with the death of his father. Pleasant conceives of his vendetta as a series of private affairs performed not only to avenge Cameron but to maintain the honor of his family, the first in the series of patriarchal organizations that constitute a proper society. This is in accordance with the moral code of the Old South, but since this is true, Cameron's actions are never totally private, and with each murder they become less so. A general and increasing sense of fear is engendered in the community, and men who hold office in the civil structure are killed.

Pleasant intends for the climax of his mission to be the death of Tyson Lovell, but when he meets Lovell late in the first half of the novel, he does not act. His motives are complicated. For one thing, he has been corrupted by all the blood he has shed. He wants, he says, to punish Lovell by letting him live for a while longer in fear for his life. But of more importance is the fact that, as Lovell informs him, the Civil War has begun. Unlike Forrest, whose private and public duties—to protect both his family and his country—led to a single line of action, Pleasant, at least instinctively, understands that his private vendetta, his conceived duty to his family, is now in conflict with his public duty, which is to help win the war. But he does not understand well enough. He joins the Confederate army, but he neglects his military duty in order to kill more of Lovell's men. His epiphany comes when his pursuit of personal vengeance causes the death of a fellow soldier who is his good friend.

The conflict between and the coincidence of public and private duty, which Lytle discovered in his life of Forrest, have remained major themes in Lytle's work throughout his career. In "Mister McGregor," which appeared a year before *The Long Night*, McGregor, like Forrest, defends both public and private order when he fights his slave Rhears. Later, Lytle developed his fiction in terms similar to those that inform *The Long Night*. Mrs. McGowan in "Jericho, Jericho, Jericho" confuses moral values in selecting flawed means to achieve her private ends, and in doing so, she offends public probity. The same is true on a much larger scale of DeSoto in *At the Moon's Inn* and of Brent in *A Name for Evil*. In *The Velvet Horn*, by far the most complex of Lytle's works, public organization is confirmed by an adherence to private familial morality after much individual failure and pain. *A Wake for the Living*, Lytle's celebration of family and community and country, confirms all the values that have informed his canon and been the moral basis of his work.

Finally, while writing his biography of Forrest, Lytle schooled himself in narrative technique. For example, his account of Forrest's pursuit of the Federal General Streight, who had been sent with a larger force than Forrest's to pursue and destroy him, is paced with skill. Part of the narrative moves as rapidly as Forrest's horsemen, but at important points Lytle pauses to anchor the general flow of the story in the lives of individual people and to increase suspense. We see two officers eating their one meal of the day on horseback. We hear the alarm in Emma Sanson's mother's voice when she sees her daughter riding off behind General Forrest. We are given the dialogue spoken by the representatives of each army at the surrender. We smell the dust and the tired horses and men, but most of the time we are watching the armies as a whole.

Lytle's sense of structure seems to indicate that he was a novelist who had not yet written a novel when he set to work on Forrest, and this conclusion is supported by his superb use of physical detail. Here is Lytle, writing history, at his concrete best.

> When [Forrest and his brother Jeffry] reached the position where the enemy was reported waiting to dispute their march, the woods were gray with the first morning light. They were on that portion of the field which had seen the most stubborn fighting. As it grew brighter, the carnage of battle appeared gradually from the dark. The faces of the dead looked gray as wood ashes lying on the white ground, drawn and tightened in an agony so intense that its silence seemed to fix time onto eternity. As if the cold winter air had suddenly frozen them in action, staring eyes, gaping mouths, curiously contracted legs writhed in a mighty effort to break apart the irresistible bond which was holding them fixed forever in a sort of abstract animation. One clutched the branch of an overhanging tree and hung half-suspended. Another with compressed mouth, a hole in his head, his hands fiercely tight about his musket, pushed against its butt, plunging the bayonet up to its hilt in the ground. One other sat against a tree and, with mouth and eyes wide open, looked up squarely at the sky, as if he were strangely amazed at the sudden approach of day.

Let mere historians read this passage and despair.

DANIEL HOFFMAN

History as Myth, Myth as History, in Faulkner's Fiction

In the empirical structures of his novels, as in his uses of motifs, characters, and conflicts from native folklore and from myth, Faulkner is truly in the American grain. He carries on into the twentieth century the experimental and experiential struggles to create new fictional forms commensurate with the contingent nature of truth that characterized the best works of Hawthorne, Melville, and Mark Twain. Allied with Joyce and Conrad in his modernism, Faulkner is at the same time in the line of these American forebears. He shares not only their improvised and unprecedented narrative forms (as in *The House of the Seven Gables* and *The Blithedale Romance*, *Moby-Dick* and *The Confidence-Man*, *The Adventures of Huckleberry Finn* and *Pudd'nhead Wilson*), but also their receptivity to the traditional materials of myth and literary expressions of the folk imagination in the exploration of his themes.

Yet, it is hard to think of an author whose own imagination is as deeply implicated in historical fact, or the appearance of fact, as is Faulkner's. Each family, each person in Yoknapatawpha is the sum of the train of events, relationships, acts, and feelings that comprise his being. Even things have their stories, which is to say their histories, whether already achieved or imagined before the occurrence of the facts. For instance, in *The Hamlet*, the voluptuous Eula Varner is courted by three country youths whose "fairly well-horsed buggies stood in steady rotation along a picket fence." But now that the pregnant Eula has been married off by her father to Flem Snopes and is about to depart on the Texas train, Ratliff, sorrowfully observing her departure, observes also the abandoned buggy of one of her unsuccessful suitors who had decamped in haste.

> Ratliff was to see it, discovered a few months afterward, standing empty and with propped shafts in a stable shed a few miles from the village, gathering dust; chickens roosted upon it, steadily streaking and marring the once-bright varnish with limelike droppings, until the next harvest, the money-time, when the father of its late driver sold it to a Negro farmhand, after which it would be seen passing through the village a few times each year, perhaps recognised, perhaps not, while its new owner married and began to get a family and then turn gray, spilling children, no longer glittering, its wheels wired upright in succession by crossed barrel staves until staves and delicate wheels both vanished, translated apparently in motion at some point into stout, not new, slightly smaller wagon wheels, giving it a list, the list too interchangeable, ranging from quarter to quarter between two of its passing appearances behind a succession of spavined and bony horses and mules in wire- and rope-patched harness, as if its owner had horsed it ten minutes ago out of a secret boneyard for this particular final swansong's apotheosis which, woefully misinformed as to its own capacities, was each time not the last.[1]

Such specificity, such a concentration upon the interaction of time with things, would seem the opposite of the mythic imagination which subsumes all actions under the patterns of the archetypes they embody. The chronicle of the suitor's wagon, writ large, comprises the composite stories, hence the history, of Yoknapatawpha County. But story becoming history, if it is to transcend the unending recital of random, disconnected, meaningless events, must participate in a discernible pattern, an inherent action larger and grander than the quotidian details of its telling. As Faulkner writes, in *A Fable*, of an interpolated folktale about a stolen three-legged racehorse, "being immortal, the story, the legend, was not to be owned by any one of the pairs [of characters] who added to its shining and tragic increment, but only to be used, passed through, by each in their doomed and homeless turn."[2]

The relationship between historical data and the transcendent and legendary meanings that inhere in them has been addressed by Nicolas Berdyaev in terms appropriate to

Faulkner's imagination. "History," says Berdyaev, "is not an objective empirical datum; it is a myth." Believing that each man contains within his inner nature "a sort of microcosm in which the whole world of reality and all the great historical epochs combine and coexist," the Russian philosopher posits the individual consciousness as a sensorium of historical knowledge; and that knowledge proves to be "immortal, the story, the legend."

> Myth is no fiction, but a reality. . . . Historical myths have a profound significance for the act of remembrance. A myth contains the story that is preserved in popular memory and that helps to bring to life some deep stratum buried in the depths of human spirit. . . . The significance of the part played by tradition in the inner comprehension of history [is that it] makes possible a great and occult act of remembrance. It represents, indeed, no external impulse or externally imposed fact alien to man, but one that is a manifestation of the inner mysteriousness of life, in which he can attain to the knowledge of himself and feel himself to be an inalienable participant.[3]

This is to say that a nation's history comprises the received and inborn pattern of knowledge with which its citizens are endowed and in which, knowingly or otherwise, they participate. The culturally received patterns of experience available to the American writer include the remembrance of national history, the Judeo-Christian tradition, the pagan past of classical and primitive myth, and the rambunctious annals of native folklore. From the beginnings of American settlement it was felt that colonial life reenacted the Bible. Governor Bradford's *Journal* and the writings of other Puritan and Quaker worthies abundantly show that the first settlers saw themselves as reliving the annals of the Israelites, who sought a Promised Land in a wilderness, or else as attempting to experience once again the primal innocence of an edenic life in a new world free from the corruptions of European civilization. Inescapably bringing with them the intellectual baggage of the Europe from which they would free themselves, Americans celebrated their heroes and the fertility of their new continent in terms borrowed from Homer, Virgil, and Bulfinch's *The Age of Fable*. In time a folk thesaurus developed here of new legendry or of inherited tales remade. Regional characters emerged as recognizable types, the Yankee and the frontiersman, cast in innumerable conflicts. Natural and human fecundity were celebrated in a folk comedy and in a supernaturalism free of Christian restraint, while the evil sides of man and of nature were expressed in the folklore of demonism and witchcraft. A bumptious lexicon of folk speech enriched the American language. Thus, in character, in sketch, in tall tale, joke lore, superstition, and folk speech a cast of characters, rudimentary plots, and metaphors explored the natural and supernatural world.

The tone of this American folklore was ebullient, self-confident, and comic. The American, as revealed in this lore, was adaptable to circumstance, undaunted by adversity, and at any moment ready to change his calling, be born into a new identity, go west and grow up with the country. Reflecting a new society in which status was achieved, not ascribed by rigid and inherited class lines, the transformations of the metamorphic hero dramatized the hope of upward mobility, while blithely ignoring the costs in human relationships of such alienations from one's beginnings. At the same time, in antebellum popular literature there emerged fictional figures who expressed the negative, irresponsible aspects of the metamorphic man, as seen in Halliburton's Sam Slick and Hooper's Simon Suggs. As I have shown in *Form and Fable in American Fiction*, the literary combination of these properties, both inherited and natively grown, prefigured in Washington Irving's stories "Rip Van Winkle" and "The Legend of Sleepy Hollow," was embodied in the romances of Hawthorne, Melville, and Mark Twain. In them we find the optimism of the metamorphic hero—Holgrave, Ishmael, and Huck Finn—and also the negative implications of metamorphosis. These include fraudulence (for when a man has so many identities, which is the real person?), which is allied with demonism in Hawthorne's Dr. Westerveldt and Melville's Confidence-Man and, parodically, with the illusions of the artist in Tom Sawyer, the Duke, and the Dauphin.[4] Faulkner's work brings into the mid-twentieth century these conventions, these mythical and folk archetypes. Yet, as is always true of him, he transformed what he borrowed.

For the nineteenth-century romancers, America represented the promises, whether delivered or betrayed by experience, of freedom, of life under unprecedented political arrangements, whereas Europe was feudalism, oppression, suffering, and defeat. American life was innocence; Europe was a past burdened with guilt, as its history, myths, and superstitions attested. Faulkner, however, had no need to turn to Europe and its past for images of tragedy or defeat, for these were the fate of the South after the Civil War. Unlike the rest of the United States, Faulkner's region—even his hometown—had known the invasion of alien armies, skirmishes and battles, destruction of homes, looting of property, the death of its young men, and, after the war, the long, difficult effort to reconstitute a society rent apart by defeat, pillage, and devastation.

The Old South differed from the rest of the United States also in that its inflexibly hierarchical social system made mobility between the classes much less feasible than elsewhere. The egalitarianism to which, at least in principle, the institutions, rhetoric, and folk fantasies of American public life in other regions were committed was, in the South, greatly compromised by a social system based upon chattel slavery. These were the social conditions that Mark Twain had represented in medieval costume in *A Connecticut Yankee in King Arthur's Court*, a book in which the simple application of egalitarian Yankee pragmatism to a feudal slavocracy leads not to a more just society but to revolt and holocaust. The intransigence of the South to the democratic dogma espoused elsewhere in the United States is what most characterized the culture and history of that region. In effect, in Faulkner's *donnée*, the values attributed to Europe by his authorial forebears were characteristic of southern history and internalized, as Berdyaev had said, in the experiences of the southern men and women aware of their own heritage.

Thus, the South had developed its own attitudes to its own historical experience, assumptions that Faulkner shared and developed further in his fiction while criticizing them at the same time. Among many commentators on this theme, Lewis P. Simpson has explored it most deeply, showing how Faulkner was anticipated by the antebellum southern writers' defense of the peculiar institutions that comprised an intrinsic part of the pastoral society they sought to regard as an earthly paradise and how, after the war, the literary memory of antebellum times was inevitably tinged by slavery— the root cause of the fall of the South. This view in truth comprises a "myth" of southern history, a secularization of the biblical theme of the Garden of Eden and the inescapable presence therein of original sin.[5] The tension is strong, in Faulkner's work, between the desire for a prelapsarian history and the realization that even before the war the seed was sown of the defeat of the South, the destruction of its way of life, and the downfall of its aristocracy.

Like Hawthorne, Poe, Melville, and Mark Twain before him, Faulkner savors imagining himself as a disinherited aristocrat. In varying degrees and ways our nineteenth-century writers made use of this theme—the obverse of the upward social mobility represented by the metamorphic hero—which the circumstances of their family histories, as they perceived them, thrust into their fictions. In works as different from one another as *The House of the Seven Gables,* "The Fall of the House of Usher," *Pierre,* and *Pudd'nhead Wilson,* whether in satire or in sorrow at their exile from man's kingly estate in the Garden, theirs was the sense of loss and diminution in the world through deprivations of rank, property, and grace. The disinherited aristocrat experienced in his personal and family history a retelling of the Fall of Man. At the same time, except for the southerner Poe, these authors were committed to the democratic spirit of the country and the age. Its leveling egalitarianism was in conflict with the vestigial aristocratic memories or hopes each could not refrain from projecting onto his characters.

Thus, like his own forebears, Hawthorne's Pyncheons seek, while his Holgrave derides, their lost deed that would confer title to an earldom in Maine. Poe, who actually was disinherited by the wealthy (though not aristocratic) Richmond merchant who had reared him, and Melville, descended from heroic generals of the Revolution to witness his father's bankruptcy and madness, made of these losses metaphoric actions in their fictions. So, too, did Mark Twain, whose father's failed law practice and bankrupt general store on the Missouri frontier seemed a bitter comedown for a Virginia gentleman with a claim to vast lands in Tennessee.

William Faulkner, too, was descended from a proud and distinguished ancestor whose present seed had come somewhat down in the world. His great-grandfather, W. C. Falkner, was a swashbuckling Confederate colonel with, it is true, a somewhat equivocal record of military achievements, but around whom an aura of heroic legend affixed itself, an aura cherished and embellished by his great-grandson who made him the model for Colonel John Sartoris in *Flags in the Dust*

and *The Unvanquished.* W. C. Falkner was Faulkner's fore-
bear not only as a hero in the war that forever dramatized the
character of the South, but also as an author. For Colonel
Falkner, ambitious on every side of his active life, wrote a
best seller, *The White Rose of Memphis.* He was at once a
frontier brawler, mixed up in several murderous shoot-outs,
in the last of which he lost his own life, and an entrepreneurial businessman who, after the debacle of the Confederate defeat, tried to revive the Mississippi economy by
rebuilding the railroad the Yankees had destroyed. He was
a complex man, fierce, competitive, sentimental, talented,
unyielding. But two generations down the line his grandson, William Faulkner's father, Murry, was something of a
bumbler, a ne'er-do-very-well whose own father set him up
in one quickly failing enterprise after another. The family, as
everyone knows, was widely ramified with siblings and in-
laws, all of whom came well connected in the decades-thin
history of antebellum Mississippi.[6]

The intensity, the amplitude of historical detail, the sympathy given by Faulkner to the theme of the ruin of the aristocratic class comes with the territory, for much more than
any other section, the South had actually experienced a class
structure in which a landed squirearchy controlled the political, economic, and personal destinies of the region. Although the antebellum planter class in Mississippi was
essentially a one- or two-generation aristocracy, in such a society the self-made man—who is in fact the basis for the
metamorphic folk hero—is by definition a parvenu. Those
who possess wealth, holdings, privilege, position, and power
are quick to erect self-protective barriers against the inter-
loper who arrives without the baggage of a history, a family,
or a past. When a man like Thomas Sutpen (in *Absalom, Absalom!*) arrives in Yoknapatawpha County with his gran-
diose plan of setting himself up as the lord of a wilderness
fiefdom—a southern analogue to the original Pyncheon
in *The House of the Seven Gables*—such an intruder will
never be accepted by those already established on their plantations, with yeomen and slaves in a hierarchy not to be disturbed by a stranger's ambition. Their own ambition, their
own fierce pursuits of land, wealth, and position, must have
been hardly less intense than his, but they got there first and
will brook no intrusion by a rootless latecomer.

The Old South placed its slave-owning whites in positions of arbitrary and unchecked power; the order pertained also to the poor whites, who owned no slaves, often no lands either, and were obliged to defer to the values as well as the persons of the master class. This aristocracy had, in the nature of things, certain high and undeviating obligations toward those it owned or led. Faulkner is quite specific in making clear the character of these obligations and the cost, not only to the aristocrats and their descendants but to the South at large, of their flouting or ignoring the obligations intrinsic to their position. At the same time, Faulkner makes it clear that the aristocratic class subscribed to its own code of honor, at once a badge of distinction and a curse, as will be seen in Faulkner's chronicle-histories of the Sartoris family in *Flags in the Dust* and *The Unvanquished,* the Compsons in *The Sound and the Fury,* and the McCaslins in *Go Down, Moses.*

At the opposite end of the social scale from these is another of Faulkner's parvenus, another self-made, chameleonic personage. Flem Snopes resembles Sutpen in that he, too, in his different fashion, is enacting the revenge of the descendant of poor white trash against the stratified society of the South. In the course of Faulkner's trilogy (*The Hamlet, The Town,* and *The Mansion*) Flem Snopes elevates himself from being the penniless son of a shiftless former horse thief and barn burner to being clerk in Varner's store; then he becomes in turn its manager and what the Irish call a gombeen man, who has all of the dirt farmers in the district in his debt; thence he is cashier in the bank in Jefferson, where he schemes to replace its president and ultimately succeeds, thus becoming a prominent citizen of the county seat. This progress from rags to riches by an ambitious, bloodless character whose wiles are as intricate as his patience is long, this fulfillment of Poor Richard's wise advice to the journeyman, Faulkner views with loathing. The Horatio Alger attributes of a Flem Snopes lead to success, but not, in Faulkner's world, to heroism. Flem as metamorphic man is Faulkner's version of the twentieth-century commercial man turned devil, a true descendant of Melville's Confidence-Man.

Another biblical theme appears as a mythical paradigm in Faulkner's work, an executive image of the human condition. This theme is the *imitatio Christi.* Several of Faulkner's fictional heroes reenact, or try to reenact, the life and sacrifice of Christ, or they are seen by their author as conforming, whether knowingly or not, to that archetype. The world being demonstrably fallen, any reprise in contemporary lives of a Gospel paradigm will of necessity be either satirical or parodic; if the parallel is intended seriously despite the evidence of historical fact to the contrary, it will be manipulated as allegory. But a version of history can include a parallel to the Gospel story, an incomplete and unsuccessful parallel; this approach would allow for the representation of historical complexity and give a tragic dignity to the character's failed attempt to imitate the example of Christ. Faulkner, typically, has written works in all these modes of mythicizing contemporary life, of imbuing biblical paradigms with the texture of historical reality and vice versa. The results are different indeed in three novels that well illustrate the risks and rewards of these strategies. I take them up thematically rather than in chronological order: the allegory of *A Fable*, the parodic grotesque of *Light in August*, and the replication, in *Go Down, Moses*, of the attempt of a man to live as it seems to him Christ would have done.

The Gospel paradigm is not treated in isolation in the two last-named novels. Faulkner's sensibility, exploring the richness of his culture, reflects the divisions defined by Matthew Arnold in "Hebraism and Hellenism." Classical antiquity, paganism, and, in the New World, primitivism provide other archetypes and executive metaphors. Here, too, the tendency is to see the Age of Fable as a golden age, and contemporary avatars as also fallen from a now unattainable grace. These energies of the pagan past do not figure in *A Fable* but are a source of images and metaphors in *Light in August*; in *Go Down, Moses* paganism is a source of pre-Christian spiritual experience.

The last-written of these novels, *A Fable* (1954), is embedded in modern history but not specifically in the history of the South; for, with the exception of the interpolated and extrinsic fable of the racehorse, all the action takes place in France during the First World War. That conflict was of course the crucial historical event that defined Faulkner's own generation, as the Civil War had defined that of his great-grandfather half a century earlier. Faulkner himself had volunteered for the RAF but was still taking flight training in Canada when the Armistice was declared. He returned to the University of Mississippi with his flight tunic, his swagger stick, and a limp, and encouraged the impression that he had been injured in a crash and was wearing a metal plate in his hip to patch a war wound.[7] The romantic young pilot eager for combat but arriving too late recurs in *A Fable*, but otherwise Faulkner's own experience does not directly figure in the work.

The principal character of *A Fable* is an unnamed French infantry corporal who, with a dozen accomplices, organizes a rebellion of an entire regiment. After four horrible years of suffering and slaughter, these soldiers disobey an order to attack; their refusal to continue the war spreads among the Allied troops and to the German side. Their general takes this mutiny as a blot on his own honor and presses the Marshal of the Army to order the execution of the entire regiment for dereliction of duty. The Marshal—the fictional equivalent of Marshal Foch—is the corporal's Adversary; in fact he is the corporal's father, having begotten him illegitimately while on duty in the Middle East. On a much grander and more ambitious scale this novel replays some of the themes and conflicts of Melville's *Billy Budd*, with the military figure of authority (like Captain Vere) representing accommodation to this world, the innocent youth representing a purity of spirit that will not accommodate the world. From this point on the replication in fiction of the Gospels is unequivocal: the corporal's execution between two thieves becomes the Crucifixion, the disappearance of his corpse during a bombardment represents the empty tomb, and so on. Faulkner adds an irony by having the corpse be the one chosen by a detail sent to find an unidentified body for interment as the Unknown Soldier.

The pattern, predictable once it is recognized, is held in abeyance for several hundred pages by a willfully obfuscatory style. Sentences a page long spin almost out of syntactical control, not as expressions of the confusion of one of the characters but as the chosen vehicle of an omniscient narrator who conceals as long as he can—by approaching the theme through the viewpoints of various other characters— that the corporal is the Prince of Peace. Other major characters are similarly nameless—the runner, the sentry—enforcing their identities as archetypal rather than individual persons. But the chief reason why this novel is Faulkner's most ambitious failure was pointed out, soon after the novel appeared, by R. W. B Lewis: "The trouble with *A Fable* is its lack of complexity in the undefiled purity of the hero, and the undefiled purity with which his person and career repeat those of Jesus. There are symbols in the book, but the corporal, the women, the disciples, the thieves, the judges are not among them. They do not *symbolize* anything; they *are* their originals." This book, Lewis avers, demonstrates "the dramatic unfitness of the unmodulated Christ figure."[8]

Thus, despite its realistic evocations of temporal reality, which in themselves comprise an imaginative feat of considerable magnitude, *A Fable* fails to enclose within its suprahuman structure what Yeats called "The fury and the mire of human veins." Elsewhere Faulkner has dramatically presented a vision of the Resurrection and an exemplar of muscular Christianity, as in the sermon of the Reverend Shegog in *The Sound and the Fury* and the character of the Reverend Goodyhay in *The Mansion*. These are minor characters whose religion, which we are to take seriously, is counterpointed against the corruption of the world around them; Faulkner does not there pretend, as the allegorical structure of *A Fable* requires him and his readers to do, that contemporary reality reveals the replication of the truth of the Gospel.

Over twenty years earlier than *A Fable*, in 1932, he had published a novel that seems designed to demonstrate just the opposite, the total inapplicability of the life of Jesus to contemporary life. For after the Fall comes exile from the Garden and man's durance in our world, the Waste Land. The novelist's invocation of mythic and biblical parallels ironically projects this diminution, the despair, the detritus of our modern condition. Hence the wild discrepancies between mythic and biblical originals and their modern instances in *Light in August* (as, also, in *Absalom, Absalom!*, *The Sound and the Fury*, *Sanctuary*, and *Requiem for a Nun*). All readers of *Light in August* have been struck by the correspondence of the initials of its hero with those of Jesus Christ; surely there is significance in his being given the name Joe Christmas when found abandoned on the orphanage steps on Christmas morning. If this line of inference has any meaning, however, we are asked to accept as a Christ surrogate a bastard and a murderer, who, far from being an ethical example and a leader of men, is an alien against whom everyone's hand is turned and who turns against everyone. His paternity is in doubt to the end—he never knows whether his father was a Negro or a white, and therefore his whole life is a desperate, futile search for wholeness, for self-acceptance. Faulkner has thrust upon this one tortured character the dilemma that Mark Twain dramatized in *Pudd'nhead Wilson* as the fate of two, the black and the white babies switched in the cradle, each growing into a false identity. Joe Christmas acts as a Negro when among whites, as a white man when among Negroes. These considerations have led us far from the Gospels, but there are other tantalizing hints and allusions to the life of Christ, all similarly fraught with contradictions.

It has been suggested that Joe's affair with the prostitute Bobbie alludes to Christ and the fallen woman. Lena Grove seems a Mary figure, a sweet, innocent country girl who carries her illegitimate child while seeking the lover who abandoned her; there is even a conflation of Lena's baby, seen in this connection as a Christ figure, with Joe Christmas, when Joe's grandmother, Mrs. Hines, who is present at Lena's delivery, confuses the new baby with her dead daughter's baby Joe. Now, at age thirty-three (or is it thirty-six?), Joe has brutally murdered Joanna Burden, the descendant of an abolitionist and carpetbagger family who had befriended him, taken him as her lover, and, learning that he may be black, turned him into a Negro she can at once patronize and use to fulfill her wild erotic fantasies. By this time Joe has become a bootlegger and has a disciple, Lucas Burch, who betrays him to the sheriff. But the biblical parallels present Lucas, the father of Lena's baby, as a prospective Joseph as well as a Judas. The role of Joseph, however, seems better filled by Byron Bunch, who accepts Lena, loves her, and at the end will doubtless marry her. Thus, the novel is riddled with touches suggesting connections between the lives of these poor Mississippi proletarians and the story of Jesus, but we are never clear what those connections can be.

In *Light in August*, Christianity is represented only in grotesque and aberrant forms. There are three ministers in the book, all of them mad. Joe's grandfather, Doc Hines, preaches a God of wrath and hatred. The God of Joe's foster-father, McEachern, is the God of vengeance. And the God of Byron Bunch's friend the Reverend Hightower is a God of self-absorption. Doc Hines, gibbering denunciations of woman filth, abomination, and bitchery, is the evil spirit who blights Joe's life. He murdered Joe's father on mere suspicion that he was black, thrust the baby into an orphanage, and became janitor there so he could watch over Joe and pursue him with the doubt of his race; in the end it is Doc Hines's preaching hatred to the crowd after Joe is in jail that leads to his being killed and mutilated by Percy Grimm. The vengeful Calvinist McEachern, taking the boy out of the orphanage, flogs him for failing to memorize passages from the Bible and forbids him all normal pleasures. When McEachern pursues and denounces Joe, who has stolen away to meet Bobbie at a dance, the youth brains him with a chair and begins his endless flight from his own past.

The past is history, and in this book history—the history of the South—is dramatized by the grim determinism with which three chief characters are caught in the toils of their grandfathers' lives. Joe Christmas can never escape from Doc Hines's baleful influence. Hightower is transfixed in time, his imagination unable to move beyond the moment when his grandfather led a doomed Confederate charge; the aging grandson, in his incomprehensible sermons, confuses cavalry with Calvary. Hightower's onanistic daydream represents, historically, the futility of the Confederacy and its irrelevance to the needs of the contemporary South. By the end of the novel Hightower has been rescued from his isolation through the friendship of Byron Bunch and by his helping to deliver Lena's baby. This suggests that he is at last redeemed or at least that his redemption is possible. The third character obsessed and undone by a grandfather's past is Joanna Burden, who cannot escape her inheritance of his willfulness, his intractability, and his fanatical espousal of the Negro as a cause.

Thus, the historicity of *Light in August* dramatizes the determinism that gives the novel its inexorable power. This naturalism, appropriate to a novel about proletarian people written during the Great Depression, would seem incompatible with the tangled hints of allusions to the Christ story. The problems encountered in trying to integrate the latter into the perceived themes of *Light in August* arise, however, from thinking of its mythical or biblical level only in terms of content. In the same year that Berdyaev defined the mythical nature of historical knowledge, T. S. Eliot in his review of *Ulysses* proposed a different yet equally integral role for myth in modern literature.[9] Myth would provide the contemporary writer with the structure of his fiction, as

Joyce had taken the form of his novel from the superimposition of contemporaneous reality upon the pattern of *The Odyssey*, each chapter of *Ulysses* being based upon the corresponding book in Homer.

That a similar use of myth informs *Light in August* is the interpretation proposed by Virginia V. Hlavsa: "Faulkner arranged his events and directed the themes in his 21 chapters to parallel the 21 chapters of the St. John Gospel. Further, he developed the stories in John by incorporating mythic figures, primitive practice and folk belief from Sir James Frazer's complete *Golden Bough*. In other words, following John sequentially, Faulkner used his chapter themes to reach for the mythic or primitive tradition which he may have thought of as lying behind each story in John, and this with considerable knowledge of Johannine scholarship."[10] She suggests that the novel is structured as is the book of John, with the coming of Lena, the introduction of a different narrator, and so on in the chapters corresponding to those in that Gospel. Further evidence of this correspondence, and of Faulkner's use of Frazer, Hlavsa discovers by searching a concordance of the novel for "key words and groups of high-frequency words," which reveal many verbal parallels, such as those in Chapter 3 between Hightower and Nicodemus and those "linking each vaguely biblical character with an appropriate mythical figure," such as Lena Grove's associations with Mary, the Corn Mother, and Isis.[11] Many of these verbal echoes seem quite tenuous, as though Faulkner were playing a private joke on his readers. Indeed, the dependence of the architecture of the whole work on the Gospel of St. John, though demonstrable, remains arcane and not, as with *Ulysses*, readily recognized once pointed out.

The source of the novel's strength, as I have indicated, lies not in its parodic distortions of the Gospel of St. John or in allusions to the corn goddess, but in its relentless determinism that so compellingly portrays a modern man torn apart by the region's inheritance of rival fanaticisms of the South and the North. The implied mythical prototype behind Joe Christmas' tragic story is the Waste Land, the ultimate disutopia we have made of our inheritance. The light at the end of the tunnel of Joe's doomed flight is cast by the departure for some other venue of Lena Grove with her newborn son and her faithful friend Byron Bunch, as told by a traveling furniture dealer, who has given them a ride in his wagon, to his wife. That a novel of such suffering and doom can end in the amused pillow talk of a happily married couple does give a ray of hope for mankind. The echoes of Christ's life in Joe's life and death were parodic, satirical, distorted, and grotesque; perhaps the new baby can lead a life more in *imitatio Christi* than had Joe Christmas. But that would be another story.

Such a story is the one Faulkner wrote and rewrote over the next eight years, culminating in the publication in 1942 of *Go Down, Moses*. Here the character whose life is reminiscent of Christ's mission and sacrifice is no bastard outcast but the heir to a plantation. Isaac McCaslin's given name suggests his role, too, as an averted sacrifice to the Lord. Faulkner in this book abandons the irony he had intended in naming Ab Snopes and calling his first chronicle of Snopesism *Father Abraham* (written by 1926, not published until 1982), in which that Abraham had as his son not an Isaac but a Flem.

In what way is Isaac McCaslin an averted sacrifice? The nearest he comes to reenacting that biblical story is in his solitary confrontation with Old Ben in which he dashes weaponless between the great bear's legs to rescue his little fyce and escapes untouched. The great bear is a complex image, representing the spirit of the wilderness, of olden times, of a primitive nobility beyond that of our world—in short, a numinous, divine essence. His priest of course is Sam Fathers, the half-Indian, half-Negro hunter who initiates Isaac into the mysteries of the big woods and the hunt. Sam Fathers is thus Isaac's spiritual father; his own name, Fathers, alludes to his Indian descent as the son of two fathers. Isaac, also, has two fathers—his natural father is Uncle Buck, the comic bachelor of *The Unvanquished* and of "Was" in the present book. Yet, Uncle Buck has left Isaac a spiritual legacy, too; for if Isaac learns of primal innocence and the divinity of nature from Sam Fathers, in deciphering the almost illiterate journal of life on the family plantation kept by Uncle Buck and his brother Uncle Buddy, he learns also of guilt, his human inheritance. Their journal gradually reveals the original sin lurking behind the prelapsarian boys' life so affectionately and comically dramatized in the opening chapter, "Was."[12] The family history is inexorably tainted by the actions of its progenitor, Carothers McCaslin—by his ownership of slaves, his seduction of his slave women, and his committing incest with his own half-breed daughter. These sins he had covertly confessed by leaving a bequest in his will to each of his black descendants; still in slavery days, his sons Buck and Buddy had carried repentance a bit further after their father's death by moving into a slave cabin, giving their blacks the run of the big house, and manumitting those who wanted to leave. Isaac, coming of age after emancipation, takes on the burden of his family's guilt. He tries to expiate these sins by renouncing his inheritance, turning carpenter like Christ, giving up his marriage, and not begetting further descendants to whom the family guilt would be passed.

In Isaac's double initiation, first into the primal world of the wilderness with its numinous values, then into the tainted world of history with its guilt and responsibilities, the imagery is drawn from both biblical and pagan sources. Unlike the satirical and sardonic employment in *Light in August* of references to *The Golden Bough*, paganism in *Go Down, Moses* is taken seriously as a sacral reality with its own rites and practices. Faulkner is not resurrecting classical antiquity but is dramatizing the historical reality of his own county, for one of the blessings he made of his *donnée* is the nearness to his own day of the time when the land was lived in by Indians with their reverence for the wilderness, their propitiation of the spirits of the game they slew. Sam Fathers is a true high priest, and Isaac proves worthy to become his spiritual heir. To be a spiritual heir of Christ, however, is more difficult still. In the end Isaac's renunciations seem rather pointless, since he has set no one else an example; his kinsman Roth Edmonds commits yet again the miscegenation and incest (with a distant mulatto cousin) of Carothers McCaslin, thus repeating the original sin of the family. And Isaac has lost something of his own humanity in his pursuit of a superhuman ideal—as dramatized when the abandoned mulatto woman reproves him, holding her baby in her arms, "Old man . . . don't you remember anything you ever knew or felt or even heard about love?"

In *Go Down, Moses* the theme of Isaac's imitation of Christ is embedded in a historical chronicle of a family over five generations, from the time Mississippi was a wilderness to the present—1942—when an alienated McCaslin Negro, fled to a northern city, is executed for murder. The novel thus complexly intertwines several mythic prototypes—the doom of an aristocratic family, exile from Eden, and the imitation of Christ—in the historical matrix of the South, with its legacy of the division between the races and its inherited burdens of lust and guilt. History becomes myth and myth becomes history in this work in which, avoiding the parodic bitterness of the earlier *Light in August* and the allegorical simplifications of the later *A Fable,* Faulkner, at the height of his creative powers, successfully fused the representation of reality with his imagination of the experience of the South.

Notes

1. William Faulkner, *The Hamlet* (New York, 1956), 147, 148.

2. William Faulkner, *A Fable* (New York, 1978), 129.

3. Nicolas Berdyaev, *The Meaning of History*, tr. George Reavey (New York, 1936), 21, 22, 23–24.

4. Daniel Hoffman, *Form and Fable in American Fiction* (New York, 1961).

5. Lewis P. Simpson, *The Man of Letters in New England and the South* (Baton Rouge, 1973), 167–91; Simpson, *The Dispossessed Garden: Pastoral and History in Southern Literature* (Athens, 1975); Simpson, "Yoknapatawpha and Faulkner's Fable of Civilization," in Evans Harrington and Ann J. Abadie (eds.), *The Maker and the Myth: Faulkner and Yoknapatawpha* (Jackson, Miss., 1978), 122–45; Simpson, *The Brazen Face of History* (Baton Rouge, 1980).

6. Biographical details of Colonel W. C. Falkner are given fully in Joseph Blotner, *Faulkner: A Biography* (2 vols.; New York, 1974), I, 14–50.

7. Blotner, *Faulkner*, I, 225–26, 229, 231–32, 324.

8. R. W. B. Lewis, *The Picaresque Saint* (Philadelphia, 1959), 218, 210.

9. T. S. Eliot, "Ulysses, Order, and Myth," *Dial*, LXXV (1923), 480–83.

10. Virginia V. Hlavsa, "St. John and Frazer in *Light in August:* Biblical Form and Mythic Function," *Bulletin of Research in the Humanities*, LXXXIII (Spring, 1980), 11; Hlavsa, "The Levity of *Light in August*," in Doreen Fowler and Ann J. Abadie (eds.), *Faulkner and Humor* (Jackson, Miss., 1986), 47–56.

11. Hlavsa, "St. John and Frazer," 13, 14.

12. I have parsed this opening chapter in "Faulkner's 'Was' and Uncle Adam's Cow," in Fowler and Abadie (eds.), *Faulkner and Humor*, 57–77.

BLYDEN JACKSON

Jane Pittman Through the Years:
A People's Tale

T*he Autobiography of Miss Jane Pittman* (here-
inafter to be known as *Pittman*), since all genuine autobiography clearly represents a form of history, is, in itself,
obviously an exercise in historiography. Of course, it is a
fake exercise. No woman who actually lived more than a
hundred years wrote (or, rather, dictated) it. But it is interesting to observe that the fictive Jane Pittman does orally communicate her resumé of her long personal past—presumably
from her own mind and in her own words—to a man who
teaches history. Ernest Gaines, the actual author of *Pittman*,
apparently wants even readers who cannot take subtle hints
to realize that Jane's life is history as well as autobiography.
He seems, however, also to want something more. He seems
to want his readers to perceive, through Jane, the entire history of a race.

Gaines takes care, with some significant and highly visible signals at the beginning of his book, to make of Jane's
memoir, for all of his emphasis upon Jane's independent
contribution to it, a collaborative act of composition. Jane's
amanuensis, for instance, the aforesaid teacher of history who
seeks her out, driven by a sense of professional duty honed
to an extra edge of keenness, it is not difficult to see, both by
his appreciation of Jane's venerability and his own simple curiosity, is white. He will, through his many weeks of association with Jane, record not only what Jane tells him, but also
what some of Jane's friends, speaking in Jane's stead, assure
him, under Jane's supervision, Jane might well have said to

him to fill in lacunae left by her in her confessions to him. Moreover, when Jane dies some months after his last interview with her, this white historian checks Jane's story with surviving neighbors of hers who, he thinks, should be able to verify or supplement Jane's legacy of anecdotes to him. Thus, in one quite discernible manner Jane's individual testimony acquires something of the character and force of the voice of a community—a community, moreover, with decidedly a distinctive identity and a strong sense of solidarity—discoursing about itself. There is, too, in the voices other than Jane's in *Pittman*, as a complementary value certainly not to be taken lightly, a reminder of an important auxiliary to the action often to be found in ancient Greek tragedy. This notable auxiliary is the chorus, which has given surely many moments of exquisite pleasure to scholars and other lovers of the drama of Old Hellas. For, frequently this Greek tragic chorus does more than say in effect, "Look, if you do not know it, this is what is going on in this play." Frequently this faithful band of devoted onlookers goes beyond its possible other functions to comment on the action in the very play it accompanies. What a sense of universality thus may be imparted to any playwright's utterance! Men do puzzle over their own lives and other human lives of concern to them, and when they do, often it is within a context of their most profound and comprehensive musings about the nature and eschatological implications of their experience of life—in other words, within a frame of reference for their thought which attention solely to an individual self could not satisfy. The voices, then, of Jane's coadjutors in her autobiography do play a role, impressively, in making of her autobiography more of the history of an entire people than her autobiography, but for them, otherwise might be.

Jane's friends and neighbors who speak for her, and of her, quantitatively expand, without a doubt, her historical voice. The choral commentary from their collective consciousness may be seen, by the same token, as qualitatively affecting that same articulation of a mere individual. And in at least one other way Gaines throws into bold relief the utility of *Pittman* as a history—a history of black America—as well as a novel. He provides a prelude for the rest of his novel with an "Introduction," placed (as an introduction should be) at the beginning of *Pittman* and serving there as exposition very much in the manner of the so-called Stage Manager's opening remarks in Thornton Wilder's play *Our Town*. This "Introduction," it should be emphasized vigorously, is not history. All of it occurs on Jane's front porch (which is truly not hers, but the property of the white man who owns the house and land where she resides). In it Jane, before a few of her regular associates, yields finally to the importunities of the white historian already mentioned here and agrees to tell him the story of her life, it may well be ultimately, because of his stress upon her absence from the history books he teaches. But after its "Introduction" *Pittman* is divided into four books, each book conforming closely in every vital essential to a chapter in a good history of black America. Even the titles of the books in *Pittman* may be easily seen as the titles of chapters in a work by John Hope Franklin or Benjamin Quarles. So, Book One is titled "The War Years"; Book Two, "Reconstruction"; Book Three, "The Plantation"; and Book Four, "The Quarters." Actually, despite the title of Book One, Jane is first encountered in "The War Years" while she is still a slave, so *Pittman* does begin its black history with slavery. At the end of "The War Years" Jane has just been freed. "Reconstruction" presents Jane, and black America, during Reconstruction. In "The Plantation" Jane ages as the nineteenth century ends, the twentieth century proceeds into and out of most of its first half, and black America suffers through the horrible era, for the majority of blacks, of "Southern Redemption" and its bitter aftermath. In "The Quarters" Jane survives into the period of civil-rights activism in the sixties. Thus *Pittman* covers, in the proper chronological order and with due regard for what might well be called "the big picture," all of Afro-American history from its inauguration until the early 1960s. The correlation of Jane's life, in *Pittman*, with the actual epochs of the Afro-American past, it may safely be conjectured, is no accident happening without Gaines's intent and his skill in making his intent come true.

Within the framework of his division of his novel into the major periods of Afro-American history Gaines, however, does not depend upon chronology alone to suggest the firm and solid nature of Jane's right to be regarded as a microcosm representing a macrocosm. A background of innuendo, intimating all that has been part of the black experience in America, tends constantly to be present in Gaines's novel (yet quite without thereby converting *Pittman* into a tract or a tour guide), if not in the guise of a sort of both injection and penumbra, a surrounding, yet also simultaneously pervading, element of implication and suggestion investing Jane's life with dimensions of historiography beyond those of ordinary biography or autobiography, then in concrete actions and incidents, none of them involving Jane directly or in any tangible way, but every one of them a factor of some strength and import in the configuration of the black world from which Jane is indivisible. So, through what might well be called Gaines's virtuosity in the manipulation of the materials of his novel, a whole context of the world as it was for blacks throughout America's past comes very much alive in *Pittman.*

To give Gaines credit he richly deserves, it does not do so at the expense of Jane's success as a fictive character. Jane, the redoubtable centenarian of Gaines's imagination, comes very much alive in *Pittman* too. She is, there, neither too wooden nor too flat. Rather, she is warmly credible, a convincing demonstration of what she might actually have been had she ever really existed in actual flesh and blood. Indeed, she is one of the finest and most memorable characters in all black fiction. Even so, convincing as she is exclusively within the confines of her own unique selfhood, she is, nevertheless, still by far sufficiently translucent to emit through the vision of herself she projects, as through a prism collecting and diffusing light, a second extensive and coherent vision, an image of the black America of her time—which is to say, since (among other things) her time was so protracted, an image, truly, of all of black America for all of black America's time. Jane, as has been earlier here observed, is not a slave for many years in *Pittman.* Moreover, of her enslaved years Jane recalls, in her reminiscence, only events which happen on two days, although those two days are a full twelve months apart. Thus, according to one method of reckoning, it may be argued that, in *Pittman,* slavery receives short shrift. On the other hand, it may be argued, as here it will be shortly, that two days of slavery, in *Pittman,* are all Gaines needs to say, *multum in parvo,* a great deal about all that slavery was. For, to make of Jane a black Everyman (and black Everywoman) Gaines does not forsake, or curtail, a diligent prosecution of his assignment at any point throughout his novel. He has in *Pittman* a people's tale. Clearly he meant so to have it. Part of the delight of reading *Pittman,* good art that it is, may be derived, therefore, from recognizing the magnificence of Gaines's performance, with true grace under tremendous pressure, of a double task within a single operation. He is a novelist who is an historian and an historian who is a novelist. And he is such at no peril to his being either.

An examination of precisely how Gaines integrates so well his black-American history with his facsimile of an autobiography in *Pittman* may be expedited by separate views of three aspects of Gaines's authorial enterprise in his portraiture of Jane. In one of these three aspects Gaines may be said to be a diarist, a preserver of copious information about the daily round of existence of a selected folk. In such an habiliment it is that he resorts profusely to the use of detail, circumstantial and otherwise, to the ambitious end that he might create, admittedly, an artifice, a copy of reality, and yet thereto a copy so persuasive as not to seem itself only a duplicate, but truly that which it affects to reproduce. His aim here is, of course, immense, albeit not singular to him either in substance or immensity. The better novelists of every race and country and creed—Dickens and Thackeray, for example, Balzac, Flaubert and Proust, the great Russians, Faulkner, especially in Yoknapatawpha, Ellison and Wright—all have shared this burning passion so to stock imaginary universes of theirs with item after item of observable fact that they may actually appear to have erased the line between the pretended and the real. In a second aspect here Gaines hopes to equip his reader with what may be conveniently termed an elevated eye, an eye from which history largely transcends the tiny segments of temporality and becomes, in effect, a huge panorama. Within the telescopic lens of this aspect the daily round of human existence sinks into almost total obscurity beneath the wider contours of history lifted to the level at which it forms itself into eras and epochs. At such an altitude history does, moreover, appear as a continuum, making inexorably its unbroken progress from each of mankind's generations to the next, and so, here, indeed, history is a wide survey, thus accomplishing here, among other things, a considerable distinction between itself and journalism. In the third of our three present aspects Gaines becomes a philosopher, a seeker, here, after answers to man's most abiding questions about the nature of his cosmos and of himself. Gaines asks tacitly, here, that his audience attribute adequate correspondence in *Pittman* to black history as black history has truly been for the lessons to be learned from the sometimes concocted and sometimes real black history in *Pittman* to possess the same authority they might well have were they being taken from a close reading of a serious, competent work on black history in which everything is documented from fact and nothing is invented from whole cloth. Historians do read history as philosophers. Gibbon wrote an entire history of Rome to announce, as he thought he had divined it, the cause for Rome's decline and fall. Gaines's awareness of racism is the great stimulant in *Pittman* for Gaines's excursion there into the groves of metaphysical meditation.

In the first of the three aspects just delineated above, that of Gaines as diarist, since it relies so much as it does on detail, and detail of every kind, some virtue there applies, in *Pittman*, merely to the raw amount of detail *Pittman* contains. For *Pittman* is packed with atomistic bits of perceptible things which give material reality to the particulars of its world. If some novels may be said to be thin, *Pittman* must be said to be thick—thick with the texture of a warp and woof of narrative spun bulkily from threads compounded of the atomistic bits just mentioned above. No reader ever finds himself in such an attenuated atmosphere in *Pittman* as not to sense the proliferation of specific entities, whether of matter or motion or mental activity, which acquaint him there with the characters and the physical scene, as well as the flow of incident, in the simulated world Gaines uses to teach his lesson in intimate history about black America's past. A gesture here, a word there, an episode recorded with a painter's avid appetite for telling idiosyncrasies of line or color—or both—all of these are instances of the detail of every conceivable sort which flourishes in *Pittman*. Given this kind of richness of texture in his novel it remains, therefore, for Gaines only to take the step of correlating his employment of detail with various signs of a time—indications which differentiate in *Pittman*, for example, a day during Reconstruction from, perhaps, a day during the years of Huey Long—for this aspect of his novel to serve him as he would wish. Gaines does take this step. Indeed, in *Pittman*, he is always taking it. Let it suffice here to confine our scrutiny of his correlation of his provision of time-telling detail with the sense he wants to give of Negro life in this, or that, black historical epoch only to his re-creation of the Negro enslaved in "The War Years." Let us moreover, for this purpose, accord him an intelligence sufficient for the recognition, by him, of the presence in the slave of forms of behavior which may fittingly be said to have become institutions of his enslavement, caused by his bondage and representative of it. Some illustrations of exemplifications of this institutionalized behavior from "The War Years" follow.

Jane, in telling the story of her own life, is not quite sure as to when she, herself, came into this world. She does not doubt that in 1864, her point of departure for her autobiographical narrative, she was ten or eleven, an indication that, insofar as her own recollection could be trusted, the year of her birth was either 1853 or 1854. Many slaves, of course, were at least as unsure about when they were born as Jane. Jane identifies her mother with confidence. She is less positive about her father. And so, concerning her parents, Jane reflects another phenomenon among slaves which may be said to be, as it were, institutionalized during slavery. Young as Jane is in 1864, she has been both a house slave and a slave in the fields. The division between house slaves and field slaves was widespread, and also institutionalized, during slavery. She is illiterate. That, too—black illiteracy—was an institution of slavery. She can neither read nor write. Nor is she always competent in her use of spoken English. To her, for instance, the sword of the officer commanding the Confederates who stop at her plantation is a "sable." Moreover, Jane's life during slavery is dictated by her attachment to an agrarian economy in which she functions at the will of others. No black freemen or black artisans appear in *Pittman* before Jane's emancipation. To that extent, at least, *Pittman* fails of comprehensiveness in its coverage of the period of slavery. Still, within the brief compass of its opening pages it conveys a good sense of life in black America until Appomattox. In 1860 not quite a half a million Negroes, almost half of them in the North, were free. At the same time four million Negroes, by far the most of them identical with Jane in all that mattered in their lives, were slaves.

On Jane's plantation there is an old Negro, Uncle Isom, who represents an additional phenomenon which tended to be institutionalized among slaves during slavery. Uncle Isoms were endemic for the antebellum South. Jane never refers to her Uncle Isom as a preacher. Many Uncle Isoms were the forerunners of the purveyors of the gospel immortalized in James Weldon Johnson's *God's Trombones*. But, though Jane's Uncle Isom lacks, apparently, a vocation as a minister of Christ, he does benefit, among Jane's contemporary fellow slaves, from his reputation as a conjure man. In Louisiana, therefore, he fits easily and swiftly into the local color of the region. Anywhere in the South, moreover, his connections with shamanism and spells would link him with Africa, the continent to which slaves could turn, in their minds, to remind themselves, if of nothing else, that they had not always been slaves. Uncle Isom was, however, not only, in his part of the world, someone to be dreaded as a possible thaumaturgist. He was also, by the voluntary agreement of his black peers, the head counselor for all of them, so that, although he was too old to work, he was not too old to play among them the role of a leader of a flock. In that capacity alone Uncle Isoms were fairly legion in the South of slavery. And he was accompanied, on Jane's plantation, by another black functionary whom slavery had more or less institutionalized, the black driver.

There is no white overseer on Jane's plantation in 1864. Perhaps there never was. Perhaps, moreover, had there been, he had gone to war. But be that as it may, the black driver over Jane in 1864 is not loved by Jane. In the scholarly literature on slavery some black drivers, like Jane's, did wear too abrasively and too spitefully, where their fellow Negroes were concerned, their white-delegated authority. Others, like the real father of the real Robert R. Moton, were not only excellent executives but so statesmanlike in their dispositions as to win, and retain, the respect and affection of all they touched, both black and white. *Pittman* does need, hence, more than a single black driver to exhaust the subject of antebellum black drivers. Even so, with his black driver Gaines supplements realistically his house slaves and field slaves and his Uncle Isom. Slaves during slavery, in spite of their defenselessness, their degradation, and the host of indignities then imposed upon them (such as, for instance, even the withholding from them, should a master so desire, of the prerogative of selecting their own names), were not all clones, carbon copies of each other in how they looked and what they did. They were human and they demonstrated their humanity in many ways, good and bad. There were distinctions of class and power among whites. There were comparable distinctions among slaves. And such distinctions were meaningful whether they were conceived by whites or initiated by the slaves themselves.

One of Jane's fellow slaves on her plantation is a half-wit. He is, however, physically robust and, even, as Jane is to discover (though, fortunately, without harm to herself) quite able, and eager, to rape a woman. As stout and huge, nevertheless, as is the physique of this half-wit, another of Jane's fellow slaves, who happens to be a woman, Big Laura, surpasses him, though altogether without his idiocy, both in size and strength. This Big Laura saves Jane from the half-wit, for it is Big Laura who has stepped into a breach and appointed herself the leader of the group of former slaves, from Jane's plantation, only hours old in their freedom, who have decided to leave their now deposed master and seek their fortunes elsewhere. Yet as forceful, and as heroic, as Big Laura is, she is to be killed, to be beaten to death, in the dawn of a day before twenty-four hours of her new freedom have elapsed, by white men who do not know her and whom she has never seen before—white men who obviously believe that nothing is of greater importance in their lives, or should be in America, than keeping Negroes in their place. Big Laura has two children, a little girl whom she is carrying in her arms when she and the group she is leading are attacked and a boy whom she has, after she pauses for rest on her first night away from the familiar vicinity where she had borne her son and daughter, temporarily entrusted to Jane. Big Laura's little girl is killed with Big Laura, although Big Laura, in defending this offspring of hers, as well as herself, does fight off for a while, and kill, some of her attackers.

Big Laura's battered corpse, and the crushed corpse of her babe, are discovered, once the attacking whites are gone, by Jane, who has managed, with Big Laura's son, to hide from Big Laura's murderers. In a manner of speaking, therefore, Jane's view of Big Laura and Big Laura's daughter, as well as of other slaughtered former slaves in the group of new black freedmen of which Jane and Big Laura had been a part, represents Jane's farewell to slavery. These now speechless former companions of hers are a bloody epitaph, perhaps more gruesome than epitaphs should ever be, to her days of slavery. Jane is no rhetorician, although, as her verbal jousting with her fellow slaves, and various whites, has already made clear, her mind is bright. She may not think of matriarchy, of a constrained labor force, of cruelty with or without a cause, of a short-sighted closed society, or of human feelings that will not be denied in terms sufficiently oracular and sophisticated to belong to the language of the learned or any other cultural elite. But her token conduct in starting to bury Big Laura's baby and, then, of replacing the dead infant within Big Laura's lifeless arms, is eloquent of her ability to engage in thoughts the full complex involutions of which she could hardly express with her limited fund of words. And Gaines's citation of this conduct of hers is of the essence of Gaines's fine performance as a diarist throughout *Pittman*. Gaines, the diarist in *Pittman*, does not stop on the outside of his people there. He goes inside of them. He is adept with *Pittman* as a costume drama. From exteriors in *Pittman* he lets us know when and where we are historically. But, most intimate of diarists that he can be, he sometimes indicates acts and deeds of people which, from within those people, serve to remind us of the permanent in humanity, of the ties which bind us to all our human ancestors and may well connect us with all humans who will come after us, and thus he adds the decisive measure of convincingness to his diary in *Pittman*. The past is past to us not only because so much of it we recognize as strange, but also because of what we feel in it is like ourselves.

In one of its aspects, we have averred, *Pittman* is a panorama. Its emphasis, in that aspect, is upon the calendar and not the clock, on time seen in large masses and on the long chain of connected events and successive social moods which binds human generations together even as it sends one human generation to its dotage and extinction while it brings another human generation to its prime. The panorama of *Pittman* is, perhaps, the easiest aspect of *Pittman* for Gaines to devise and place before his readers. He does not, incidentally, in crafting his panorama, resort much to the introduction of famous historical figures into his novel, as does, for instance, Tolstoi in *War and Peace* or Thackeray in *Henry Esmond*. He does not even use many characters that are only thinly disguised from the real people on whom they are modeled, as in a *roman à clef*. But he does advertise *Pittman* as panorama in at least two ways, one of them quite simple, the other somewhat more complex.

Throughout *Pittman* Gaines plays what may well be

called a dating game. This is his simple way with his pan-orama. The detachment of Confederate soldiers who stop at Jane's plantation at the beginning of "The War Years," it can be calculated quickly, are phenomena of 1864, if only because Gaines makes it clear that they appear in *Pittman* one year before Jane's master assembles his slaves to tell them they are free. Jane goes to western Louisiana with Joe Pittman in the late 1870s, after Big Laura's boy, whom she has raised, has become old enough, although not yet in his twenties, to join the Exodusters of the late 1870s and the early 1880s in Kansas. This boy, when Jane shepherds him away from his slain mother, is merely Ned. He becomes Ned Brown. Jane is, at one time, Jane Brown. Before he goes to Kansas he has become Edward Stephen Douglass in honor of Frederick Douglass. He fights in the Spanish-American War. One year later, in 1899, he returns to Louisiana and the locality on the St. Charles River where Jane now lives alone and spends much of her time fishing. He is killed, after the passage of still another year, by the white paid assassin, the Cajun Albert Cluveau, who dies himself in terror, believing that he expires the victim of a curse from Jane, in 1912. All of the dates given above are explicit in Gaines's text. And there is more, in *Pittman*, of dates given no less explicitly. Equally ascertainable, however, in *Pittman*, through statements in the text not so explicit are surmisable dates which would indicate when the panoramic effect of *Pittman* has reached the 1920s, when it moves through the 1930s and 1940s, and when, at last, it arrives into the early 1960s, to witness the civil-rights activism which will engulf the South, lead to the killing of Jimmy, Jane's second surrogate son, and see the end of Jane's own life at approximately the age of 110. It appears beyond doubt that this dating game in *Pittman* is deliberate. It certainly requires no genius to figure it out. It does not harm the art of *Pittman*, for it interferes with no effect of value in *Pittman* and obvious as it is, yet is not clumsy.

Somewhat more complicated than its dating game is the way in *Pittman* in which its panoramic effect is supported by intimations of epochal change—that is, by representations within the novel which differentiate Reconstruction from the period in national black life succeeding it, and so on into the period of SNCC, SCLC, and the other demonstrators of the 1960s. Dates alone do not suffice for this element in the panorama, although a sense of dates does enter into the impressions emanating from it. What does suffice here (and so provides here an additional demonstration of Gaines's excellence as a literary artist) is Gaines's ability to capture the distinctive tempers of successive, yet at least somewhat disparate, historical epochs.

Thus, after his quick reprise of slavery, it behooves Gaines to move the panorama of *Pittman* into Reconstruction, a time, for Negroes, of some confusion. Many Negroes, hitherto immobile quite simply because of slavery, celebrated their freedom and sometimes sought their own new horizons by taking to the road, even if they did not always know where they were going. There are Negroes, including Jane, on the road in *Pittman* during its "Reconstruction," and the black hunter Jane meets as she indulges herself in her vain search for Ohio is not an unhistorical figure among the actual Negroes of Reconstruction. He is trying to find his parents, and many Negroes, during Reconstruction, did exactly what he was doing, set out to trace what leads they could to try to bring together again their families of lost relatives. There was a Freedmen's Bureau during Reconstruction. Jane and Ned benefit from it. The Redemptioners, in Reconstruction, as soon as possible, got rid of the Freedmen's Bureau and Jane and Ned, in *Pittman*, are very much around to watch the bureau's end and become involved, though neither voluntarily nor agreeably, in the restorations of feudalism which follow the bureau's demise. For no single thing, of course, was more tragic for the postbellum South than its refusal to share ownership of its land with its former slaves and thus to give its neophytes in citizenship at least some help in establishing themselves as independent Americans. Jane, it will be noticed, does want land. She hopes to get it, but does not, with Joe Pittman, whose dangerous trade of horse-breaking, good for his sense of manhood, leads to his death. Some blacks actually received an education during Reconstruction, often from teachers, white and black, who came South from the North. That identifiable mark of Reconstruction appears in *Pittman*. Ned is taught by a black teacher from the North. There were Republicans and so-called scalawags and carpetbaggers in the South during Reconstruction. Gaines does not scant them, although he certainly views them with an eye less jaundiced than that of a Claude Bowers in *The Tragic Era* or George Fort Milton in *The Age of Hate*.

But there was also terrorism in the South against blacks, during Reconstruction, violence by whites to intimidate any Negro who really wanted to help make the South abide by the "Negro" amendments to the American Constitution and Gaines, without the biases of a Bowers or a Milton, puts that terrorism into *Pittman*, too.

For at least a half of a century after its sabotage of Reconstruction the South seemed static. Its whites had retrieved their land, some even before President Hayes withdrew the last federal soldiers from the states of Louisiana and Florida, but many influential southerners had neither abandoned their antebellum dream of a feudalistic agrarian empire based on the cultivation of a staple crop (and a docile and exploited labor force) nor made an effort properly to understand and appreciate the urbanization and industrialization which were transforming the North into a human (and economic) scene far different from that in which Yankee peddlers and clipper ships, small artisans and old-fashioned financiers, Federalists and Whigs, Transcendentalists and Unitarians once had thrived. If "progress" had meant nothing else to the North, it had meant change, and not only the change in which, for instance, the France of Louis XIV differed from the France of the French Revolution, but the other kind of change in which change itself becomes a constant factor of daily life in the consciousness of many people. So, relatively speaking, from about 1880 until about World War II, in the North an external world seemed always composed of shifting circumstances along almost every front. In the South time seemed always caught in its own immobility. And in *Pittman* a sense of life in a world where authority decrees tomorrows like today pervades some of "Reconstruction" and "The Quarters" and all of "The Plantation."

The longest and darkest years of denial, indeed, for blacks in America after slavery were those in which the first generation of black *freemen* (as distinct from *freedmen*) grew up, wrestled as best they could with America's racism, bred their children for what they hoped would be a better future, and died themselves with only the bitter knowledge of how little they had done to aggrandize their own status in the social order of which they were a part. *Pittman* recreates the world of this generation of freemen, especially in "The Plantation," the section of *Pittman* which deals with Jane's years on the Samson estate before she becomes, as it were, super-

annuated. At Samson, tilled by black labor when Jane moves
there, years come and go, Mr. Robert succeeds his father as
the Mr. Samson, and everything remains the same until the
decade before World War II. Rumors from the outside world
do penetrate the wall of silence which engulfs the South. But
the outside world (with its possible agitations and "agi-
tators") is, apparently, remote from Samson. Even so, all is
not as tranquil, as fixed, as impervious to what Spenser
called mutability, at Samson as it may seem. The outside
world, for instance, does come to Samson if only in the mag-
netism it exerts upon the young of Samson's blacks. In "The
Quarters" Samson's blacks are virtually nothing but a community of the elderly. Other things have changed, too, at
Samson, including its labor force, most of whom, by World
War II, are white, much more independent of Mr. Robert than
Mr. Robert's blacks once were, and all of whom tend to have
mechanized their farming. Dates alone, then, do not tell the
history of Samson. Characterization and incident do, as well,
with a power and intimacy unavailable to any simple recital
of given years. On every page in *Pittman* the muse of history
proceeds apace, reconstructing in landscape, dialogue, and
incident the nature of experience as it may well have been for
selected people in various epochs of America's past. But the
novel focuses on blacks, and so it maintains one of its methods by which it pursues its goal to be, among other things, a
history of black America.

Historians, like many nonhistorians, tend to be interested in causes as well as effects. Gaines, the novelist-histo-
rian, in *Pittman* is not satisfied merely to attempt the re-
vocation of a past essentially as it was. As has been said
earlier here, he seeks a meaning in that past, an indication of
how and why it assumed the form it has today. He broods,
indeed, over what may be gained from his didactic scrutiny
of history with much of the intensity and fervor with which
Faulkner peers into the southern past in Faulkner's Yoknapatawpha novels. This brooding, this peering, in *Pittman*
appears hardly to be an exercise in futility. Quite to the contrary, the results from it well may be, in *Pittman*, the crown-
ing achievement of a major piece of fiction. They certainly
belong to the third, and final, aspect of *Pittman* to be noticed here.

In the final analysis Gaines wrote *Pittman* to insist to his readers that a credo common among American whites and the injustices that credo has occasioned American whites to perpetrate upon American blacks has accounted almost as unequivocally for the major problems of black America as, according to St. Augustine, the Good Lord accounts for the City of God. Why does a woman of Jane's human stature, a woman who has so much to give, who, though barren, can play so well the surrogate mother of two remarkable men, whose sense of humor is matched in its abundance, its acuteness, and its lack of sour self-defensiveness, only by her propensity for compassion, who is respected by all who get to know her well, be they black or white, or magnates or nonentities, and who has lived so long that her age alone has made her a fondly beloved figure truly admired in her community—why does such a person find herself calumniated as she is in America? How has her life been so unnecessarily (as well as, sometimes, so venomously) circumscribed? And why is she, even at her advanced age, treated by whites as if she were still a child? Is she responsible for the indignities heaped upon her? If she is not, who is? And has a system, a prescribed routine, rather than individuals reacting to their own observations and following their own leads, been her bane, and if a system, what is its nature and what, principally, the thing that makes it work? Jane's problem, and the one she shares with all black Americans, Gaines does say in *Pittman*, is indeed with a system. That system works, along with other reasons, Gaines does also say, because of its simplicity. And it has worked so well that not only whites contribute to its success. So do blacks. And if that system is to end, whites must free themselves of their willingness to maintain its vitality, but so, also, must blacks.

The system, of course, as Gaines makes clear in *Pittman*, is color caste, a very unesoteric thing, which has as its object the setting apart from the rest of society, in a way that hopelessly subordinates them, a group of people stigmatized by one criterion, their color. In America that color is black, a stipulation even an idiot can remember. Caste differs from class, and is so hopeless as it is, because people may change classes. They may move from poor to rich, from the proletariat to the bourgeoisie, from illiteracy to literacy, and even from humble learning into the circles of the intellectually elite, as well as reverse the order of progress in each class just cited here. But people cannot change their caste. From a caste—any and every caste—there must be no movement, no escape. Ideally, where caste is concerned, people must die within the caste into which they were born. The easiest and most understandable means, obviously, to keep them within their caste is to prevent their marriage outside of it. So, in America, for generations, marriage between whites and blacks has been a sin when it has not also been a crime. "Would you want your daughter to marry a nigger?" has been a rhetorical question with only one answer—an answer easily taught. Thus, in America, a caste has been created and isolated and then used shamefully by a social order which has institutionalized segregation, discrimination, and an etiquette of behavior to exploit the caste which its ban against intermarriage (but not, under the right circumstances, against miscegenation) has conspicuously identified as a collection of victims whom anyone other than the victims themselves may abuse and humiliate at will.

Pittman notes the presence, and the significance, of color caste in America. It may do so at approximately the right level of insistence, not too strenuously, yet, also, not too pusillanimously. It does not fail to address the crucial importance to the prosperity of color caste of America's prescriptions on intermarriage. It recounts, for instance, with some fullness, the case of Timmy and Tee Bob, the two sons of Robert Samson. They are half-brothers. Timmy's mother is black. Tee Bob's mother is white. So Tee Bob's mother, Miss Amma Dean, is married to Robert Samson and lives in the big house of the Samson plantation. Timmy's mother, whose connection with Timmy and Robert Samson "everybody" knows, lives, during Timmy's boyhood, in a house in the black "quarters" of the Samson holdings. The pretense is never made that she is married to Robert Samson or that Robert Samson ever considered it an obligation of his to legitimate his carnal relation with her or include any offspring of hers by him in the division, after his death, of his estate. Yet, Timmy resembles Robert more, both in appearance and disposition, than Tee Bob, although eventually it is Timmy who is exiled from the Samson plantation, by Robert Samson himself, because Timmy refuses to remain peaceful as he is physically mistreated by a white man.

If Timmy and Tee Bob illustrate vividly color caste—in

so doing simultaneously performing a similar office for all of American racism—they are, nevertheless, not Gaines's ultimate pronouncement on color caste and racism in his role as an interpreter of history in *Pittman.*

The Gaines who conceived and executed *Pittman* was an artist of a large and unclouded vision. In *Pittman* he sees his whites and blacks not only intimately, but also clear and whole. In *Pittman* neither whites nor blacks are perfect. Both are capable of human failings as well as of human heroics. Still, no reader should turn away from *Pittman* without vowing never to forget Tee Bob and the girl named LeFabre who comes to Samson to teach the black children there. LeFabre is a creole, which often means, as it does with her, that she is much more white than black, a decided octoroon with Caucasian features and virtually no visible signs of African ancestors in anything about her. Born into a black family whose white progenitor was a man of means and high social position sufficiently enamored of his black paramour to provide almost lavishly for his black progeny, LeFabre is really, at Samson, something of a missionary in the mold of the New England schoolmarms of Reconstruction. She idealizes her work. But she is also bewitching to the sight. Tee Bob falls in love with her, romantically, deeply, and, being the genuine gentleman that he is, as honorably as he would with any woman in the world, whatever her color. Eventually, Tee Bob declares his love for her to LeFabre, in so doing making it clear that he wants to take her far away from Samson and marry her. LeFabre then cites to him the first and great commandment of color caste, its prohibition of intermarriage. In the library of the big house at Samson Tee Bob stabs himself to death.

But afterwards Jules Reynard, Tee Bob's *parrain,* or godfather, discusses Tee Bob's last colloquy with LeFabre in a very private tête-à-tête with Jane. Reynard admits his absence from the colloquy. But he insists he knows, at least enough to explain Tee Bob's suicide, what happened there. Reynard, incidentally, is himself a genuine gentleman. It is he, indeed, who plays the leading role in arranging LeFabre's spiriting away from Samson as part of his determination to prevent her exposure to a fabricated charge of murder. For Tee Bob's statement of his intentions, and his wishes, he corners LeFabre in her room in the quarters of his father's plantation.

He would never harm LeFabre, as LeFabre knows. But he is rendered distraught by LeFabre's reaction to his proposal. He rushes upon her for a moment. With her in his arms, although never really so not himself as to rape her, he overpowers her, causing her to fall to the floor with himself looming, it might seem menacingly, above her. In that moment, Reynard assures Jane, for a fleeting fraction of a second, Tee Bob saw in LeFabre's eyes a sudden, servile acquiescence to him—or, actually, to the white man he would be were he like most white men—a loss of her pride, usually so stalwart a part of her, and a willingness, as of a person doomed, to behave in any way, however shriven of her self-respect, to comply with his whims and gratify his lustful desires. From that fleeting fraction of a second, from what it tells him of the conditioning force of color caste, Tee Bob rushes away, his own life in ashes, to his own suicide. We are all, Reynard tells Jane, responsible for Tee Bob's death. It is Reynard's way of informing Jane that, culpable as are American whites for American racism, blacks share with whites the blame for black complicities in this particularly noxious form of man's inhumanity to man. And Reynard speaks for Gaines.

The black American past reveals, in the racism inseparable from it, limitations of conduct not white alone. If the whites have sinned more, as they probably have, in the business of excluding blacks from full participation in American democracy, blacks are not consequently thereby absolved from making their own contributions to an elimination, in America, of the color line. Ned Douglass, in *Pittman*, is very much Gaines's man. For Ned speaks impartially, as it were, to his pupils about both blacks and whites. Of Ned's disposition, furthermore, is the anonymous and kindly white male recluse who treats Jane, the naïve young inquirer of him for a traveler's direction to Ohio, as he would any wayfarer to whom he could be considerate and civil. And so, to some extent, *Pittman* is, above all, a morality play. It speaks of the past not only in order that the past may come alive, exhumed from its grave without serious loss of its true character, but also to the end that the future may be conceived in terms corrective of the wrongs which a close study of the past can, thankfully, reveal. *Pittman* is the story of a life and a history of a people; yet, too, like the medieval *Everyman*, also a message meant for those who have ears to hear about their own salvation. Water to be drunk plays a role, in *Pittman*, at both the novel's end and its beginning. Would that some water, Gaines seems to say throughout *Pittman*, would be the well of a new life for all Americans, especially in their relations, if they are white, with blacks, but no less, if they are black, with whites.

The Principal Writings of
Lewis P. Simpson: A Bibliography

This selective bibliography includes books, edited works, essays in books, and articles and long book reviews in periodicals. It leaves out of account Professor Simpson's many short introductions, editorial notes, brief book reviews, and remarks in published transcriptions of panel discussions.

BOOKS

The Brazen Face of History: Studies in the Literary Consciousness in America. Baton Rouge, 1980.
The Dispossessed Garden: Pastoral and History in Southern Literature. Athens, 1975.
The Man of Letters in New England and the South: Essays on the Literary Vocation in America. Baton Rouge, 1973.

EDITED BOOKS

The History of Southern Literature (with Louis D. Rubin, Jr., Blyden Jackson, Rayburn S. Moore, and Thomas D. Young). Baton Rouge, 1985.
The Possibilities of Order: Cleanth Brooks and His Work. Baton Rouge, 1975.
The Poetry of Community: Essays on the Southern Sensibility of History and Literature. Atlanta, 1972.
Profile of Robert Frost. Columbus, Ohio, 1971.
The Federalist Literary Mind. Baton Rouge, 1962.

ESSAYS IN BOOKS

"The Ideology of Revolution" and "The Mind of the Ante-
    bellum South." In *The History of Southern Literature*,
    edited by Louis D. Rubin, Jr., Blyden Jackson, Rayburn S.
    Moore, Lewis P. Simpson, Thomas Daniel Young (Baton
    Rouge, 1985), 57–67, 164–74.
"The Concept of the Historical Self." In *Robert Penn War-
    ren's Brother to Dragons: A Discussion*, edited by
    James A. Grimshaw (Baton Rouge, 1983), 244–49.
"Home by Way of California: The Southerner as the Last
    European." In *Southern Literature in Transition: Heri-
    tage and Promise*, edited by Philip Castile and William
    Osborne (Memphis, 1983), 55–70.
"The Southern Republic of Letters and *I'll Take My Stand.*"
    In *A Band of Prophets: The Nashville Agrarians After
    Fifty Years*, edited by William C. Havard and Walter
    Sullivan (Baton Rouge, 1982), 65–91.
"The Fable of the Writer in Southern Fiction." In *Prospects:
    The Annual of American Cultural Studies*, edited by
    Jack Salzman (New York, 1982), 249–66.
Introduction to *James Russell Lowell*, by Edward Everett
    Hale (New York, 1980), v–xii.
Preface to *The Collected Works of Ada Jack Carver*, edited
    by Mary Dell Fletcher (Natchitoches, La., 1980), xv–
    xviii.
"William Faulkner of Yoknapatawpha." In *The American
    South: Portrait of a Culture*, edited by Louis D. Rubin, Jr.
    (Baton Rouge, 1980), 227–44.
"The Southern Literary Vocation." In *Toward a New Ameri-
    can Literary History: Essays in Honor of Arlin Turner*,
    edited by Louis J. Budd, Edwin H. Cady, and Carl L.
    Anderson (Durham, N.C., 1980), 19–35.
"Roark Whitney Bradford (1896–1948)" and "George Fitz-
    hugh (1806–1881)." In *Southern Writers: A Biographi-
    cal Dictionary*, edited by Robert Bain, Joseph M. Flora,
    and Louis D. Rubin, Jr. (Baton Rouge, 1979), 44–45,
    156–57.
"Southern Fiction." In *Harvard Guide to Contemporary
    American Writing*, edited by Daniel Hoffman (Cam-
    bridge, Mass., 1979), 153–90.
"The Fugitives" and "[Southern] Periodicals." In *The Ency-
    clopedia of Southern History*, edited by David C. Roller

and Robert W. Twyman (Baton Rouge, 1979), 498, 968–69.

"*The Southern Review* and a Post-Southern American Letters." In *The Little Magazine in America,* edited by Eliott Anderson and Mary Kinzie (New York, 1978), 78–99.

"The Southern Aesthetic of Memory." In *Essays in American Literature in Honor of Richard P. Adams,* edited by Donald Pizer (New Orleans, 1978), 207–27.

"Sex and History: Origins of Faulkner's Apocrypha" and "Yoknapatawpha and Faulkner's Fable of Civilization." In *The Maker and the Myth: Faulkner and Yoknapatawpha,* edited by Evans Harrington and Ann J. Abadie (Jackson, Miss., 1978), 43–70, 122–45.

"The Symbolism of Literary Alienation in the Revolutionary Age." In *Two Hundred Years of the Republic in Retrospect,* edited by William C. Havard and Joseph L. Bernd (Charlottesville, 1976), 79–100.

"Faulkner and the Legend of the Artist." In *Fifty Years After "The Marble Faun,"* edited by George H. Wolfe (Tuscaloosa, 1976), 69–100.

"The Printer as Man of Letters: Franklin and the Symbolism of the Third Realm." In *The Oldest Revolutionary,* edited by J. A. Leo Lemay (Philadelphia, 1976), 3–20.

"The Children of Pride." In *Literary Annual,* edited by Frank N. Magill (Englewood Cliffs, N.J., 1975), 72–77.

"William Faulkner Writes *The Sound and the Fury.*" In *Great Events in American History,* edited by Frank N. Magill and John Loos (Englewood Cliffs, N.J., 1975), 1571–76.

"The Southern Reaction to Modernism." In *Southern Literary Study: Problems and Possibilities,* edited by Louis D. Rubin, Jr., and C. Hugh Holman (Chapel Hill, 1975), 48–68.

"The Satiric Mode: The Early National Wits." In *The Comic Imagination in American Literature,* edited by Louis D. Rubin, Jr. (New Brunswick, N.J., 1973), 49–61.

"Donald Davidson and the Southern Defense of Poetry." Introduction to *Still Rebels, Still Yankees,* by Donald Davidson (Baton Rouge, 1972), v–xvi.

"Southern Spiritual Nationalism: Notes on the Background of Modern Southern Fiction." In *The Cry of Home: Cultural Nationalism and the Modern Writer,* edited by H. Ernest Lewald (Knoxville, 1972), 189–210.

"James McBride Dabbs." In *Contemporary Literature Supplement*, edited by Ralph McGill (Englewood Cliffs, N.J., 1972), 288–91.

"Ruth McEnery Stuart." In *Notable American Women, 1607–1950*, edited by Edward T. James and Paul S. Boyer (Cambridge, Mass., 1972), 407–408.

"The Crisis of Alienation in Emerson's Early Thought." In *Emerson's Relevance Today*, edited by Eric W. Carlson and J. Lasley Dameron (Hartford, Conn., 1971), 35–43.

"Literary Ecumenicalism of the American Enlightenment." In *The Ibero-American Enlightenment*, edited by Alfred Owen Aldridge (Urbana, 1971), 317–32.

"Joseph Stevens Buckminster and the New England Clerisy." In *Essays in Honor of Esmond L. Marilla*, edited by Thomas A. Kirby and William J. Olive (Baton Rouge, 1970), 259–82.

"Roark Bradford (1896–1948)" and "Lafcadio Hearn (1850–1904)." In *A Bibliographical Guide to Southern Literature*, edited by Louis D. Rubin, Jr. (Baton Rouge, 1969), 159–60, 217–19.

"Yoknapatawpha and the World of Murry Falkner." Foreword to *The Falkners of Mississippi: A Memoir*, by Murry C. Falkner (Baton Rouge, 1967), vi–xv.

"Isaac McCaslin and Temple Drake: The Fall of New World Man." In *Nine Essays in Modern Literature*, edited by Donald E. Stanford (Baton Rouge, 1965), 88–106.

"Touching the Stylus: Notes on Poe's Vision of Literary Order." In *Studies in American Literature*, edited by Waldo McNeir and Leo B. Levy (Baton Rouge, 1960), 33–48.

ESSAYS AND LONG BOOK REVIEWS IN PERIODICALS

"The Last Casualty of the Civil War." *Sewanee Review*, XCV (1987), 149–62.

"Lionel Trilling and the Agency of Terror." *Partisan Review*, LVII (1987), 18–35.

"The Critics Who Made Us: Allen Tate." *Sewanee Review*, XCIV (1986), 471–85.

"The Ferocity of Self: History and Consciousness in Southern Literature." *South Central Review*, I (1984), 67–84.

"The Sexuality of History." *Southern Review*, n.s., XX (1984), 785–802.

"A Procession of Visionaries." *New England Quarterly*, LVII (1984), 567–73.

"The Southern Writer and the Economy of Leisure." *Sewanee Review*, XCI (1983), 512–18.

"The Sorrows of John Peale Bishop." *Sewanee Review*, XC (1982), 480–84.

"Faulkner and the Comedy of History." *Michigan Quarterly Review*, XXI (1982), 365–72.

"Cowley's Odyssey: Literature and Faith in the Thirties." *Sewanee Review*, LXXXIX (1981), 520–39.

"The Inwardness of History." *Virginia Quarterly Review*, LVII (1982), 158–67.

"The Saints Marching In." *Sewanee Review*, LXXXVIII (1980), 70–77.

"Arlin Turner, 1909–1980." *Resources for American Literary Study*, X (1980), 117–20.

"The Antebellum South as a Symbol of Mind." *Southern Literary Journal*, XII (1980), 125–36.

"The Act of Thought in Virginia." *Early American Literature*, XIV (1980), 253–68.

"A Note on Allen Tate." *Southern Review*, n.s., XVI (1979), ix, 519–20.

"The *Southern Review* and a Post-Southern American Letters." *Triquarterly*, XLIII (1978), 78–99.

"The Decorum of the Writer." *Sewanee Review*, LXXXVI (1978), 566–71.

"A Necrology of Modern Southern Fiction." *Southern Literary Journal*, IX (1977), 150–59.

"The Southern Literary Imagination and the Pastoral Mode." *Southern Humanities Review*, X (1976), 13–21.

"John Adams and Hawthorne: The Fiction of the Real American Revolution." *Studies in the Literary Imagination*, IX (1976), 1–17.

"The Identity of the Writer." *Southern Review*, n.s., XII (1976), xii.

"Malcolm Cowley and the American Writer." *Sewanee Review*, LXXXIV (1976), 22–47.

"The Symbolism of Alienation in the Revolutionary Age." *Journal of Politics*, XXXVIII (1976), 79–100.

Foreword to "Kate Chopin," by Robert D. Arner. *Louisiana Studies*, XIV (1975), 5–10.

"The Loneliness of William Faulkner." *Southern Literary Journal*, VIII (1975), 126–43.

"Faulkner and the Symbolism of Pastoral." *Mississippi Quarterly*, XXVIII (1975), 401–15.

"The Civil War: Written and Unwritten." *Southern Literary Journal*, VII (1974), 132–45.

"The Southern Recovery of Memory and History." *Sewanee Review*, LXXXII (1974), 1–32.

"A Tribute to Theodore Hornberger." *Early American Literature*, VII (1973), 257–60.

"Walter Sullivan and the Southern Possibility." *Southern Literary Journal*, V (1973), 88–101.

"A New Prospectus for Louisiana Studies." *Louisiana Studies*, IX (1972), 186–87.

"William Byrd and the South." *Early American Literature*, VII (1972), 187–95.

"On Garnishing and Peopling a Void." *Southern Review*, n.s., VIII (1972), xv–xix.

"Poet-Critics and a Critic." *Southern Review*, n.s., VIII (1972), xv–xix.

"Mark Twain and the Pathos of Regeneration: A Second Look at Geismar's Mark Twain." *Southern Literary Journal*, IV (1972), 93–106.

"The Crisis of Alienation in Emerson's Early Thought." *American Transcendental Quarterly*, IX (1971), 35–43.

"The Southern Writer and the Great Literary Secession." *Georgia Review*, XXIV (1970), 393–412.

"O'Donnell's Wall." *Southern Review*, n.s., VI (1970), xix–xxvii.

"The Chosen People." *Southern Review*, n.s., VI (1970), xvii–xxiii.

"The Poetry of New Orleans." *Southern Review*, n.s., IV (1968), xiii–xv.

"Mark Twain: Critical Perspectives." *Southern Review*, n.s., IV (1968), 491–92.

"Boston Ice and Letters in the Age of Jefferson." *Midcontinent American Studies Journal*, IX (1968), 58–76.

"The Short, Desperate Life of Henry Thoreau." *Emerson Society Quarterly*, XLII (1966), 45–56.

"The Humor of the Old Southwest." *Mississippi Quarterly*, XVII (1964), 63–66.

"Poe and the Literary Vocation in America." *Emerson Society Quarterly*, XXXI (1963), 11–14.

"Federalism and the Crisis of Literary Order." *American Literature*, XXXII (1960), 253–66.

"The City and the Symbolism of Literary Community in the United States." *Texas Quarterly*, III (1960), 97–111.

"Emerson and the Myth of New England's Intellectual Lapse." *Emerson Society Quarterly*, X (1958), 28–31.

"A Literary Adventure of the Early Republic: The Anthology Society and the *Monthly Anthology*." *New England Quarterly*, XXVII (1954), 168–90.

"William (Alias Joseph Brown) Ladd: A Spurious Biography in the Bieber Collection." *Library Chronicle of the University of Texas*, V (1954), 28–33.

"Not Men, But Books." *Boston Public Library Quarterly*, IV (1952), 167–84.

"The Intercommunity of the Learned: Boston and Cambridge in 1800." *New England Quarterly*, XXIII (1950), 491–503.

"*The Literary Miscellany* and *The General Repository*: Two Cambridge Periodicals of the Early Republic." *Library Chronicle of the University of Texas*, III (1950), 177–90.

The Contributors

Daniel Aaron, Victor S. Thomas Professor of English and American Literature, Emeritus, at Harvard University and President of the Library of America, is the author of *Writers on the Left* (1961) and *The Unwritten War: American Writers and the Civil War* (1973).

Sacvan Bercovitch, Charles E. Carswell Professor of English and American Literature at Harvard University, has written *The Puritan Origins of the American Self* (1975) and *The American Jeremiad* (1978).

Cleanth Brooks, Gray Professor of Rhetoric, Emeritus, at Yale University, helped to establish the practice of New Criticism and is best known for *The Well Wrought Urn* (1947) and *William Faulkner: The Yoknapatawpha Country* (1963).

Louise Cowan, Professor of English Emeritus at the University of Dallas and Founding Fellow of the Dallas Institute of Humanities and Culture, is the author of *The Fugitive Group* (1959) and editor of *The Terrain of Comedy* (1984).

James M. Cox, Professor of English and Avalon Professor in the Humanities at Dartmouth College, has written *Mark Twain: The Fate of Humor* (1966), as well as the many essays to appear in a forthcoming collection, *Recovering Literature's Lost Ground*.

DANIEL MARK FOGEL, Professor of English at Louisiana State University, has published *Henry James and the Structure of the Romantic Imagination* (1981) and is founding editor of the *Henry James Review.*

ELIZABETH FOX-GENOVESE is Professor of History and Director of Women's Studies at Emory University. EUGENE D. GENOVESE is Distinguished Professor of Arts and Sciences at the University of Rochester. They are coauthors of *Fruits of Merchant Capital: Slavery and Bourgeois Property in the Rise and Expansion of Capitalism* (1983).

DANIEL HOFFMAN, Poet in Residence and Felix E. Schelling Professor of English at the University of Pennsylvania, is the author of *Poe Poe Poe Poe Poe Poe Poe* (1972) and editor of the *Harvard Guide to Contemporary American Writing* (1979).

BLYDEN JACKSON, Professor of English, Emeritus, at the University of North Carolina, is coauthor (with Louis D. Rubin, Jr.) of *Black Poetry in America* (1974) and author of *The Waiting Years: Essays on American Negro Literature* (1976).

J. GERALD KENNEDY, Professor of English at Louisiana State University, is the author of *The Astonished Traveler: William Darby, Frontier Geographer and Man of Letters* (1981) and *Poe, Death, and the Life of Writing* (1987).

J. A. LEO LEMAY, H. F. du Pont Winterthur Professor of English at the University of Delaware, is the author of *"New England's Annoyances": America's First Folksong* (1985) and *The Canon of Benjamin Franklin, 1721–1776: New Additions and Reconsiderations* (1986).

TERENCE MARTIN, Distinguished Professor of English at Indiana University, is the author of *The Instructed Vision* (1968) and *Nathaniel Hawthorne* (1983).

LOUIS D. RUBIN, JR., University Distinguished Professor of English at the University of North Carolina and editorial director of Algonquin Books, has published *The Wary Fugitives* (1978) and *A Gallery of Southerners* (1982).

WALTER SULLIVAN, Professor of English at Vanderbilt University, is the author of *Death by Melancholy: Essays on Modern Southern Fiction* (1972) and *A Requiem for the Renascence: The State of Fiction in the Modern South* (1976).